THE SLAVONIC
& EAST EUROPEAN
REVIEW

Volume 101, Number 4 — October 2023

ARTICLES

Literature, Film and Culture

Authenticity, Facts and Politics in the Fin-de-Siècle Pushkin Debate

ANNA SCHUR

In 1893, *Severnyi vestnik*, a leading outlet of Russian decadence, began serializing *Zapiski A. O. Smirnovoi (Neizdannye istoricheskie dokumenty)* (Notes of A. O. Smirnova [Unpublished historical documents]).[1] Aleksandra Smirnova (née Rosset), a lady-in-waiting to two Russian empresses who had a personal relationship with Nicholas I, was also a friend of Pushkin, Zhukovskii, Viazemskii, Gogol´ and other literary luminaries of the 1820s–40s. Smirnova's *Notes* were obtained for *Severnyi vestnik* posthumously from Aleksandra's daughter Ol´ga by Liubov´ Gurevich, the journal's publisher, who made a special trip to Paris where Ol´ga resided and where she kept her mother's extensive archive. In 1895, Smirnova's *Notes* appeared as a separate edition.

From its first appearance in *Severnyi vestnik*, Smirnova's *Notes* was surrounded with suspicion about its authenticity.[2] Focused in large part on Pushkin, the memoir was riddled with factual errors that suggested forgery, while the sentiments and statements attributed to Pushkin pointed to Ol´ga as their source. Pushkin's supposed opinions struck the critics as more

Anna Schur is a Professor in the Department of English at Keene State College, New Hampshire.

With thanks to the anonymous referees for their valuable criticisms and suggestions.

[1]   The full title under which Smirnova's work appeared in *Severnyi vestnik* was *Zapiski A. O. Smirnovoi. (Neizdannye istoricheskie dokumenty). Iz zapisnykh knizhek 1826–1845 gg.* The journal ran Smirnova's *Notes* from March 1893 to September 1894 with one interruption in July 1894.

[2]   For a comprehensive history of Smirnova's archive, see S. V. Zhitomirskaia, 'K istorii memuarnogo naslediia A. O. Smirnovoi-Rosset', in R. V. Iezuitova et al. (eds), *Pushkin, issledovaniia i materialy*, Moscow and Leningrad, 1979, vol. 9, pp. 329–45; Zhitomirskaia, 'A. O. Smirnova-Rosset i ee memuarnoe nasledstvo', in A. O. Smirnova-Rosset, *Dnevnik. Vospominaniia*, ed. S. V. Zhitomirskaia, Moscow, 1989, pp. 579–632. See also, A. V. Koshelev, '"Zapiski A. O. Smirnovoi": k istorii izucheniia' <https://cyberleninka.ru/article/n/zapiski-a-o-smirnovoy-k-istorii-izucheniya> [accessed 15 March 2023].

redolent of Smirnova's own views and habits of expression than consistent with what was known of Pushkin's. There were also glaring anachronisms. The list included such blunders as Pushkin's alleged comments on Alexander Dumas's *Les Trois Mousquetaires* (*The Three Musketeers*, 1844) and on Stendhal's *La Chartreuse de Parme* (*The Charterhouse of Parma*, 1839), both published after Pushkin's death in 1837.

For other readers, none of this was a problem. For them, Smirnova's *Notes* accurately captured Pushkin's spirit and possessed a type of higher-order authenticity that rendered factual errors irrelevant. Among those who embraced Smirnova's memoir was the writer and early exponent of Russian symbolism, Dmitri Merezhkovskii. In his 1896 essay, 'Pushkin', originally published in Petr Pertsov's *Filosofskie techeniia russkoi poezii* (Philosophical Currents of Russian Poetry, 1896), Merezhkovskii extolled Smirnova's *Notes* and relied on it to paint his own portrait of the poet. Soon after, 'Pushkin' was included, with slight changes and omissions, in Merezhkovskii's *Vechnye sputniki* (The Eternal Companions, 1896), where it retained its position as the collection's culminating essay in all subsequent editions which otherwise were subjected to multiple reshufflings and revisions.

Responding to Merezhkovskii's *Companions* in a long review that appeared in the liberal *Vestnik Evropy*, the lawyer and literary critic Vladimir Spasovich (Russified version of the Polish Włodzimierz Spasowicz) sided with those who challenged the credibility of Smirnova's *Notes*. To him, the memoir was inauthentic in origin, reference and style, and thus an unacceptable basis for Merezhkovskii's conception of Pushkin. Spasovich's review, and particularly his own account of Pushkin, provoked a new round of controversy which involved some of the period's leading intellectuals. Divided in their response to Spasovich's view of Pushkin, they were also split over the importance of historical authenticity.

In this article, I draw on this protracted and tangled debate to explore ideas about historical authenticity and the importance of factual accuracy in fin-de-siècle Russia. From recent research, authenticity in the Russian context emerges as an unsettled — even messy — issue. In part, the difficulty has to do with the capaciousness of the English term that encompasses several Russian meanings, occasionally, but far from always, adjacent. For those interested in authenticity as proximate to *iskrennost'* (sincerity), it is above all a moral category, even if sometimes it straddles the aesthetic realm.[3] For other scholars, the term's primary connotations

---

[3] Anna Fishzon, 'The Operatics of Everyday Life, or, How Authenticity Was Defined

are epistemological and ontological ones, best captured by *podlinnost'* and *dostovernost'*, although these, too, can cross into the domains of both aesthetics and morality.[4] How, according to these studies, the fin-de-siècle understanding of authenticity, especially in art, was impacted by technological modernization is hardly settled either. If some associate authentic artistic expression with non-technological and non-automatized, in the vein of Walter Benjamin,[5] others have argued that new technologies transformed the relationship between the original and the copy, thus giving rise to new conceptions of authenticity.[6] In this article, I seek to contribute to this growing investigation by focusing on the attitudes toward historical authenticity.

The sense of authenticity I explore relates to the notions of origin, provenance and credibility of sources and facts (conveyed by *podlinnost'* and *dostovernost'*), not authenticity as sincerity (conveyed primarily by *iskrennost'*). My focus will be on journalistic criticism in the popular press, not on academic Pushkin study that at this time was beginning to take shape as a formal field of scholarship. As Frances Nethercott and Andy Byford have argued, academic study of the humanities underwent, over the course of the nineteenth century, a shift away from the romantic ethos of 'subjective aestheticism' toward more empirically grounded modes of inquiry that had a literary counterpart in realism (even if the romantic current was never fully purged).[7] This meant, among other things, a greater investment in determining authenticity of sources, materials and facts than was typical of the earlier decades.

On the pages of literary journalism, however, historical authenticity was a polarizing issue, as the Smirnova controversy, which soon morphed

in Late Imperial Russia', *Slavic Review*, 70, 4, 2011, pp. 795–818; Ellen Rutten, *Sincerity after Communism: A Cultural History*, New Haven, CT, 2017, pp. 59–61.

[4] Ekaterina Pravilova, 'Truth, Facts, and Authenticity in Russian Imperial Jurisprudence and Historiography', *Kritika: Explorations in Russian and Eurasian History*, 21, 1, 2020, pp. 7–39.

[5] Rutten, *Sincerity after Communism*, p. 60.

[6] Ekaterina Pravilova, 'The Trouble with Authenticity: Backwardness, Imitation, and the Politics of Art in Late Imperial Russia', *The Journal of Modern History*, 90, 3, 2018, pp. 536–79. I am grateful to the author for bringing this important study to my attention. Also see Fishzon, 'The Operatics of Everyday Life', especially pp. 810–11.

[7] Frances Nethercott, *Writing History in Late Imperial Russia: Scholarship and the Literary Canon*, London, 2021, pp. 58, 165; Andy Byford, *Literary Scholarship in Late Imperial Russia: Rituals of Academic Institutionalisation*, London, 2007, pp. 4, 30. For an account that explores the subsequent shift from positivism to other methodologies of humanistic study in the late nineteenth–early twentieth century, see O. B. Leont'eva, *Istoricheskaia pamiat' i obrazy proshlogo v Rossiiskoi kul'ture XIX - nachala XX vv.*, Samara, 2011, pp. 25–81.

into a debate on Pushkin, reveals. At first blush, it hardly seems surprising that a writer and a lawyer may have different levels of tolerance for factual looseness and even outright fabrication. Moreover, in Merezhkovskii's and Spasovich's case, their positions reflected more than professional habits of mind. They were also consonant with their aesthetic tastes, which in turn loosely tracked generational preferences. As a key exponent of symbolism, with its anti-rationalist and anti-positivistic rebellion against mimetic realism and the vision of the artist as a type of miracle-worker transfiguring existence itself, the thirty-one-year-old Merezhkovskii revived the spirit of romantic historiography to give precedence to creation over discovery, including in his approach to literary criticism. Concerns about credibility of evidence and historical authenticity of sources had no place in his programme. A representative of the older generation, Spasovich, in contrast, had little patience for modern art and was much more at home with traditional realist forms. His position on facts and sources reflects both his commitment to positivism and realism and a keen understanding of their limits. The first half of the article is devoted to mapping out Merezhkovskii's and Spasovich's views.

In the article's second half, I examine reverberations of the Merezhkovskii-Spasovich exchange throughout the Pushkin debate that it triggered. What this subsequent debate demonstrates is that the contributors' professional identities, aesthetic tastes and generational differences do not fully account for their methods of engaging with the past. As prominent intellectuals rallied on both sides, this ensuing polemic made clear that the participants' clashing views on fact and authenticity were also dictated by their politics.[8] The official patriotic and conservative nationalist narratives, which identified Pushkin with Russia and the Russian national identity, called for an idealization that had little use for historical fact, whereas the dissenting narrative that displayed more care and interest in historical authenticity and in getting facts right eschewed the nationalist fervour and was vilified by the opponents as an attack on Russia itself.

Merezhkovskii: Pushkin and 'subjective' criticism
According to Merezhkovskii, the fundamental reason why Smirnova's memoir was challenged by the critics was not the errors it contained. The main problem was that the portrait of Pushkin as a sage and philosopher

[8] This loosely corresponds to Pravilova's recent suggestion that fin-de-siècle authenticity took a number of shapes: 'of form, impression, material, and so on.' Pravilova, 'The Trouble with Authenticity', p. 576.

that emerged from Smirnova's *Notes* disrupted the reigning understanding of him as 'a *mere* poet', 'a *mere* artist' shared even by Pushkin's admirers. And it entirely subverted the earlier but still influential view of detractors like Pisarev who dismissed Pushkin as a frivolous versifier of an antiquated past with nothing to say to modernity. It was, in other words, the strangeness and novelty of the image put forth by Smirnova — and the challenge to the consensus it represented — that drove the search for factual errors. Merezhkovskii was incensed by the reception accorded to Smirnova's memoir, a work that in any other land would have had, so he believed, epochal significance. To Merezhkovskii himself the errors were nothing more than 'small inaccuracies'. Searching for them was not merely a mark of pedantry but also of indecency.[9] It resembled literary libel in the vein of Faddei Bulgarin.

As to Merezhkovskii's Pushkin, he is, first and foremost, a reconciler of world contradictions: Apollonian order and Dionysian exuberance, spirit and flesh, art and life. Above all, he unites in his genius what Merezhkovskii sees as the two elemental strains of Russian and European culture: the Christian ideal of renouncing one's own self and losing it in the divine, and the pagan impulse of deification of oneself in the heroic. The sermon of humility, mercy and chastity is harmonized in Pushkin's poetry and personality with a demigod's challenge to the corrupt civilization. A harbinger of the spiritual and religious renaissance that is yet to come, in Merezhkovskii's Nietzschean scheme, Pushkin is both the past and the future.[10] He is, in Gogol''s iconic phrase that opens Merezhkovskii's essay, 'a Russian person in his development, how he will appear in two hundred years'.[11]

If this description sounds familiar, it is not because it resembles Smirnova's. What we recognize here are the echoes of Dostoevskii's 1880 'Pushkin speech' (down to Gogol''s quotation that opens both Merezhkovskii's and Dostoevskii's texts). For Dostoevskii, the ability for reconciling contradictions, for alleviating all strife was related to the alleged quality of unique 'responsiveness' to other cultures and nations which he attributed to the Russian people and which he found embodied in Pushkin. Dostoevskii's Pushkin foreshadows the Russian mission of renewing the

---

[9] D. S. Merezhkovskii, *Vechnye sputniki. Portrety iz vsemirnoi literatury*, ed. E. A. Andrushchenko, St Petersburg, 2007, p. 231.

[10] On the Nietzschean categories in Merezhkovskii's conception of Pushkin, see Irina Paperno, 'Pushkin v zhizni cheloveka serebriannogo veka', in Boris Gasparov, Robert P. Hughes and Irina Paperno (eds), *Cultural Mythologies of Russian Modernism: From the Golden Age to the Silver Age*, Berkeley, CA, 1992, pp. 19–51, especially pp. 20–21.

[11] Merezhkovskii, *Vechnye sputniki*, p. 229.

West under the banner of the Russian idea: through a 'reconciliation of European contradictions' and by uttering the 'ultimate word of the great, universal harmony, of the ultimate brotherly communion of all tribes in accordance with the law of the Gospel of Christ!'[12]

Merezhkovskii's very understanding of Pushkin as a genius of harmony, of bringing into balance a whole host of seemingly irreconcilable values and principles thus echoes one of Dostoevskii's central points. Indeed, Merezhkovskii's very language is redolent of Dostoevskii. When we read that for him, too, Pushkin was the first to lay bare 'in the depth of the Russian world-view [...] the makings of the future Renaissance — of that spiritual harmony which represents the rarest fulfilment of all nations' millennia-old aspirations', we realize the full extent of Dostoevskii's influence.[13] Despite his criticism of Dostoevskii's Slavophilism, Merezhkovskii's Pushkin is as much of an embodiment of the Russian idealized spirit as he was for Dostoevskii.

As concerns Smirnova's *Notes*, her memoir seems less like a source of concrete detail than something of a pretext for Merezhkovskii to create his own portrait of Pushkin. This may have something to do with Merezhkovskii's ways of reading and with his attitude to historical fact. For Merezhkovskii, historical accuracy took the backseat to personal impression. In the 'Preface' to the *Companions*, he made a point of laying out his purposely subjectivist approach. 'The author's goal', he wrote in the Preface, 'is not to give a more or less objective and complete picture of his chosen topics'. His goal is 'openly subjective': 'to show behind a book the living soul of the writer — an idiosyncratic, unique, inimitable form of being' and its impact 'on the intellect, will, heart, the whole inner life of a critic, as a representative of a given generation'.[14] In the essay 'Cervantes', Merezhkovskii further noted that subjective criticism is a superior method of arriving at 'the inner meaning' (*vnutrennii smysl*) of a literary work, because, unlike 'objective' criticism, which 'strives only toward dispassionate historical authenticity' (*besstrastnaia istoricheskaia dostovernost'*), it operates through 'empathetic excitement' and 'living impressions'.[15] Meant by Merezhkovskii as a description of his approach

[12] F. M. Dostoevskii, 'Pushkin', in *Polnoe sobranie sochinenii v tridsati tomakh*, ed. G. M. Fridlender et al., 30 vols, Leningrad, 1972–90, 26, pp. 136–40, 148.

[13] Merezhkovskii, *Vechnye sputniki*, p. 285. By expunging the references to Peter I, Goethe and Leonardo Da Vinci from the previous version of this passage, Merezhkovskii made the echo of Dostoevskii still more audible. See note 167 in *Vechnye sputniki*, pp. 822–23.

[14] Ibid., pp. 5–6.

[15] Ibid., p. 86.

to the 'companions', these remarks summarize equally well his use of Smirnova's memoir.

Merezhkovskii's critical method was a natural extension of his overall aesthetic programme. His series of lectures, 'O prichinakh upadka i o novykh techeniyakh sovremennoi russkoi literatury' (On the Reasons for the Decline and on the New Tendencies in Russian Literature, 1893), delivered around the same time and widely considered as the first theoretical statement of Russian symbolism, reveals a connection between Merezhkovskii's unapologetically subjectivist method of literary criticism and his rejection of mimetic realism. As 'the dominant taste of the mob', realism, for Merezhkovskii, is a quintessence of banality, vulgarity and tastelessness. It represents the denial of a 'higher ideal culture' and is an artistic equivalent to scientific and 'moral materialism'.[16] Merezhkovskii, of course, minimizes the symbiosis of the real and the ideal, of the objective and the subjective that was fundamental to realism. In fact, his very efforts to rebrand Dostoevskii, Turgenev, Goncharov and Tolstoi as 'idealists' owe to the fact that realism has never been merely what he claims. Nevertheless, however polemical and one-sided, his view of realism is in line with his position on traditional criticism, including its concern with historical authenticity.

If new art was to be characterized by 'mystical content, symbols, and the widening of artistic impressionability', new criticism was to become 'poetry' in its own right.[17] The old critic who had long transformed criticism into a podium for journalistic sermonizing was to give way to the 'poet-critic'. An inspired creator himself, 'the poet-critic' is attuned to the mysteries of artistic creation and capable of achieving spiritual unity with the soul of the poet he reads. The higher mission of 'the poet-critic', concerned with uncovering the spark of 'divine idealism' animating a true work of art, is at odds with the pedestrian ways of customary criticism dominating Russian literary scene.

Part and parcel of the materialist and positivist programme, concern with fact and authenticity is, for Merezhkovskii, a sign of the shallow mind and desiccated spirit. Worries about genuineness and provenance of documents get especially short shrift. Regarding a recent debate about Lermontov's manuscripts, Merezhkovskii writes:

How thoroughly and painstakingly the responsible publishers compared the drafts of the sketches, how much paper was wasted on the fierce

[16] Ibid., p. 455.
[17] Ibid., p. 459.

polemics among serious academics and journalists *a propos* of insignificant variants! And all these researchers were merely walking 'around' the artist, no one has tried and succeeded in entering *his interior world* [...], to no one was Lermontov simply a living, kindred, and close person.

Merezhkovskii dismisses these efforts as 'dead bookish erudition', as he would soon dismiss the efforts to ascertain the authenticity of Smirnova's memoir. Such efforts are the province of the plodding 'eunuchs of poetry', not of the inspired 'poet-critic', an emerging breed, whose spiritual communion with the beloved artist has little use for any objective anchors.[18]

The distinction between information that is 'dead' and knowledge that is 'living' was a common trope that predated Merezhkovskii, but he made it a cornerstone of his approach to history, as did other writers of the Silver Age. Elaborating on the peculiarity of history in a later essay, Merezhkovskii pointed out that unlike the fields that study 'what is', history deals with 'with what was'. Historians are separated from their subject by 'the abyss of time', which is 'deeper and more irremediable [*bezvozvratnee*] than any abyss of space. [...] The abyss of time is the abyss of death; to fly over it one needs the wings of love'. Only love can bring true knowledge: not data (*svedeniia*) one gets from 'touching, palpating, and seeing the subject from the outside', but knowledge from 'the inside', yielded by a special 'inner vision, clairvoyance', by 'the experience of co-feeling, the experience of love'. The proper task of history is to defy death itself: 'history is resurrection of the dead — the last miracle of knowledge, the miracle of love.'[19]

Everything here, from the rhetoric of 'resurrection' as the goal of historical memory to the evocation of love and 'co-feeling' as a key to the recovery of the past, is part of the standard arsenal of early twentieth-century Russian historiosophy, which itself was a form of historical revival. In its vocabulary of 'immersion' (*pogruzhenie*), of 'living-' and 'feeling-into' (*vzhivanie* and *vchuvstvovanie*), in its reliance on visions, clairvoyance, epiphanies and mystical connections, Russian Silver Age historiosophers revived the anti-rationalist, anti-Enlightenment, intuitivist aspects of romantic historiography.[20] And just as their intellectual predecessors,

---

[18] Ibid., pp. 498, 497.

[19] Dmitrii Merezhkovskii, 'Aleksandr I', in Merezhkovskii, *Bylo i budet. Dnevnik 1910–1914*, Moscow, 1915, pp. 125–38 (pp. 127, 128).

[20] I. M. Savel'eva, A. V. Poletaev, *Istoriia i intuitsiia: nasledie romantikov*, Moscow, 2003, especially pp. 24–25; M. A. Voskresenskaia, 'Istoriosofskie vozzreniia tvortsov Serebriannogo veka', 2008 <https://cyberleninka.ru/article/n/istoriosofskie-vozzreniya-

Silver Age thinkers dismissed the importance of historical authenticity as a property belonging to the realm of the 'dead' externals: of 'cold' reason, pedantic factuality, and uninspired objectivity.[21] Consider, for instance, how the familiar distinction between the internals and externals is mobilized by the philosopher Semen Frank to justify his own reliance on Smirnova's *Notes*. Quoting from the memoir (as cited by Merezhkovskii in his *Companions*) in a Pushkin essay of his own, Frank noted that the authenticity of the quoted material is 'perfectly evident for *inner* reasons, however inauthentic the many testimonies of this dubious memoir may be'.[22] Despite italicizing the word 'inner' to give it special weightiness, Frank does not explain what the phrase means. It is clear, however, that Frank's 'inner authenticity' does not refer to historical authenticity in a standard sense but signifies, as it does for Merezhkovskii, the material's consonance with his own vision of Pushkin.

Spasovich: Facts and fantasizing

The seeds of the ideas central to the Silver Age historiosophy were contained, as we have seen, already in Merehzkovskii's early lectures, where he first formulated the principles of his 'subjective' criticism, conceived as a counter — and a refutation — to its positivistic, utility-oriented and morality-centred foil. Notably, among the still rare breed of the emerging critic, Merezhkovskii included none other than Spasovich. In his last lecture, he praised Spasovich's treatment of Lermontov upholding it as an example of the subjective criticism he advocated. But Merezhkovskii underestimated how profoundly different from his own Spasovich's views on art and reality were. A self-described 'man of the nineteenth century, and not even of its end, but of its middle', Spasovich rejected modernist art as unintelligible and puerile and, like many lawyers of his generation, was much more at home with traditional artistic forms. It is just such forms that stand as an unnamed foil to modernist aesthetics in the following excerpt from a 1901 speech:

> When they take me to a canvas and show some stains and doodles, as if drawn by a child, and tell me that it is beautiful or at least symbolic;

tvortsov-serebryanogo-veka/viewer> [accessed 15 March 2023]. See also, Leont'eva, *Istoricheskaia pamiat' i obrazy proshlogo*.

[21] Savel'eva and Poletaev, *Istoriia i intuitsiia*, p. 25.

[22] Semen Frank, 'Pushkin kak politicheskii myslitel'', in A. E. Tarkhov (ed.), *Pushkin v russkoi filosofkoi kritike: Konets XIX – pervaia polovina XX v.*, Moscow, 1990, pp. 396–422 (p. 413).

when they give me not lucid discourses and stories but abruptly changing moods, without connection or logic, and assure me that that these are revelations of the bared soul; when I seek in a literary work some idea, meaning, but it turns out that they are not needed, that they have no place here — I cannot reconcile myself to it.[23]

Spasovich's rejection of modernist forms had a natural counterpart in his rejection of Merezhkovskii's subjectivist epistemology that, among other things, defined his approach to sources. To begin with, Spasovich was unconvinced by Merezhkovskii's claim to the novelty of his 'subjective' criticism. All criticism, Spasovich argued in his review of *Companions*, passes works of literature through the critic's intellect and emotion and thus cannot be anything other than subjective. At the same time, criticism, according to Spasovich, is a type of science, and science concerns itself only with truth and nothing else. Its goal is to reproduce 'the real writer' as 'he is known in reality'. Spasovich does not explain what exactly 'the real' writer or 'reality' may mean, but the 'historical truth', to which the scientific critic should aspire, and which precludes invention and 'fantasizing', seems to emerge from the aggregation of the existing information, including perceptions of prior observers.[24] Later in the essay, Spasovich speaks of 'the real Pushkin', that is Pushkin 'as he is perceived not from some but from all of his works and letters' and that is a far cry from the Pushkin 'composed' by Merezhkovskii after his own likeness.[25]

Despite some holes in this argument, it is easy to recognize here the general shape of Spasovich's approach to truth and reality traceable to earlier writings, where he dwelled on these issues at a greater length. Like any lawyer of his time, in his courtroom speeches, Spasovich could shuttle, depending on the need of the moment, between positions that were at least in tension, if not in direct conflict, sometimes in the same trial. Nevertheless, with due allowances for the pragmatic pressures of the courtroom contest, Spasovich's writings disclose an adherence to a set of attitudes, positions and tropes that cut across decades and genres. Especially useful in this regard are the works free of immediate pragmatic concerns, like his writings on legal theory and literary criticism which

---

[23] *Zastol'nye rechi V. D. Spasovicha v sobraniiakh sosloviia prisiazhnykh poverennykh okruga S.-Peterburgskoi sudebnoi palaty, 1873–1901*, Leipzig, 1903, pp. 78–79.

[24] V. Spasovich, 'D. S. Merezhkovskii i ego *Vechnye sputniki*', in D. S. Merezhkovskii, *Vechnye sputniki. Portrety iz vsemirnoi literatury*, ed. E. A. Andrushchenko, St Petersburg, 2007, p. 643.

[25] Spasovich, *Vechnye sputniki*, p. 674.

offer a window onto his views and confirm their considerable consistency. On the whole, Spasovich's views are characterized by a belief in the objective reality of truth tempered by an appreciation of the inescapably subjective nature of experience, a position consonant with his preference for realism. The symbiosis of the objective and the subjective, the awareness that one cannot reach unmediated reality, the task of doing one's best nonetheless, the casting of this task as a moral enterprise, the view of language as a means of recording our perceptions of reality rather than reality itself — all central concepts of nineteenth-century realism — find a reflection in Spasovich's views.

Thus, already in *O teorii sudebno-ugolovnykh dokazatel'stv v sviazi s sudoustroistvom i sudoproizvodstvom* (Theory of Criminal Evidence in the Judicial System and in Legal Proceedings), a series of lectures delivered in 1860, when Spasovich was still a university professor, he defined truth as 'an accurate reflection of reality in human consciousness; it is the most perfect, as far as it is possible, identity of our impressions of an object with the object as it is in reality'.[26] Although it is not the literary critic but the judge who is compared in this instance to the natural scientist, here, too, Spasovich recognizes the impossibility of escaping the subjective dimension of knowledge, even as he insists on the existence of objective reality. In fact, as he puts in one of his more famous cases, language itself inevitably interposes itself between us and reality, because what it represents is not reality but only our perceptions 'coloured by our "I", suffused with our subjectivity'.[27] Nevertheless, 'Reality, exists on its own, independently of the judge's conviction. It belongs to all thinking people, and anyone can check if in actuality it corresponds to its reflection in the judge's conscience'.[28] For Spasovich, truth 'has two sides: one objective, independent of the inquiring person, and the other subjective, dependent on this person's characteristics'.[29] Relying solely on an 'unaccountable individual conviction', on 'instinct', 'hunch' and 'inspiration' means giving up on the difference between conviction (*ubezhdenie*) and prejudice (*predubezhdenie*), between truth and untruth.[30]

[26] V. D. Spasovich, *O teorii sudebno-ugolovnykh dokazatel'stv v sviazi s sudoustroistvom i sudoproizvodstvom. Publichnye lektsii, chitannye v S.-Peterburgskom universitete (sentiabr' i oktiabr' 1860 g.)*, Moscow, 2001, p. 64.

[27] V. Spasovich, 'Rech' po delu Davida i Nikolaia Chkhotua i dr.', p. 136 <https://cyberleninka.ru/article/n/rech-po-delu-davida-i-nikolaya-chhotua-i-dr-tiflisskoe-delo/viewer> [accessed 15 March 2023].

[28] Spasovich, *O teorii*, p. 66.

[29] Ibid. p. 65.

[30] Ibid. pp. 63, 67, 61.

To Spasovich, such surrender to subjective impression, unconstrained by 'a reasonable critical conviction' represents 'a step back' in the civilizational process.[31] Spasovich speaks here of the legal context, but Aleksandr Pypin's 1897 lecture on literary fakes, delivered to the Imperial Society of the Lovers of Ancient Writing, clarifies the relevance of this remark to the field of literary study. Although Pypin never mentions Smirnova's *Notes* — his topic was the fakes of ancient manuscripts fabricated earlier in the century — the controversy surrounding the memoir may be seen as an unspoken background to Pypin's lecture. Explaining why fabrications of ancient Russian texts could inspire, in earlier decades, widespread belief in their authenticity, including among luminaries of Gavriil Derzhavin's and Nikolai Kostomarov's calibre, Pypin attributed it to 'insufficient knowledge of authentic (*podlinnykh*) facts', on the one hand, and a shortage of 'people capable of scientific criticism', on the other.[32] Sounding much like Spasovich, his one-time collaborator and close associate in the *Vestnik Evropy* circles, by scientific criticism Pypin understood a strict adherence to 'a fully authentic [*vpolne udostoverennyi*] fact' to the exclusion of all 'fantasizing where no such data were available'.[33]

Pypin's observation is in line with modern scholars' accounts of the growing professionalization of both academic historiography and literary scholarship.[34] As both fields were shifting away from the aesthetic subjectivism of romanticism toward more rigorous, evidence-based forms of inquiry, they were also growing more attentive to historical and philological analysis of textual materials than their romantic predecessors.[35] This explains why in Spasovich's (and Pypin's) scheme, Merezhkovskii's militantly subjective method, as well as his approach to a literary-historical document, represents a throwback to an earlier time. Merezhkovskii's claims to novelty notwithstanding, Spasovich correctly identified in his method a revival of the romantic paradigm. Having decided to use Smirnova's *Notes* as a 'lever' for advancing his own conception of Pushkin, Merezhkovskii neglected to pass it through what Spasovich called the 'filter of criticism'. Instead, he took it 'in its entirety at faith, as real truth'.[36] And such filter, Spasovich noted already in his *Theory of Proof*,

---

[31] Ibid. p. 67.

[32] A. N. Pypin, *Poddelki rukopisei i narodnykh pesen*, St Petersburg, 1898, pp. 22, 23 <https://upload.wikimedia.org/wikipedia/commons/5/5a/Подделки_рукописей_и_народных_песен_%28Пыпин%29.pdf> [accessed 15 March 2023].

[33] Ibid.

[34] Nerthercott, *Writing History*; Byford, *Literary Scholarship*.

[35] Ibid., pp. 4, 30.

[36] Spasovich, *Vechnye sputniki*, p. 660.

is especially needed when evidence takes the form of *predanie* (legend), that is a narrative of the past passed through and coloured by the 'prism of the other's conviction'.[37] In light of these reflections, Merezhkovskii's foreswearing of critical judgement must have struck Spasovich as especially reckless. After all, in Smirnova's memoir the truth of the 'real' Pushkin passes not through one but 'through two consecutive prisms: intelligence and consciousness first of the mother and then of the daughter'.[38]

Spasovich devoted considerable efforts to cataloguing the various instances of inauthenticity plaguing Smirnova's *Notes* and to establishing its apocryphal status.[39] He patiently laid out a whole litany of chronological errors, demonstrable misattributions of words and ideas, and evident misstatements of widely known or easily discoverable facts. Nor did he shy away from making less straightforwardly factual judgements. For instance, the dull and pedantic harangues to which Smirnova's Pushkin treats his interlocutors have, according to Spasovich, no trace of Pushkin's sparkling intelligence. And the prim tastes, demure persona and fervent religiosity displayed by Smirnova's Pushkin misrepresent and diminish the real one.

Spasovich also made a point of highlighting Smirnova's naive stratagems. He comments, for instance, on her practice of repeating a falsity as a way of asserting its authenticity. And he points out the absurdity of insisting that the memoir, written in French and translated into Russian in the offices of *Severnyi vestnik*, captured accurately and contemporaneously the Russian of Aleksandra's illustrious acquaintances. Although the *Notes* keeps suggesting that what it offers is 'truth not only in content but in form, that Smirnova documented everything Pushkin said exactly as he said it, in reality, under Madame Smirnova's pen Pushkin as we know from his own letters and from the tales of his friends and contemporaries vanishes altogether'.[40] Moreover, to Spasovich's mind, the fact that no one has ever seen Aleksandra's original records or even copies of those records renders Ol′ga's obviously flawed process even more problematic. Whether in origins, style or reference, in Spasovich's view, Smirnova's *Notes* brims with inauthenticity.

Still, Spasovich does not counter Merezhkovskii's in toto acceptance of Smirnova's memoir with its in toto rejection. Such a move, too, would be historically regressive. If earlier in the century, the formal theory of evidence dictated automatic dismissal of untrustworthy sources, with the

---

[37] Spasovich, *O teorii*, p. 8.
[38] Spasovich, *Vechnye sputniki*, p. 664.
[39] Zhitomirskaia, 'K istorii memuarnogo naslediia', p. 330.
[40] Spasovich, *Vechnye sputniki*, p. 665.

passage of time historians came to rely on reason and analysis to plumb even less than reliable documents and artefacts for hidden rudiments of historical truth.[41] This is the spirit in which Spasovich approaches Smirnova's *Notes*. When he argues that 'at present, the 1895 *Notes* of A. O. Smirnova as they have been managed by her daughter Ol´ga Nikolaevna Smirnova will not do as a historical source', the implication is that a more analytically minded researcher and scrupulous editor could produce a different result.[42] To Spasovich, the memoir represents a complex fusion of 'the undoubtedly authentic' (*nesomnenno dostovernoe*) with 'the fabled' (*skazochnoe*) which, in his view, was to a large extent enabled by the disorderliness of the records.[43] A careful analysis and rigorous examination of the documents — including of the kind Merezhkovskii especially despised: tracing their provenance, comparing physical copies, verifying dates and authorship — could reclaim the deposits of historical truth and free 'the genuine remembrances of the past' from the layers of later incrustations.[44]

Engelhardt and Rozanov: 'We are not in court'
Spasovich's review of Merezhkovskii's *Companions* caused a controversy of its own. Much of the response, however, was triggered not by Spasovich's critique of Merezhkovskii — Spasovich was hardly alone in criticizing the *Companions* — but by his representation of Pushkin. Some, like the writers Nikolai Engelhardt and Vasilii Rozanov, responded to Spasovich directly. Others, like the lawyer Anatolii Koni and the philosopher Vladimir Solov´ev, did so without acknowledging him by name. In the process, by implication, and sometimes even explicitly, they also took a position on Smirnova's memoir and on the problem of fact and authenticity.

This subsequent debate reveals that the clash between the approaches to historical authenticity reflected more than generational tastes or professional dispositions and habits of the mind. As we will see, the lawyer Koni, a member of the older generation and no admirer of modernism, shared Merezhkovskii's position on the memoir's authenticity. On the other

---

[41] Pravilova, 'Truth, Facts, and Authenticity'.
[42] Spasovich, *Vechnye sputniki*, p. 675.
[43] Ibid., p. 663.
[44] The view that proving inauthenticity of the *Notes* was not the end but the beginning of their study and of the efforts to reclaim it for scholarly use was later shared by generations of scholars, from P. E. Shcheglov, one of the first professional 'Pushkinists', to S. V. Zhitomirskaia, the foremost Soviet expert on the Smirnova archive. Zhitomirskaia ultimately prepared the scholarly edition of *The Notes* as part of the 'Literaturnye pamiatniki' series. See A. O. Smirnova-Rosset, *Dnevnik. Vospominaniia*.

hand, Solov'ev, often regarded as the progenitor of Russian symbolism, opposed the cavalier approach to fact typical of the new brand of literary criticism. As Rozanov's and Engelhardt's indignant reactions to Spasovich make especially clear, an important dividing line in this round of the debate was politics. Central to their outrage was Spasovich's Polish origins and his profession as a lawyer, both of which presumably predisposed him to needless quibbling about facts which went hand in hand with a disparaging view of Pushkin and of Russia itself.

To Spasovich's mind, Smirnova's Pushkin comes across as something of Tsar Nicholas's pet, a proper and docile courtier much like Smirnova herself. Merezhkovskii, too, 'composes his own Pushkin, after his own taste, after his own likeness', blatantly disregarding any fact, testimony, or other kind of historical evidence that may get in the way of his preconceived idea.[45] Both produce simplifying idealizations that fail to capture the 'real' Pushkin in all the complexity of his genius, personality and biography. In Merezhkovskii's case in particular, the portrait of Pushkin as a never-changing, radiant Apollo, exuding only cheerfulness and gaiety passes over in silence the tragedy of his position after the Decembrist revolt when he was forced to pay for Nicholas's magnanimity (the tsar forgave Pushkin for his ties with the Decembrists) with self-censorship and even with loyalist, chauvinistic verse.[46] Spasovich also went on to challenge Merezhkovskii's restatement of the prevalent view that Pushkin's death in his duel with d'Anthès was an inevitable result of the vicious society's persecution of unappreciated genius. Ever since the publication of 'Ruslan and Liudmila' (1820), Spasovich argues, Pushkin enjoyed the stature of Russia's greatest poetic talent until his early death, so the complaints about the hostile and stifling environment should be checked into the archive, 'along with the whole romantic wardrobe'.[47] As to the public's eventual cooling toward Pushkin in the 1830s, Spasovich puts the blame for it at Pushkin's own feet. Quoting Adam Mickiewicz, Spasovich suggests that the public ceased seeing Pushkin as its 'spiritual guide' because he stopped nourishing it with the kinds of ideas and emotions that it craved during the dark years of Nicholas's reign.[48]

---

[45] Spasovich, *Vechnye sputniki*, p. 676.

[46] Boris Eikhenbaum echoed Spasovich's point in 'D. S. Merezhkovskii kak kritik', in *D. S. Merezhkovskii. Pro et contra: lichnost' i tvorchestvo Dmitriia Merezhkovskogo v otsenke sovremennikov*, St Petersburg, 2001, pp. 324–25.

[47] Spasovich, *Vechnye sputniki*, p. 680.

[48] Ibid. p. 681.

At the time when the cult of Pushkin was taking hold of Russian educated society, Spasovich's essay was perceived by many as an outright assault on the poet's reputation. The reaction was as swift as it was negative. Within weeks of Spasovich's publication, Nikolai Engelhardt, the conservative writer and future co-founder of 'The Russian Assembly' (Russkoe sobranie), a right-wing nationalist organization, came out with a response in the politically like-minded newspaper, *New Time*. Titled 'Spasovich o Pushkine' (Spasovich on Pushkin, 1897), the article pays only cursory attention to Merezhkovskii. Engelhardt's focus is on discrediting Spasovich's method and on replacing his slanderous portrait of Pushkin with an admiring one of Engelhardt's own making. Despite the purely literary nature of Spasovich's contribution, Engelhardt made a point of emphasizing his career as a lawyer.

Engelhardt's opening gambit is to remind the reader of the derogatory moniker 'sophist' used in reference to defence attorneys and first introduced by Evgenii Markov in his 1875 article, 'Sofisty XIX veka' (The Sophists of the Nineteenth Century). The article eviscerated the legal profession and installed in the public mind the image of the lawyer as the modern sophist, the cynical and amoral 'adulterer of thought' (the term later used by Dostoevskii in *The Brothers Karamazov* in reference to Fetiukovich, an unprincipled defence attorney partially based on none other than Spasovich). For Engelhardt, however, even the word 'sophist' is not pejorative enough to reflect the full extent of Spasovich's corruption. Spasovich is a practitioner of eristic, a combative and dishonest style of argumentation that is even less concerned with truth than sophistry. 'A daughter of the vulgar street, not of philosophical porticos', eristic is interested merely in 'shutting the opponent's trap'.[49] In Engelhardt's telling, Spasovich's only goal was to diminish Pushkin, which he did by importing from his legal practice the strategy of witness smearing and of quibbling with facts. According to Engelhardt, in questioning the authenticity of Smirnova's memoirs or pointing out flaws in Merezhkovskii's cogitations, Spasovich was aiming to deny Pushkin's greatness. If both 'witnesses' are wrong in their portrayals of Pushkin, their praise must be groundless, and Pushkin never was the sage and the prophet they claim. This tactic, Engelhardt notes, might be successful in court. 'But we are not in court', he observes tersely. 'We are talking about Pushkin. We can form our opinion independently of Mr Spasovich.'[50]

---

[49] Nikolai Engelhardt, 'Spasovich o Pushkine', *Novoe Vremia*, 7661, 27 June 1897.
[50] Engelhardt, 'Spasovich o Pushkine'.

Spasovich's legal career was also a salient point for Vasilii Rozanov, who positioned his contribution, the article titled 'Dva vida "pravitel´stva"' (The Two Types of 'Government') which also appeared in *New Time*, as a follow-up and an extension to Engelhardt's. Like Engelhardt, Rozanov was incensed with Spasovich's assault on Pushkin, especially with the suggestion of Pushkin's servility to Nicholas and dishonourableness toward the Decembrists. And like Englehardt, he focused his attack not on disproving this view but on setting the record straight regarding Spasovich's main occupation. Whatever ambitions he may have as a literary critic, in Rozanov's estimation, Spasovich cannot be regarded as a fellow contributor to Russian letters, let alone as someone who can sit in judgement of Pushkin. It is not merely that decades of Spasovich's literary contributions cannot come close to the value of one throwaway line from Pushkin. Spasovich 'is not worthy of the name [of a writer] genuinely lofty in its meaning' because he lacks talent, originality and conviction. He is nothing more than a dilettante and an impostor, 'a well-fed and self-satisfied attorney, whose opera omnia could be conveniently titled "In the Hours of Leisure"'.[51]

In Rozanov's presentation, Spasovich's 'main' profession is key to his approach both to Pushkin and to his own writing. In accusing Pushkin of servile submission to power, Spasovich is merely channelling his own subjection: both to his clients' interests and to his readers' tastes. Not a real writer himself, Spasovich cannot comprehend that Pushkin retained the only freedom that mattered: his independence from his reading audience. As an illustration and proof of Spasovich's baseness, Rozanov reminds the reader of what many saw as the lowest point of Spasovich's legal career — his defence of one Stanislav Kronenberg in a scandalous child abuse case two decades earlier. Spasovich's defence of Kronenberg, on trial for cruel beatings of his young daughter with a switch, turned on the definition of torture and of parental punishment. Whereas in court, in the interest of the case, Spasovich went to extreme lengths to defend the conservative view of patriarchal authority and to whitewash the use of the switch, in print he projected a liberal attitude demanded by his readership. Someone this unprincipled and a lawyer to boot, Rozanov suggests, is in no position to make moral pronouncements about Pushkin.

To Rozanov, Spasovich's approach to Pushkin reveals his hatred for Russia. Spasovich, according to Rozanov, belongs to 'those segments of

---

[51] V. V. Rozanov, 'Dva vida "pravitel´stva"', in *O pisatel´stve i pisateliakh*, ed. A. N. Nikoliukin, *Sobranie sochinenii*, Moscow, 1994–2009, vol. 4, pp. 20–26 (p. 21).

society and literature of which the late Dostoevskii said [...] that they are brimming with "animal malice" toward Russia'.[52] Like Engelhardt, Rozanov never directly mentions Spasovich's Polish origins. But the reference to his profession as a lawyer (often demonized as quintessentially un- and even anti-Russian), the details of the Kronenberg case Rozanov chooses to recall, as well as the direct and indirect allusions to Dostoevskii, whose anti-Polish prejudice informed, at least in part, his critique of Spasovich, leave no doubt that Spasovich's presumed foreignness is a key trigger behind Rozanov's — and Engelhardt's — outraged response. Focused more on discrediting Spasovich than on offering a different conception of Pushkin (whom elsewhere Rozanov dismissed as irrelevant and obsolete), 'The Two Types of "Government"', is prompted by Rozanov's hostility toward the Pole Spasovich daring to sully the national treasure like Pushkin.

Solov'ev: 'False judgments' vs 'false facts'
That Spasovich's Polish origins motivated many of his critics was publicly noted by Vladimir Solov'ev when, in 'Osoboe chestvovanie Pushkina. Pis'mo v redaktsiiu *Vestnika Evropy*' (A Peculiar Celebration of Pushkin: A Letter to the Editorial Board of *The European Messenger*), he commented on the three lonely voices (Spasovich's, Tolstoi's and his own) that dared to desist from an all-out Pushkin worship. While Tolstoi's opinion was, in Solov'ev's words, surrounded with 'deferential silence', Spasovich's take on Pushkin 'was immediately attributed to his Polish bias'.[53]

'A Peculiar Celebration' was published in 1899, the year of the Pushkin centennial. It was the second in what became a three-essay series with 'Sud'ba Pushkina' (Pushkin's Fate) the first and the most controversial of the three appearing in 1897, and the last one, 'Znachenie poezii v stikhotvoreniiakh Pushkina' (The Significance of Poetry in Pushkin's Verse) five months after 'A Peculiar Celebration'.[54] 'A Peculiar Celebration' was a response to the Jubilee issue of *Mir iskusstva*, the main outlet of Russian symbolism, which marked the anniversary with the articles by Merezhkovskii, Rozanov and other Silver Age modernists.

---

[52] Ibid.

[53] V. Solov'ev, 'Osoboe chestvovanie Pushkina', in S. M. Solov'ev and E. L. Radlov (eds), *Sobranie sochinenii Vladimira Sergeevicha Solov'eva*, 2nd edn, 9 vols, St Petersburg, 1911–13, 9, pp. 277–87 (p. 286).

[54] On Solov'ev's Pushkin essays, see William Mills Todd III, 'Vladimir Solov'ev's Pushkin Triptych: Toward a Modern Reading of the Lyrics', in Gasparov, Hughes and Paperno (eds), *Cultural Mythologies of Russian Modernism*, pp. 253–63.

As the intellectual forerunner of Russian symbolism, Solov'ev would seemingly be their natural ally. But this was not the case. Both in his views on art and in his approach to fact, Solov'ev was leagues apart from his intellectual heirs, as the debate on Pushkin demonstrates.

It was not merely that Solov'ev had a general antipathy toward Nietzsche-inspired visions of art, which decoupled the good and the beautiful, embraced by Merezhkovskii and like-minded critics. He also objected to what he saw as a cult-like idealization of Pushkin and insisted on the need to separate Pushkin-the-poet from Pushkin-the-man, arguing that his poetic genius far outstripped his moral virtues. To Merezhkovskii's worshipful vision of Pushkin as a sage, prophet and key figure of Russian spiritual revival, who overcame the pagan-Christian divide and absorbed into himself the very essence of the Russian national spirit, Solov'ev counterposed a portrait of a morally flawed and often frivolous man, even as he recognized Pushkin as a great poet.

All three of Solov'ev's Pushkin articles post-dated Spasovich's response to the *Companions* and came out in *Vestnik Evropy*, the same outlet where Spasovich's review had earlier appeared. But with the exception of 'A Peculiar Celebration', where he called out the nationalist animus as the main motivation of Spasovich's critics, Solov'ev made no other direct reference to Spasovich. Nevertheless, both in his assessment of Pushkin's biography and his insistence on the importance of fact, Solov'ev quietly but firmly sided with the famous lawyer. Especially redolent of Spasovich is 'Pushkin's Fate', the first essay of the series, that appeared in print a mere three months after Spasovich's review.

Like Spasovich, Solov'ev outraged the public by challenging the notion that Pushkin was a victim of fate, where fate was understood as a mean and uncomprehending 'crowd' persecuting the unappreciated genius. The facts of Pushkin's biography, Solov'ev argued, stubbornly resist this interpretation of his life and death. Using language identical to Spasovich's, Solov'ev contrasted the 'real, historical Pushkin', whose portrait emerges from the totality of known 'facts' and 'details', to various Pushkins composed by other critics after 'their own image and likeness'.[55]

That among such 'composers' of personal Pushkins Solov'ev counted Merezhkovskii is evident from his discussion of their critical approach. Solov'ev rejects it precisely for its subjectivity, which was, we remember, the self-proclaimed hallmark of Merezhkovskii's critical method. The image of Pushkin as 'a teacher of paganism's cheerful wisdom and a prophet of

---

[55] Solov'ev, 'Sud'ba Pushkina', in *Sobranie sochinenii*, vol. 9, pp. 33–60 (pp. 49, 36, 57).

[...] the renewed cult of heroes', which Solov'ev dismissed for its frivolity and arbitrariness, is also an obvious swipe at Merezhkovskii. And so is an unexpected comparison between Pushkin admirers and Pushkin hecklers, who, according to Solov'ev, rely on the same bag of tricks. If Merezhkovskii cast Pushkin's foremost detractor Pisarev as the ultimate symbol of growing barbarism and degradation, Solov'ev tauntingly argued that 'the present-day adorers of Pushkin' apply to their idol Pisarev's own method — 'but from the other end and in a far more ridiculous fashion'. What makes the adorers' method more ludicrous (if also more pernicious) is its utter disregard for facts. To highlight the distinction, Solov'ev lays bare the logic behind each approach. Pisarev rejected Pushkin because he was not a social reformer. The demand, Solov'ev notes, was arbitrary, but the fact was correct. The new 'Pushkomaniacs', in contrast, while preserving the bad habit of making subjective demands and applying arbitrary criteria, implement an even worse scheme. Having declared Nietzschean philosophy the measure of true greatness and Pushkin a great man, they conclude that Pushkin was a Nietzschean *avant la lettre*. If Pisarev's conclusion was merely 'a false judgement', the Pushkomaniacs assert 'a false fact'.[56]

Facts and logic are also a topic in 'A Peculiar Celebration'. While the contributors to the Jubilee issue differed in their views on Pushkin, they all shared a type of intuitive, reason-defying approach which Solov'ev described as 'logic-transcending'.[57] And while he chided all of them, including Merezhkovskii, for flippancy, incoherence and obscurity, Solov'ev's main target this time was Rozanov. Again, among Solov'ev's chief concerns was Rozanov's irresponsible attitude toward fact. Thus, musing about the well-known episode when the young Nikolai Gogol', freshly arrived in St Petersburg, attempted to visit Pushkin, Rozanov asked if this might have been the same night when Mikhail Lermontov wrote his famous poem, 'Vykhozhu odin ia na dorogu' ('I Go Out On the Road Alone'), a lyrical meditation on existential themes inspired by the sight of a star-studded sky. 'Who knows?' Rozanov asks cryptically, suggesting the possibility.[58]

---

[56] Ibid., pp. 48, 49.

[57] Solov'ev coined the terms 'sverkhlogichnyi' and 'sverkhlogichnost' as a pun on Nietzsche's 'sverkhchelovek' to describe the methods of *Mir iskusstva* contributors who wrote on the Pushkin jubilee. See 'V. S. Solov'ev protiv Ispolnitel'nogo lista', *Sobranie sochinenii*, vol. 9. pp. 288–93 (pp. 292, 288).

[58] V. V. Rozanov, 'Zametka o Pushkine', in *Sobranie sochinenii*, vol. 7, pp. 420–26 (p. 424).

To Solov'ev, Rozanov's 'Who knows?' sounds like so much pompous nonsense. 'Well, anyone knows, and if one does not, one can make necessary inquiries and easily find out when exactly Gogol´ met Pushkin, and to which period Lermontov's poem dates back', Solov'ev retorts. 'And having found this out, *anyone* can see that at issue are two facts separated by long years, and that the Petersburg autumn night' when Gogol´ visited Pushkin 'could not possibly have been the same sparkling night that inspired Lermontov [...] many years after Pushkin's death'.[59] For Solov'ev, Rozanov's glaring disregard for even the modicum of historical accuracy is a trademark of the 'reason-transcending' approach of the new critics-'orgiasts'.[60]

Although Solov'ev refrained from expressing his solidarity with Spasovich directly, his portrait of Pushkin and the way he went about constructing it was met with a similar rebuke. Of course, unlike Spasovich, Solov'ev could not be attacked for his ethnic, religious, or professional background. Instead, his depiction of Pushkin's persona, grounded, as he argued, in a careful attention to fact, was perceived as an extension of his anti-nationalist views which began to take shape already in the 1880s. For example, in his 'Sud nad Pushkinym' (The Trial of Pushkin, 1901), the lawyer and literary critic Boris Nikol´skii expressed outrage with what he saw as Solov'ev's denigration of the poet, whom he described as 'an unimpeachably, gallantly noble man whose lofty character remains beautiful even in his deepest delusions'.[61] For the ultra-right nationalist, Orthodox monarchist, and the future Black Hundreds member Nikol´skii, Solov'ev's view of Pushkin was inseparable from his rejection of Russian nationalism and exclusivism. 'An inveterate slanderer of Russia', Solov'ev, according to Nikol´skii, was defaming not only Pushkin but Russia itself. For Nikol´skii, 'Solov'evshchina' figures next to positivism, 'zhidovshchina' and other 'swinish elements' plaguing Russian life.[62]

---

[59] V. Solov'ev, 'Osoboe chestvovanie Pushkina. Pis´mo v redaktsiiu *Vestnika Evropy*', in *Sobranie sochinenii*, p. 281.

[60] 'V. S. Solov'ev protiv Ispolnitel´nogo lista', p. 292; Solov'ev, 'Osoboe chestvovanie Pushkina', p. 277 and *passim*.

[61] Boris Nikol´skii, 'Sud nad Pushkinym', in *Sokrushit´ kramoly*, ed. O. A. Platonov, Moscow, 2009, pp. 312–39, 333. Nikol´skii's language echoed that of St Petersburg metropolitan. See Jeffrey Brooks, 'Russian Nationalism and Russian Literature: Canonization of the Classics', in I. Banac et al (eds), *Nation and Ideology: Essays in Honor of Wayne S. Vucinich*, Boulder, CO, 1981, pp. 315–34, especially p. 322.

[62] Quoted in Dmitry Stogov, 'Predislovie', in *Sokrushit´ kramoly*, p. 32.

Koni: The 'official' Pushkin and 'retrospective intuition'

If Solov'ev quietly sided with Spasovich and demanded respect for facts, the lawyer Anatolii Koni took the opposite view. One of the most prominent jurists of his era, Koni, like Spasovich, was also a literary critic with a special interest in Pushkin. His 1899 lecture 'Nravstvennyi oblik Pushkina' (The Moral Persona of Pushkin), delivered to the academy of sciences during the days of the Pushkin centennial, was a central event of the official festivities and was attended by a contingent of ministers and members of the imperial court and family.[63] Composed in the key of official patriotism, the lecture was a veiled response both to Spasovich and to Solov'ev.

Whereas Solov'ev's Pushkin is an artistic genius but a morally flawed man, Koni's Pushkin is a devout Christian, a good husband and a loyal subject. He combines in himself humility and benevolence and dedicates his gift to 'the spiritual service to the people'.[64] He exudes the spirit of tolerance and is concerned with the rights of women and humane treatment of the criminal. His, in short, are the virtues cherished by the mainstream Russian intelligentsia to which Koni himself belonged. Even in his legal views, Koni's Pushkin is his intellectual ally. The primacy of 'higher justice' over law and freedom in evidence interpretation are said to be Pushkin's deeply held convictions as they were Koni's own.[65] When Solov'ev later observed that it was sometimes hard to tell whether Pushkin admirers wanted 'to do the honour to Pushkin by counting him among such superb people as [themselves] or to do the honour to [themselves] by claiming like-mindedness with Pushkin', Koni might well have been among the admirers Solov'ev had in mind.[66]

Significantly, one of the sources for Koni's lecture was Smirnova's *Notes*. Koni made a point of announcing this from the outset and of using Smirnova's name throughout. As was fitting for the official celebration, Koni never mentioned the controversy surrounding the memoir. But Spasovich was as much of a foil for Koni as was Solov'ev. Years after Spasovich challenged the memoir's authenticity, Koni validated it once again by openly drawing on it in his lecture. As if to pre-empt potential

[63] On the Pushkin centennial, see Marcus C. Levitt, 'Pushkin in 1899', in Gasparov, Hughes and Paperno (eds), *Cultural Mythologies of Russian Modernism*, pp. 183–203.

[64] A. F. Koni, 'Nravstvennyi oblik Pushkina', in *Sobranie sochinenii v vos'mi tomakh*, 8 vols, Moscow, 1966–69, 6, pp. 24–59 (p. 52).

[65] Ibid., p. 48.

[66] Solov'ev, 'Znachenie poezii v stikhotvoreniiakh Pushkina', in *Sobranie sochinenii*, vol. 9, pp. 294–347 (p. 298).

complaints about his relaxed attitude toward historical authenticity, Koni enlisted Pushkin as an ally.

In the lecture, Koni praised what he called Pushkin's 'retrospective intuition', by which he meant something like a gift for discerning historical truths intuitively rather than through conventional academic research.[67] In Koni's mind, 'retrospective intuition' bypasses the search for historical facts to activate a type of artistic perception necessary for accessing the past. Elsewhere, Koni used 'retrospective intuition' interchangeably with 'poetic intuition', defining it as an ability to enliven the past by feeling one's way into it and thereby making the reader co-feel it as well.[68] In Koni's view, for 'the artist of the past' to remain neutral to his subject is tantamount to withdrawal 'into dead objectivity'. It is not enough, according to Koni, 'to furnish — fruitlessly and mechanically — the reader's mind and memory with numerous ethnographic, historical and archaeological facts'. The place to look for the past is 'one's own heart. The past that is contained in reason alone is dead', Koni wrote citing the Goncourt brothers.[69]

In denigrating 'dead' objectivity and equally 'dead' reason, in prioritizing personal intuition over the search for historical fact, and in speaking of 'enlivening' the past by 'feeling' one's way into it, Koni sounds like Merezhkovskii or any number of the Silver Age intellectuals, as we have seen. To be sure, it would be a mistake to see Koni as Merezhkovskii's all-out ally. Like Spasovich, he disliked modern art in general and had a strong antipathy to Merezhkovskii in particular.[70] Nevertheless, whatever distance might have separated the lawyer and traditionalist Koni from the writer and experimentalist Merezhkovskii, in the context of the Pushkin debate, Koni proved closer to Merezhkovskii than to his fellow-lawyer Spasovich.

Although Koni's Pushkin bears little resemblance to Merezhkovskii's, the two portraits share an important commonality: both emerge from a relaxed approach to historical fact. That the neo-romantic programme of privileging what Merezhkovskii called 'empathetic excitement' and intuitively grasped 'inner' meanings over 'dispassionate historical authenticity' would appeal to Koni is not especially surprising. It gave cover to his voluntaristic re-invention of Pushkin into a late nineteenth-century model Russian *intelligent* of loyalist persuasion suitable, as Koni

---

[67] Ibid., vol. 6, p. 37.
[68] A. F. Koni, 'Baron N. N. Vrangel´ i russkoe proshloe', in *Starye usad´by. Ocherki istorii russkoi dvorianskoi kul´tury*, St Petersburg, 1999, pp. 298, 300.
[69] Ibid., pp. 303, 297–98.
[70] A. F. Koni, *Sobranie sochinenii*, 6, pp. 641–42.

believed, for the official celebration.[71] But in joining with the likes of Merezhkovskii, Engelhardt and Rozanov, Koni was also giving vent to his ideological disapproval of Spasovich. For even Koni, whose middle-of-the-road liberalism entailed a milder form of nationalism than Rozanov's or Engelhardt's, regarded Spasovich's approach to Pushkin as a form of anti-Russian prejudice. Although in the lecture (and elsewhere) Koni refrained from expressing his disapproval publicly, privately, he, too, considered Spasovich's departure from Pushkin worship as a moral stain on his colleague's reputation on a par with his defence of Kronenberg. And like Rozanov and Engelhardt, he, too, linked it to Spasovich's Polishness.[72]

Conclusion

The Pushkin Myth began taking shape since Gogol' first declared him the national poet in 1835.[73] Following Dostoevskii's 1880 speech, where he amplified Gogol''s identification of Pushkin with Russia and Russian national identity, Pushkin became increasingly politicized, as various parties vied with each other over control of his image to lay claims to particular visions of the past, present and future and to validate their political and cultural agendas. The fin-de-siècle Pushkin debate further contributed to the politicization of Pushkin's image. However different in tone and tenor, the reverential portraits of the poet produced by the intellectuals of the era generally agreed on Pushkin's centrality to Russian culture and national identity. In contrast, even if they acknowledged the supreme quality of Pushkin's artistic genius, the accounts that were less laudatory of his life and persona, eschewed such nationalist inflection.

What distinguishes the Smirnova controversy and especially the surrounding Pushkin debate from earlier disputes about the poet's legacy and reputation is a greater transparency of the link between the participants' politics and their modes of engaging with the past. The fusion of Pushkin with Russia, typical of nationalist and official patriotic narratives, was aligned with the neo-romantic revival of subjective intuition as a basis for historical depiction, an approach that had little interest in facts, especially when they could get in the way of ritualized reverence. Conversely, accounts devoid of nationalist fervour were more attuned to positivist methods of inquiry, and they put greater stock in facts and historical authenticity. As these accounts tended to depart from the

[71] Todd makes a similar observation in note 3 to 'Vladimir Solov'ev's Pushkin Triptych', p. 261.

[72] See Koni's letter to V. D. Komarova in Koni, *Sobranie sochinenii*, vol. 8, pp. 191, 400.

[73] N. V. Gogol', 'Neskol´ko slov o Pushkine' (A Few Words about Pushkin).

rapidly crystallizing Pushkin Myth, they quickly came under fire for their methods as much as for their substance. Not only were they perceived as unpatriotic assaults on Pushkin as the repository of an idealized national identity; they were also condemned as un-Russian in their fixation on facts. In this sense, the fin-de-siècle Pushkin polemic both prefigures the patterns of Pushkin debates to come,[74] and illustrates how in politicized, nationalist narratives, concern with historical authenticity yields to an intuitivist approach to the past, bolstered, when needed, by apocryphal and partisan sources.[75]

[74] For an informative discussion of how, in the context of the late-Soviet *russkost'* debates, reason-guided, evidence-based knowledge in Pushkin scholarship was demonized by nationalist literary critics as unpatriotic, unspiritual and un-Russian, see Kathleen Parthé, *Russia's Dangerous Texts: Politics Between the Lines*, New Haven, CT, 2004, chapter 4. See also, Wendy Slater, 'The Patriots' Pushkin', *Slavic Review*, 58, 2, 1999, pp. 407–27.

[75] In this sense, the fin-de-siècle debate offers an illustration to Savel´eva and Poletaev's assertion that the intuitivist approach to 'constructing the past' (which in their history of academic historiography was fully replaced by positivism already in the middle of the nineteenth century) remains operative in the 'extremely ideologized nationalist histories oriented toward irrational stereotypes'. Savel´eva and Poletaev, *Istoriia i intuitsiia*, p. 47.

Nabokov's Cinematic Sensibility and Film Strategy in *The Defense*

BARBARA WYLLIE

> You will see that this little clicking contraption will make a
> revolution in our life — in the life of writers. [...] We shall
> have to adapt ourselves to the shadowy screen and to the
> cold machine. A new form of writing will be necessary.[1]

Introduction

Lev Tolstoi's comments on the importance of film and the challenges it
presented to literary convention were made just over a decade after the
first screenings of moving pictures, his words anticipating the role cinema
was to play in modernist art in both Russia and the West in the first
decades of the twentieth century. In terms of its role in Nabokov's fiction,
critical studies have so far concentrated on the influence of cinema that
was immediately contemporary to particular works, for example, German
Expressionist and Soviet silent film on *The Eye* and *Despair*, or American
film noir on *Lolita*.[2] This article, however, will explore a broader range
of cinematic influence that extends back to Nabokov's formative years in
pre-revolutionary Russia. It will argue that his cinematic sensibility was

Barbara Wyllie is Managing Editor of the *Slavonic and East European Review* and is based
at the School of Slavonic and East European Studies, University College London.

    This article began as a talk given in October 2021 at the international symposium,
'Nabokov and Cinema', at l'Université de Paris-Sorbonne. I would like to thank the
Editorial Board of the *Slavonic and East European Review* for steering it through the
submissions process. I am particularly grateful to the *SEER* readers for their helpful
comments and suggestions, and to Professor Julian Graffy for his support, encouragement
and invaluable insights. I would also like to thank Thomas Straker, at the University of
Bristol Library's Special Collections, for his assistance in accessing copies of the German
film paper, *Licht-Bild-Bühne*.

[1] 'Lev Tolstoy: A record by I. Teneromo of a conversation with Tolstoy on his eightieth
birthday, August 1908', quoted in Jay Leyda, *Kino: A History of the Russian and Soviet Film*,
3rd edn, London, 1983, pp. 410–11 (p. 410). English translation by David Bernstein first
published in the *New York Times*, 31 January 1937 (hereafter, 'Conversation with Tolstoy').
[2] See, for example, Alfred Appel, Jr., *Nabokov's Dark Cinema*, New York, 1974, and
Barbara Wyllie, *Nabokov at the Movies: Film Perspectives in Fiction*, Jefferson, NC, 2003.

not only formed long before his arrival in émigré Berlin, but was also foundational to an interaction with cinema that continued throughout his career. At the same time it will focus on his third novel, *The Defense* (*Zashchita Luzhina*), a work that has not yet been explored in terms of cinema, to reveal the ways in which he deployed the themes, styles and techniques of film in his portrayal of a protagonist who has until now been considered primarily in terms of chess.

The 'story of a chess player who [is] crushed by his genius'[3] was written between February and August 1929, published serially in the émigré quarterly, *Sovremennye zapiski*, in October 1929 and in book form by Slovo in 1930. That Nabokov should have chosen to write a novel that focused on the struggles of a chess genius is unsurprising, considering that he had been involved in the game from a young age, not merely as a casual player, but as someone who, during his time in Berlin, participated in tournaments and published chess problems in the émigré press.[4] While planning his second novel, *Korol', Dama, Valet* (*King, Queen, Knave*), during the autumn of 1927, Nabokov was already conjuring ideas for new protagonists, inspired by the battle taking place between José Capablanca and Alexander Alekhine at the World Chess Championship in Buenos Aires.[5] In October, he composed a poem about a chess grandmaster, who as he plays becomes 'part of the sixty-four-celled black and white world of the chessboard'.[6] By the time *King, Queen, Knave* came out the following

---

[3]   Letter from Vladimir Nabokov to James Laughlin, 27 November 1941, in Dmitri Nabokov and Matthew J. Bruccoli (eds), *Vladimir Nabokov: Selected Letters 1940–77*, London, 1991, p. 39. In his foreword to the 1964 English translation of *Zashchita Luzhina*, Nabokov described Luzhin's genius as 'sterile' and 'recondite' (*The Defense*, New York, 1990, p. 10), echoing Vladislav Khodasevich some thirty years before, who 'perceptively remarked [that] Luzhin's tragedy lies in the fact that he is a "talent" and not a genius' ('V. Sirin. "Zashchita Luzhina"', *Vozrozhdenie*, 11 October 1930). See Aleksandr Dolinin, 'Istinnaia zhizn´ pisatelia Sirina: pervye romany', in Vladimir Nabokov (V. Sirin´), *Sobranie sochinenii russkogo perioda v piati tomakh: Stoletie so dnia rozhdeniia, 1899–1999. Tom. 2: 1926–1930*, compiled by N. I. Artemenko-Tolstoi, St Petersburg, 1999, p. 35.

[4]   The chess theme first appears in 'Christmas', a story written at the end of 1924, which Nabokov described as 'oddly resembl[ing] the type of chess problem called "selfmate"'. Vladimir Nabokov, *Collected Stories*, London, 2001, p. 647. Nabokov refers to Luzhin's suicide as a form of selfmate, or 'sui-mate'. *The Defense*, New York, 1990, p. 8. All subsequent references are to this edition.

[5]   Nabokov played Alekhine, as well as the grandmaster Aron Nimzowitsch, in Berlin in 1926. See Brian Boyd, *Vladimir Nabokov: The Russian Years*, London, 1993, p. 259. Alekhine won the World Championship in 1927.

[6]   James Murray Slater, 'Chess as a Key to Solving Nabokov's *Korol', Dama, Valet*', unpublished MA thesis, University of North Carolina at Chapel Hill, NC, 2009, pp. 46–47 (p. 1) <https://core.ac.uk/download/pdf/210603874.pdf> [accessed 9 April 2023]. 'Shakhmatnyi kon´' ('The Chess Knight', 1927) was first published in *Rul'*, 23 October

autumn, however, Nabokov was thinking not only about chess, but also about film. He tried writing an article,[7] but turned instead to a poem, 'Kinematograf' ('The Cinematograph'),[8] which he published in the émigré newspaper, *Rul'*, on 25 November 1928,[9] just two months before he began working on *The Defense*.

While Nabokov's more implicit treatment of film in *The Defense* sets it apart from the other more explictly cinematic early novels — *Mary* (*Mashen'ka*, 1926), *King, Queen, Knave* and *The Eye* (*Sogliadatai*, 1930)[10] — its particular manipulation of camera eye perspective establishes it as a direct precursor to *The Eye*. *The Defense* can therefore be considered as one of a sequence of works in which Nabokov explores the creative implications of cinema, encompassing style, narrative technique and characterization, inspired by a fascination with film that extended from contemporary cinematic culture to film technology and its impact on ways of seeing.

Key to understanding Nabokov's relationship with film is to recognize that his fascination with the medium began in St Petersburg before the revolution. In terms of *The Defense*, it is important to place it, as an example of Nabokov's early cinematic work, within a late-nineteenth-century movement that began to privilege the visual and which developed into an explicit response to and direct engagement with cinema in the

---

1927. Also collected in Vladimir Nabokov, *Stikhotvoreniia i poemy*, Moscow, 1997, pp. 410–11, and Nabokov, *Sobranie sochinenii russkogo perioda*, pp. 558–59. For commentary on this and a set of three chess sonnets Nabokov wrote in 1924, see 'Cards and Chess: *King, Queen, Knave* and *The Luzhin Defense*', in Thomas Karshan, *Nabokov and the Art of Play*, Oxford and New York, 2011, pp. 82–106 (pp. 92–95). For background on the genesis of the novel and commentary, see Boyd, *The Russian Years*, pp. 275, 289, 321–40, and Dolinin, 'Istinnaia zhizn' pisatelia Sirina', pp. 26–41. For commentaries on *The Defense* as a 'chess novel', see Brian Boyd, 'The Problem of Pattern: Nabokov's *Defense*', *Modern Fiction Studies*, 33, 4, 1987, pp. 575–604; 'Text and Pre-Text in *The Defense*', in D. Barton Johnson, *Worlds in Regression: Some Novels of Vladimir Nabokov*, Ann Arbor, MI, 1985, pp. 83–92; '*The Defense*: Secret Asymmetries', in Leona Toker, *Nabokov: The Mystery of Literary Structures*, Ithaca, NY, 1989, pp. 67–87; '*The Defense*', in Vladimir E. Alexandrov, *Nabokov's Otherworld*, Princeton, NJ, 1991, pp. 58–83; 'The Evil Differentiation of Shadows', in Julian Connolly, *Nabokov's Early Fiction: Patterns of Self and Other*, Cambridge and New York, 1992, pp. 75–100; Strother B. Purdy, 'Solus Rex: Nabokov and the Chess Novel', *Modern Fiction Studies*, 14, 4, 1968–69, pp. 379–95, and Luke Parker, 'The Gambit: Chess and the Art of Competition in *The Luzhin Defense*', *Russian Review*, 76, 2017, pp. 438–57.

[7] See Luke Parker, *Nabokov Noir: Cinematic Culture and the Art of Exile*, Ithaca, NY, 2022, pp. 55 and 209, n. 98.

[8] Rather than the non-literal translation, 'Cinema'. 'Cinematograph' is the original term for 'a motion-picture camera, projector, theater, or show'. Mirriam-Webster online <https://www.merriam-webster.com/dictionary/cinematograph> [accessed 14 October 2023].

[9] See Nabokov, *Stikhotvoreniia i poemy*, pp. 412–13, and Nabokov, *Sobranie sochinenii russkogo perioda*, pp. 595–96. Future references will be to this edition.

[10] For commentary, see Wyllie, *Nabokov at the Movies*, chapters 2–3.

early modernist era. In order to demonstrate this, the article will begin with a discussion of critical responses to cinema in Nabokov's work in the light of his comments on film and the record of his own movie-going. It will then turn to an exploration of the origins of Nabokov's cinematic sensibility in pre-revolutionary Russia, set against Russian and European literary responses to the advent of cinema at the turn of the twentieth century. The second half of the article will focus on *The Defense*, discussing the contemporary influence of Pudovkin and Shpikovskii's *Chess Fever* (*Shakhmatnaia goriachka*, 1925) and American slapstick comedy, concluding, by way of 'Kinematograf', with an analysis of Nabokov's deployment of cinematic technique in the novel, paying particular attention to the close-up, the novel's image system and camera eye perspective.

Nabokov's cinema: Reference and influence
Responding to Alfred Appel Jr.'s 1974 study of film in his fiction, Nabokov remarked that '[y]our basic idea, my constantly introducing cinema themes, and cinema lore, and cinema-metaphors into my literary compositions cannot be contested of course'.[11] Despite a number of subsequent studies ranging from textual and theoretical analyses to comparisons of the cinematic adaptations of *Lolita* with both novel and screenplay,[12] critics

---

[11] Letter to Alfred Appel, Jr. dated 8 November 1974 in Nabokov and Bruccoli (eds), *Selected Letters*, p. 537. See also, Appel, *Nabokov's Dark Cinema*.

[12] See Beverly Gray Bienstock, 'Focus Pocus: Film Imagery in *Bend Sinister*', in J. E. Rivers and Charles Nicol (eds), *Nabokov's Fifth Arc: Nabokov and Others on His Life's Work*, Austin, TX, 1982, pp. 125–38; Marie Bouchet, '"L'image-mouvement" nabokovienne: paradoxes de l'écriture cinématique à travers l'étude des œuvres de Vladimir Nabokov', in J. Nacache and J. L. Bourget (eds), *Cinématismes: La littérature au prisme du cinema*, Bern, 2012, pp. 293–313; Yannicke Chupin, '"A Most Pleasurable Antiphony": Dialogues d'auteurs et aspects de la réflexivité dans *Lolita* de Vladimir Nabokov et Stanley Kubrick', *Études anglaises*, 62, 4, 2009, pp. 415–27; Lara Delage-Toriel, *Lolita de Vladimir Nabokov et Stanley Kubrick*, Paris, 2009; Galya Diment, 'From Bauer's Li to Nabokov's Lo: *Lolita* and Early Russian Film', *Cycnos*, 24, 1, 2006 <https://epi-revel.univ-cotedazur.fr/publication/item/582>; Tatyana Gershkovich, 'Self-Translation and the Transformation of Nabokov's Aesthetics from *Kamera Obskura* to *Laughter in the Dark*', *Slavic and East European Journal*, 63, 2, 2019, pp. 206–25; Marina Grishakova, *The Models of Space, Time and Vision in V. Nabokov's Fiction: Narrative Strategies and Cultural Frames*, Tartu, 2012; Yuri Leving, 'Filming Nabokov: On the Visual Poetics of the Text', *Russian Studies in Literature*, 40, 3, 2004, pp. 6–31; Yuri Leving, 'Eystein or Eisenstein? Tricking the Eye in Nabokov's *Pale Fire*', *Nabokov Online Journal*, 6, 2012 <http://www.nabokovonline.com/uploads/2/3/7/7/23779748/26_leving_nabokov_and_eisenstein_pdf.pdf>; Gavriel Moses, *The Nickel Was for the Movies: Film in the Novel from Pirandello to Puig*, Los Angeles, CA, 2005; Thomas Allen Nelson, 'Kubrick in Nabokovland', in *Kubrick: Inside the Film Artist's Maze*, Bloomington, IN, 2000, pp. 56–81; Parker, *Nabokov Noir*; Péter Tamás, 'The Attraction of Montages: Cinematic Writing Style in Nabokov's *Lolita*', *Nabokov*

hesitate to acknowledge the extent of Nabokov's engagement with the medium, tending instead to focus on the tension between cinema and literature as valuable and enduring artistic forms, as he expressed, for example, in a 1931 essay:

> People like to say to themselves that the most impersonal writer, making the best possible portrait of his century, cannot tell us as much as the little gray gleam of an old-fashioned film. Wrong. Contemporary cinematographic methods which seem to our eyes to give a perfectly exact image of life will probably be so different from the methods used by our great-great-nephews that the impression that they will give of the movement of our era [...] will be rendered false by the very style of the photography.[13]

Nabokov's primary concerns were that the worlds of his novels should be true — 'the good memoirist [...] does his best to preserve the utmost truth of the detail' — and that his art should not date: 'there can be no question that what makes a work of fiction safe from larvae and rust is not its social importance but its art, only its art.'[14] Here he demonstrates a key understanding of cinema and photography as evolving forms, as technologies that are constantly changing and adapting, but which, in doing so, can render their past incarnations 'false', or redundant. Literature, he contends, has a greater ability to offer a more accurate and vital record of time and place, as it does not rely on equipment that is subject to the vagaries of 'style', as well as physical deterioration or obsolescence. Critics, however, seem to be more comfortable with the idea of film as 'insidious technology' that 'bolster[s] memory artificially'[15] (even though Nabokov

Online Journal, 10, 2016 <http://www.nabokovonline.com/uploads/2/3/7/7/23779748/5_tamas.pdf>; Barbara Wyllie, 'Experiments in Perspective: Cinematics in Nabokov's Russian Fiction', *New Zealand Slavonic Journal*, 2002, pp. 277–88; Wyllie, *Nabokov at the Movies*; Barbara Wyllie, 'Nabokov and Cinema', in Julian Connolly (ed.), *The Cambridge Companion to Nabokov*, Cambridge and New York, 2005, pp. 215–31; Barbara Wyllie, '"My Age of Innocence Girl": Humbert, Chaplin, Lita and Lo', *Nabokov Online Journal*, 9, 2015 <http://www.nabokovonline.com/uploads/2/3/7/7/23779748/4_9_2015_barbara_wyllie_age_of_innocence_girl.pdf>.

[13] Vladimir Nabokov, 'Writers and the Era' (1931), in Brian Boyd and Anastasia Tolstoy (eds), *Think, Write, Speak: Uncollected Essays, Reviews, Interviews, and Letters to the Editor*, London, 2019, p. 105. Luke Parker argues that '"the little gray gleam of an old-fashioned film" is echoed across [Nabokov's] work of the 1930s', with its origins in 'Tolstoi', a poem written in 1928, in which 'Tolstoy's fiction is more real than the illusory verisimilitude of technologically mediated reproductions of his image'. See *Nabokov Noir*, pp. 17–19.

[14] Vladimir Nabokov, *Strong Opinions*, New York, 1990, pp. 186 and 33.

[15] 'Tolstoi', quoted in Parker, *Nabokov Noir*, p. 17.

qualifies this statement with the word 'sometimes'), and on the notion that cinema is an artistically valueless form of commercialized mass entertainment (Nabokov 'is usually remembered for the broad satire he aims at the surface contents of popular cinema — "for it is always windy in filmland"'),[16] than acknowledging the multidimensional role that film plays in his art, as he also openly stated.[17]

This position could be said to have emerged from the first critical responses to film, and particularly the intense debates amongst Russian émigré intellectuals during the 1920s,[18] yet there is no evidence that Nabokov participated directly in these arguments. Nevertheless, this tendency to focus on the dissenting voices, to which Nabokov may or may not have aligned himself, exemplifies a reluctance to concede that he had a genuine artistic interest in film. Similar presumptions have been made about other contemporary modernist writers, for example, T. S. Eliot. David Trotter has pointed out that critics have tended to take one of two positions, either to insist on the absence of any 'formative effect' of cinema on his writing, or to emphasize Eliot's 'powerful aversion to cinema', ultimately choosing 'to quote his remarks about cinema at their most dismissive, and in isolation'.[19] Yet, Trotter argues, Eliot 'was a good deal more interested in cinema [...] than he was in film. The genres which most exercised his imagination — the Western; slapstick comedy — were all in the mainstream; indeed, they *were* the mainstream'. Not only this, but he '*chose*, in certain texts, or in certain episodes or scenes, the "disembodiment of perception by technique"', that is, to deploy the mechanisms of film in his work.[20]

---

[16] Moses, *The Nickel Was for the Movies*, p. 43, quoting Vladimir Nabokov, *Laughter in the Dark*, New York, 1991, p. 118.

[17] Parker, for example, contends that '[m]uch of Nabokov's engagement as a writer with the cinema was practical and strategic, and [...] directly related to the rapidly changing material circumstances of exile in interwar Europe. At the same time, this writerly engagement certainly includes within it his stylistic and intellectual engagement with the medium of film' — essentially in terms of 'the roles of spectator and actor', and 'how studio and screen interact as a metaphor of exile'. *Nabokov Noir*, pp. 20–21.

[18] For commentary, see ibid., ch. 2.

[19] David Trotter, 'T.S. Eliot and Cinema', *Modernism/Modernity*, 13, 2, April 2006, pp. 237–65 (p. 237). Emphasis in the original.

[20] Ibid., p. 241, quoting from 'Tradition and the Individual Talent', 1919. Emphasis in the original. The notion of the 'disembodiment of perception by technique' echoes Viktor Shklovskii's theory of 'ostranenie', or 'making strange' (a term he first used in 1917 in the essay, 'Art as Device' ['Iskusstvo kak priem']), which was 'first and foremost an urgently required and utterly relevant theoretical answer to the tremendous impact early cinema had on the early avant-garde movements in pre-revolutionary Russia'. Annie van den Oever, 'Introduction: Ostran(n)enie as an "Attractive" Concept', in eadem (ed.), *Ostrannenie: On*

It is important, therefore, to acknowledge the distinction between Nabokov's response to cinema as a popular medium of inconsistent quality and an unreliable means of recording time, and his interest in film, which through its privileging of vision and its mechanistic extension of visual capacity, tests and expands our sensory experience such that our way of interacting with the world is both profoundly challenged and radically altered.

Another problem hindering investigation of cinema in Nabokov's work is the difficulty in identifying specific allusions to contemporary films. Nabokov's single objection to Appel's study was that:

> You and I and other Nabokovians will readily realize that stylistically you are slanting my works movieward in pursuit of your main thought; yet it would be rather unfair if less subtle people [...] were to conclude I had simply lifted my characters [...] from films which you know and I don't.[21]

This level of doubt, and there being barely any record of what Nabokov had seen — in interviews he listed a handful of American comedies from the 1920s and '30s, as well as a few silent French and German films from the same era, one American *film noir*, one Lubitsch and one Hitchcock comedy[22] — has served as a major disincentive for scholars, who have found the process of mining literary allusion in Nabokov's work far more productive than searching in vain for references to particular films. There is the description of the instantly recognizable image of Harold Lloyd in *The Defense*, for example,[23] while Charlie Chaplin makes appearances in Nabokov's work from the early poetry and short stories to *Lolita* and *Pnin*,[24] but otherwise the allusions are more oblique — to Edward G.

'Strangeness' and the Moving Image, The History, Reception, and Relevance of a Concept, Amsterdam, 2010, pp. 11–18 (p. 11). See also, 'Art as Device (1917/1919)', in Alexandra Berlina (ed., trans.), *Viktor Shklovsky: A Reader*, New York and London, 2017, pp. 73–96.

[21] Nabokov, *Selected Letters*, p. 538.

[22] Buster Keaton, Harold Lloyd, Charlie Chaplin, the Marx Brothers, Laurel and Hardy; Carl Theodor Dreyer's *La Passion de Jeanne d'Arc* (1928) and René Clair's *Sous les toits de Paris* (1930), *Le Million* (1931) and *À Nous la Liberté* (1931), all of which Nabokov described as 'a new world, a new trend in cinema' (*Strong Opinions*, pp. 163–64); F. W. Murnau's *The Last Laugh* (1924), Robert Weine's *The Hands of Orlac* (1924) and Josef von Sternberg's 1932 *Shanghai Express* (Appel, *Nabokov's Dark Cinema*, pp. 137 and 58); Greta Garbo in Ernst Lubitsch's 1939 *Ninotchka* (although Véra remembered them also seeing her in Clarence Brown's 1926 *Flesh and the Devil*); Robert Siodmak's *The Killers* (1946), and Alfred Hitchcock's 1955 *The Trouble with Harry* (Appel, *Nabokov's Dark Cinema*, pp. 41, 187, 208, 129).

[23] Nabokov, *The Defense*, p. 247.

[24] See Wyllie, '"My Age of Innocence Girl"', pp. 10–11.

Robinson in *Transparent Things*, or to what appears to be a film by either Pudovkin or Eizenshtein in *The Gift*.[25] Elsewhere there are only indications of general film genres, for example in *Lolita* to gangster movies, musicals and Westerns, and references that are 'almost exclusively the product of secondary sources', as in *Ada*.[26] Yet in 1932 when confronted by the real prospect of turning one of his stories into a Hollywood film, Nabokov remarked that he 'literally adored the cinema and watched motion pictures with great keenness'.[27] In his first decade in Berlin, Nabokov and his wife Véra would go 'about once a fortnight [...] to the cheap corner [movie] theatre',[28] and on trips to Paris during the 1930s he would visit a cinema owned by an old school friend.[29] In Berlin he would go even more frequently with another friend, Georgii Gessen, who wrote film reviews for *Rul'*, taking advantage of the free tickets on offer.[30] Apart from being an audience member, Nabokov worked as a film extra, at one time considered becoming a movie star, wrote slapstick-inspired scenarios with his friend, Ivan Lukash, for Berlin's Bluebird cabaret theatre, and negotiated the rights to his novels and stories with film producers and agents.[31]

Nabokov's son Dmitri also confirmed that his father 'loved the cinema', and remembered going with him to local movie theatres in Boston and Cambridge when they were first in America, especially the Saturday morning screenings of comedy 'shorts' featuring the Marx Brothers, the Three Stooges, Abbot and Costello, and 'an occasional Buster Keaton'.[32] Nabokov may have claimed to have a 'rotten memory' when it came to recalling 'names and numbers',[33] but biographers have described him being able to cite specific films and scenes in precise detail,[34] indicating that

[25] See Wyllie, 'Nabokov and Cinema', p. 221.

[26] Vladimir Nabokov, *The Annotated Lolita*, edited by Alfred Appel, Jr, New York, 1991, p. 170, and Appel, *Nabokov's Dark Cinema*, p. 59.

[27] Boyd, *The Russian Years*, p. 376. Nabokov also discussed the possibility of turning *The Defense* into a film with the émigré Russian theatre director Nikolai Evreinov in Paris in 1932: 'I'll talk with [...] Evreinov about the chess film.' See Nabokov, *Letters to Véra*, 1 November 1932, p. 202. It was eventually adapted by director Marleen Gorris and screenwriter Peter Berry as *The Luzhin Defence* (2000).

[28] Boyd, *The Russian Years*, p. 363. See also, Parker, *Nabokov Noir*, pp. 32–34.

[29] Leving, 'Filming Nabokov', p. 7.

[30] See Parker, *Nabokov Noir*, pp. 30–37, and 'Appendix: Georgy Gessen's Film Reviews for *Rul'* (1924–1931)', pp. 187–94.

[31] See Boyd, *The Russian Years*, pp. 205, 232–33, 227, 231, 233–34, 254 and 376. Also, Parker, *Nabokov Noir*, chapters 3 and 4.

[32] Dmitri Nabokov, correspondence with the author, 1 July 1996.

[33] Nabokov, *Strong Opinions*, p. 140.

[34] Ibid., pp. 163–64, and Appel, *Nabokov's Dark Cinema*, p. 206, where Appel describes Nabokov re-enacting the opening of Siodmak's *The Killers*.

he was paying far more attention than has generally been acknowledged, which also becomes apparent when looking back to his accounts of his experiences of film in pre-revolutionary Russia.

Nabokov's cinematic sensibility: Origins and context

While Nabokov may have been a regular film-goer in Berlin and Paris, his interest in the industry and its product did not begin in emigration. In his autobiography, he introduces a key connection between film technology, memory and art by depicting the succession of tutors hired by his parents between 1900 and 1911 as a sequence of magic lantern shows. These culminate in the rather chaotic, and not particularly adept, 'Educational Magic Lantern Projections'[35] that his last tutor, Lenski, would subject them to on winter Sunday afternoons in St Petersburg. Nabokov describes how they commandeered a disused nursery, and moved various pieces of furniture out to make space for the projector at one end, with seating 'arranged for a score of spectators' and curtains drawn to block out the light.[36] Although Lenski is projecting slides rather than film, this arrangement typifies the initial use of private homes for screenings, where rooms were turned into nascent cinema auditoria by tearing down walls and introducing heavy black-out curtains. It is interesting that Nabokov mentions the 'fire-hazard considerations' of using this kind of equipment, revealing his awareness of the frequent and sometimes serious cinema fires caused at the time by highly combustible film stock and faulty projectors.[37] Despite the boredom Nabokov describes during these 'sessions', he nevertheless concludes the episode by drawing an explicit link, retrospectively, between the magic lantern and the microscope that establishes the critical role of optical tools in his art:

> Now that I come to think of it, how tawdry and tumid they looked, those jellylike pictures, projected upon the damp linen screen [...] but, on the other hand, what loveliness the glass slides as such revealed when simply held between finger and thumb and raised to the light. [...] In later years, I rediscovered the same precise and silent beauty at the radiant bottom of the microscope's magic shaft. [...] There is, it would seem, in the

---

[35] Vladimir Nabokov, *Speak, Memory: An Autobiography Revisited*, New York and Toronto, 1999, p. 124.

[36] Ibid., p. 125.

[37] Ibid. See Yuri Tsivian, *Early Cinema in Russia and Its Cultural Reception*, Chicago, IL and London, 1994, pp. 51–52, and Denise J. Youngblood, *The Magic Mirror: Moviemaking in Russia, 1908–1018*, Madison, WI, 1999, pp. 36–38.

dimensional scale of the world a kind of delicate meeting place between imagination and knowledge, a point, arrived at by diminishing large things and enlarging small ones, that is intrinsically artistic.[38]

Gavriel Moses has argued that Nabokov's already acute visual sensitivity, nurtured during his childhood by his mother and his art teacher, Mstislav Dobuzhinskii, and further refined by his early lepidopteral pursuits, is enhanced by his interest in 'the mediating optical apparatus'.[39] Here, it is a magic lantern slide, but elsewhere it could be any number of optical tools, used consistently to extend and intensify the experience of vision, and especially the potency of memory. Moses also makes the connection between Nabokov's deployment of optical media in his work and the manner in which he presents the operation of artistic consciousness — the poet's 'capacity of thinking of several things at a time', or 'cosmic synchronization'.[40] Drawing on a 1969 interview, in which Nabokov outlined the close association between the 'power of pure imagination' and the 'apparatus to reproduce those events optically within the frame of one screen', i.e. a 'video camera',[41] Moses shows how Nabokov 'transcends the traditional opposition between seeing with the eyes of a scientist and seeing with the eyes of an artist'.[42] This ability to synchronize visually and then project a simultaneously-generated collection of images as a coherent, imagined construct also enables Nabokov to accumulate details that reinforce the significance of particular individuals and events in his autobiography. It is a process epitomised by an episode at a St Petersburg cinema in 1915.

As a teenager, Nabokov frequented the numerous cinemas that sprang up during the 1910s in pre-revolutionary St Petersburg, a city that was equally charged with the cosmopolitan cinematic glamour of 1920s Berlin, which was described by a British visitor as 'one big movie, like an impossible dream'.[43] Similarly, but over a decade earlier, Nevskii Prospekt

---

[38] Nabokov, *Speak, Memory*, p. 128.

[39] Moses, *The Nickel Was for the Movies*, p. 45. Greta Slobin similarly argues that in *The Gift* (*Dar*, 1937), the mnemonic 'device of [cinematic] double exposure, discovered by Khodasevich a decade earlier', had become 'a part of the writer's arsenal'. Greta N. Slobin, *Russians Abroad: Literary and Cultural Politics of Diaspora (1919–1939)*, Boston, MA, 2013, pp. 86–90 (p. 89).

[40] Nabokov, *Speak, Memory*, p. 169.

[41] Nabokov, *Strong Opinions*, p. 154.

[42] Moses, *The Nickel Was for the Movies*, pp. 45–46.

[43] Laura Marcus, *The Tenth Muse: Writing About Cinema in the Modernist Period*, Oxford and New York, 2007, p. 333, quoting film critic Kenneth Macpherson writing to the American writer and poet, H.D., in October 1927. Both wrote for *Close Up* (1927–33),

had turned into 'a continuous strip of cinemas extend[ing] from Nikolaev Station to Anichkov Bridge':

> In the evening, when the noisy, brightly lit Nevsky Prospect hardly contains an infinite flow of people, among the uncountable lights of cinemas the bright electric star on one of the enormous central buildings of the needle-shaped avenue remains visible from the distance. This star is the 'mark' of one of the best cinemas in Russia, The Royal Star.[44]

The Royal Star, which opened in 1909, was one of the first of a number of lavish cinemas that introduced a level of luxury and spectacle which for most could only be dreamt of. This boom in cinema-building democratized movie-going, making not only film — national and international — but the cinematic environment, complete with state-of-the-art technology, available to all.[45] The popularity of this new film culture was even sanctioned by the imperial family, who had their own cinema constructed at Tsarskoe selo.[46] By 1914, St Petersburg/Petrograd had 229 cinemas, with '15 on Nevskii Prospect alone'.[47] Nabokov mentions two of them in his autobiography, the Parisiana and the Piccadilly,[48] where he would

the English-language journal which focused on film as an art form.

[44] Quoted in Anna Kovalova, 'The Film Palaces of Nevsky Prospect: A History of St Petersburg's Cinemas, 1900–1910', in Birgit Beumers (ed.), *A Companion to Russian Cinema*, Chichester, 2016, pp. 21–44 (pp. 23 and 27). The Royal Star (Roial Star, no. 48 Nevskii prospekt) changed its name in 1911 to the Soleil', and continued to function until 1917. See Anna Kovalova, *Kinematograf v Peterburge 1907–1917: Kinoproizvodstvo i fil'mografiia*, St Petersburg, 2012, pp. 365 and 367, and Kovalova, 'The Film Palaces of Nevsky Prospect', pp. 26–28, 38.

[45] See Tsivian, *Early Cinema in Russia*, pp. 19–20.

[46] Leyda, *Kino*, p. 67. See also, Oksana Chefranova, 'The Tsar and The Kinematograph: Film as History and the Chronicle of the Russian Monarchy', in M. Braun, C. Keil, R. King, P. Moore and L. Pelletier (eds), *Beyond the Screen: Institutions, Networks and Publics of Early Cinema*, Bloomington, IN, 2012, pp. 63–70.

[47] Youngblood, *The Magic Mirror*, p. 12. In comparison, 'before 1910, Charlottenburg [where Nabokov lived in the 1920s and '30s] had been a quiet and distinguished bourgeois residential area, but by the end of the decade it developed into a cinema centre second only to Potsdamer Platz (Berlin-Mitte), with eight picture palaces of more than 1000 seats and ten other cinemas.' Brigitte Flickinger, 'Cinemas in the City: Berlin's Public Space in the 1910s and 1920s', *Film Studies*, 10, Spring 2007, pp 72–86 (p. 80). By 1925, Berlin had 342 cinemas, nearly 40 of which were located in Charlottenburg. See Parker, *Nabokov Noir*, pp. 32–34.

[48] See Kovalova, 'The Film Palaces of Nevsky Prospect', pp. 28–32. The Parisiana (1914), at no. 80, is also mentioned in Nabokov's 1933 story, 'The Admiralty Spire', in which the narrator 'remember[s] dressing like Max Linder'. Nabokov, *Collected Stories*, p. 350. Linder, the world-famous French film comedian, visited St Petersburg in 1913. On Linder as a popular phenomenon in pre-revolutionary Russia, see Yuri Tsivian, 'Russia

settle into the 'last row of seats' on winter afternoons with his girlfriend, Valentina Shul'gina ('Tamara').[49] By choosing what would have been the cheap seats at the back of the stalls (presumably for privacy) rather than the more exclusive, expensive seats higher up in the auditorium, Nabokov participated directly in the democratic turn of St Petersburg film-going:

> The cost of tickets on Nevsky certainly blocked access for the 'common people,' but in the halls of first-rate cinemas an officer and a milliner, a student and a salesman, an official and a lady of light conduct would sit next to each other. Such combinations were most of all characteristic for the tram. [...] In front of the screen everyone had equal rights, and class and property distinctions were insignificant.[50]

Nabokov's focus when recalling this episode with Tamara is not on her, however, or their interactions, or their surroundings, or even the films being shown, but on the current state of Russian cinema:

> The art was progressing. Sea waves were tinted a sickly blue and as they rode in and burst into foam against a black, remembered rock (Rocher de la Vierge, Biarritz — funny, I thought, to see again the beach of my cosmopolitan childhood), there was a special machine that imitated the sound of the surf, making a kind of washy swish that never quite managed to stop short with the scene but for three or four seconds accompanied the next feature — a brisk funeral, say, or shabby prisoners of war with their dapper captors. As often as not, the title of the main picture was a quotation from some popular poem or song and might be quite long-winded, such as *The Chrysanthemums Blossom No More in the Garden* or *Her Heart Was a Toy in His Hands and Like a Toy It Got Broken*. Female stars had low foreheads, magnificent eyebrows, lavishly shaded eyes. One famous director had acquired in the Moscow countryside a white-pillared

---

1913: Cinema in the Cultural Landscape', in Richard Abel, *Silent Film*, London, 1999, pp. 194–214 (pp. 198–203). Pnin favoured Linder, along with his compatriot, André Deed (aka Pan Glupishkin), over the 'clown', Charlie Chaplin (Vladimir Nabokov, *Pnin*, London, 1960, p. 67). The Piccadilly (1913), nicknamed the '*bonbonnière*', was the first purpose-built cinema on Nevskii Prospekt (at no. 60). It had an 800-seat auditorium, designed so that the screen could be seen from anywhere, a ventilation system that pumped air through the ceiling, purple ramp lights and a state-of-the-art projection booth. See Kovalova, 'The Film Palaces of Nevsky Prospect', p. 30, and Anna Kovalova, 'Avenue du cinema: Nevskii Prospekt (1896–1917 godov)', *Seans*, 20 April 2011 <https://seance.ru/articles/avenue-du-cinema/> [accessed 20 October 2022].

[49] Nabokov, *Speak, Memory*, p. 184.

[50] Edgar Arnoldi [Arnol'di], quoted in Kovalova, 'The Film Palaces of Nevsky Prospect', pp. 37–38.

mansion (not unlike that of my uncle),[51] and it appeared in all the pictures he made. Mozzhuhin would drive up to it in a smart sleigh and fix a steely eye on a light in one window while a celebrated little muscle twitched under the tight skin of his jaw.[52]

It is easy to dismiss this description as Nabokov denigrating what at first seems to be a primitive, unsophisticated, rather hackneyed medium (a perfect example of his 'poshlust'),[53] but the passage contains a number of elements that reveal a close engagement with its every aspect, from technology to styles of directing, even to identifying Russia's most famous star, Ivan Mozzhukhin, by his signature 'steely eye' and the 'celebrated' twitch of his jaw. Not only this, but the film titles Nabokov refers to were actual releases. The first, *Ottsveli uzh davno khrizantemy v sadu* (1915) was adapted from a *romans* written in 1910, directed by Aleksandr Arkatov and starring Mozzhukhin and Zoia Karabanova,[54] while *I serdtsem, kak kukloi, igraia, on serdtse, kak kuklu, razbil* was made in 1916 by Czesław Sabiński, also with Karabanova in the lead female role.[55]

Although Nabokov's opening statement could be read as ironic, it could equally be read literally, demonstrative of his awareness of the actual development of film technology in two key areas; first, film colouring and second, the use of sound. Technicians had been experimenting with colour and sound since the mid 1900s.[56] Tinting film stock was a common

[51] Nabokov is referring to Rozhdestveno, the 'neo-classical manor' belonging to his uncle, Vasily Ivanovich Rukavishnikov (Uncle Ruka), which was left to Nabokov in 1916 as part of the inheritance he was never able to claim. See Boyd, *The Russian Years*, p. 121.

[52] Nabokov, *Speak, Memory*, pp. 184–85.

[53] Nabokov's transcription of *poshlost'* (vulgarity), which he defined as 'not only the obviously trashy but also the falsely important, the falsely beautiful, the falsely clever, the falsely attractive'. Vladimir Nabokov, *Nikolai Gogol*, New York, 1961, pp. 63–74 (p. 70). See also his definition in *Strong Opinions*, pp. 100–01: 'Corny trash, vulgar cliches, Philistinism in all its phases, imitations of imitations, bogus profundities [etc.]' (p. 101).

[54] See Veniamin Vishnevskii, *Khudozhestvennye fil'my dorevoliutsionnoi Rossii (Fil'mograficheskoe opisanie)*, Moscow, 1945, p. 72, entry 841. By 1916, Mozzhukhin's 'fame reached its apogee', while 'film entrepreneurs [were] throwing onto the market in immense quantities [...] dramatizations of the most popular romances like "Chrysanthemums"'. A. Garri, *I. I. Mozzhukhin*, 2nd edn, Moscow and Leningrad, 1927, pp. 7–8. With thanks to Julian Graffy for locating these sources.

[55] See Vishnevskii, *Khudozhestvennye fil'my dorevoliutsionnoi Rossii*, p. 97, entry 1151. Karabanova left Russia in 1920 and eventually went to America, where she continued her acting career. In 1957 she played Mrs Volotoff in fellow émigré Rouben Mamoulian's *Silk Stockings* (a remake of Lubitsch's *Ninotchka* — one of Nabokov's favourite films), with Cyd Charisse and Fred Astaire. She died in Los Angeles in 1960. With thanks to Julian Graffy for identifying these two films.

[56] See Tsivian, *Early Cinema in Russia*, pp. 97–98 and 100–03, and Philip Cavendish, 'The Hand that Turns the Handle: Camera Operators and the Poetics of the Camera in

practice, so the 'sickly blue' that Nabokov describes would have been a familiar sight. That he recognized the extent to which it typified the visual style of film at that time is confirmed by his transposition of this same scene into 'The Assistant Producer', a story written some thirty years later. Here the projectionist/narrator describes himself 'technicoloring and sonorizing' his memories, as if they were 'some very ancient motion picture where life had been a gray vibration [...] where only the sea had been tinted (a sickly blue), while some hand machine imitated offstage the hiss of the asynchronous surf'.[57] Meanwhile, Nabokov's memory of the 'special machine' at the cinema on Nevskii Prospekt almost exactly replicates its description in a 1916 publication:

> If at the moment when a wave on the screen was about to crash on the shore you flexed a piece of tin rapidly back and forth with both hands, and at the same time someone else turned the handle of the box, you would get the sound of breaking waves. If you then rapidly tipped the box in the opposite direction the stones would slide down, striking the nails and producing a noise that sounded just like waves ebbing back into the sea, taking pebbles and shells with them.[58]

Despite the difficulty in controlling the timing of the sound with such a cumbersome piece of equipment, this particular machine was expensive, and generally used only in larger cinemas, such as the Piccadilly or the Parisiana. 'The smaller cinemas', as Yuri Tsivian points out, 'made do with a metal bowl, a toy pistol and a police whistle'.[59] However, by 1916 Nabokov's 'special machine' had been succeeded by a new 'universal sound machine', which not only resolved the problem of synchronization, but could also reproduce the sound of thunder and cannon-fire, breaking glass, the 'chugging' of a car, the trampling of hoofs, horses neighing, dogs barking, cats meowing, all contained in something the size of a typewriter.[60] That the difference in the sophistication of sound-effect technology could be measured in only a matter of a year confirms both the accuracy of Nabokov's depiction of the cinema experience in 1915 and the attention he was paying to its means of production.

Pre-Revolutionary Russian Film', *Slavonic and East European Review*, 82, 2, 2004, pp. 201–45 (p. 210).

[57] Nabokov, *Collected Stories*, p. 551.

[58] See Evgenii Maurin', *Kinematograf v prakticheskoi zhizni*, Petrograd, 1916, pp. 181–82 (p. 182), quoted in Tsivian, *Early Cinema in Russia*, p. 100.

[59] Ibid.

[60] Maurin', *Kinematograf v prakticheskoi zhizni*, p. 182.

Nabokov also demonstrates sufficient knowledge of the contemporary Russian cinema industry to recognize the style of director Evgenii Bauer, who was renowned for his grand sets and outdoor locations.[61] Galya Diment has commented that '[a]mong all the directors working at the time, Bauer was probably the closest to young Nabokov's sensibilities and interests'.[62] Nabokov's oblique allusion to Bauer, which establishes a link to his Uncle Ruka via the film-maker's opulent settings, triggers the revelation of a mnemonic system whereby Nabokov uses seemingly random visual details to trace the patterns of his life. Childhood summers on the beach at Biarritz and at his uncle's estate are made vividly present by the moving images on the screen, both to Nabokov as a 16-year-old spectator and to the middle-aged writer sitting in his 'lawn chair at Ithaca, N.Y.'. The images transcend time, interconnecting like the 'tentacles' of consciousness that 'reach out and grope' for meaning in the pattern.[63] Compounding this is the vision of Mozzhukhin, whom Nabokov was to encounter in real life on a film-shoot in Crimea less than three years later,[64] and thus an additional future aspect, embedded within a past moment already brought vividly into the present, is introduced. The cinema screen, therefore, is the vehicle that generates Nabokov's 'cosmic synchronisation', offering him, in all his past, present and even future incarnations, an 'instantaneous and transparent organism of events' in which he, 'the poet, is the nucleus'.[65]

Nabokov's experience of pre-revolutionary Russian cinema, which was technically 'on a par with the American and European industries by the middle of the 1910s',[66] served as the foundation of his experience of silent

---

[61] One critic, reviewing Bauer's A Life for a Life (1916), commented on the film's 'colossal extravagance': 'Columns, columns and more columns... Columns in the drawing-room, by the fire in the office, columns here there and everywhere.' See Silent Witnesses: Russian Films 1908–1919, eds Paolo Cherchi Usai, Lorenzo Codelli, Carlo Montanaro and David Robinson, London and Pordenone, 1989, pp. 326–28 (p. 326). Bauer's columns had a practical function, however, as they 'were used to hide the equipment of the auxiliary lighting'. Yuri Tsivian, 'Evgenii Frantsevich Bauer', in ibid., p. 548.

[62] Diment, 'From Bauer's Li to Nabokov's Lo', p. 4 of 9.

[63] Nabokov, Speak, Memory, p. 169. Moses refers to this process as 'self-projections', and focuses his analysis on Speak, Memory's Biarritz episode. See The Nickel Was for the Movies, pp. 51–58.

[64] Speak, Memory, p. 193. During the revolution most of the Russian film industry decamped to Crimea, which had served until then as an ideal place for location shooting because of its climate and light.

[65] Ibid., p. 169.

[66] Cavendish, 'The Hand that Turns the Handle', p. 203. Cavendish focuses on the innovations of camera operators in terms of set design, lighting, tracking and panning shots, whilst directors like Bauer and Iakov Protazanov experimented with cross-cutting, flashbacks and close-ups. See Youngblood, The Magic Mirror, p. 66; Rachel Morley,

era film in emigration, from London and Cambridge to Berlin.[67] Silent film, 'in the absence of spoken dialogue', naturally 'placed tremendous emphasis on the visual'.[68] It was the form that Nabokov preferred: 'The viewer of a silent film has the opportunity of adding a good deal of his own inner verbal treasure to the silence of the picture', he commented.[69] Not only this, but the visual poetics of silent film also complemented the privileging of vision in Nabokov's art. 'I think in images', he stated. 'Images are mute, but presently the silent cinema begins to talk and I recognize its language.'[70] *The Defense* was written before the first fully synchronized sound film, or 'talkie', came to Berlin in late 1929,[71] so still very much belongs to the silent era, but the range of cinematic devices it deploys, particularly related to point of view, and specifically, the camera eye, which are expressive of early twentieth-century modernism, can also be traced back to a movement that began over two decades before. As Christian Quendler contends:

The camera eye has become emblematic of cinematic modernism, which regards cinema as a hub that connects to a great variety of intellectual inquiries and aspects of cultural life. At the turn from the nineteenth to the twentieth century, psychology, theories of art and literature, philosophy, sociology and cultural theory evolved in mutual exchanges with cinema.[72]

'Gender Relations in the Films of Evgenii Bauer', *Slavonic and East European Review*, 81, 1, 2003, pp. 32–69, and Rachel Morley, *Performing Femininity: Woman as Performer in Early Russian Cinema*, London, New York and Dublin, 2017.

[67] See, for example, stanza 6 of 'Universitetskaia Poema' ('The University Poem', 1926) in Nabokov, *Sobranie sochinenii russkogo perioda*, pp. 560–86 (p. 562), and Vladimir Nabokov, *Collected Poems*, trans. Dmitri Nabokov, ed. Thomas Karshan, London, 2012, pp. 29–54 (p. 31), in which Nabokov describes visiting the cinema in Cambridge as a student.

[68] Cavendish, 'The Hand that Turns the Handle', p. 210.

[69] Nabokov, *Strong Opinions*, p. 165.

[70] From a February 1977 interview. Nabokov, *Think, Write, Speak*, pp. 479–80. See also, *Strong Opinions*, p. 14.

[71] Alan Crosland's *The Jazz Singer* (1927), starring Al Jolson. See Thomas J. Saunders, *Hollywood in Berlin: American Cinema and Weimar Germany*, Berkeley and Los Angeles, CA and London, 1994, p. 224. The film was reviewed by Gessen on 27 November 1929 for *Rul'*. See Parker, *Nabokov Noir*, p. 193.

[72] Christian Quendler, *The Camera-Eye Metaphor in Cinema*, London and New York, 2017, p. 4. The camera-eye metaphor has its origins in Dziga Vertov's 'theoretical manifesto', 'Kinoks: A Revolution' (1923) — 'I am kino-eye, I am a mechanical eye. I, a machine, show you the world as only I can see it' — first demonstrated in the 1924 film, *Kinoglaz* (Kino-Eye). See Annette Michelson (ed.), *Kino-Eye: The Writings of Dziga Vertov*, trans. Kevin O'Brien, Berkeley & Los Angeles, CA and London, 1984, pp. xxiv, 11–21 (p. 17). As Levora Gruic Grmusa and Kiene Brillenburg Wurth argue, '[t]he emergence of the modernist novel is roughly contemporaneous with the birth of film — and with a modernist "frame" of mind that casts the mind as "cinematographic."' 'Cinematography

The advent of cinema at the end of the nineteenth century coincided with an 'onslaught of [sensory] stimulation' brought about by rapid industrialization, urbanization, technological advances and burgeoning commercialization. These elements combined to 'generate a perceptual climate of overstimulation, distraction and sensation', characterized by 'the rapid crowding of changing images, the sharp discontinuity in the grasp of a single glance, and the unexpectedness of onrushing impressions'.[73] This emphasis on the predominantly visual aspect of the 'hypersensory' state recalls the rush of images on a cinema screen, their fleeting, jerky, elusive quality expressive of the 'mobility and ephemerality' that was to become the essence of modernity.[74] Nabokov, however, posited that the emergence of a refined visual perspective, operating not merely as a mode of sensory experience but also as a medium of artistic expression, pre-dated the modern era:

> the development of the art of description throughout the centuries may be profitably treated in terms of vision, the faceted eye becoming a unified and prodigiously complex organ and the dead dim 'accepted colors' (in the sense of 'idées reçues') yielding gradually their subtle shades and allowing new wonders of application.[75]

'All the great writers', he continued, 'have good eyes'.[76]

---

as a Literary Concept in the (Post)Modern Age: From Pirandello to Pynchon', in Kiene Brillenburg Wurth (ed.), *Between Page and Screen: Remaking Literature through Cinema and Cyberspace*, New York, 2012, pp. 184–200 (p. 186). See also, 'Beginnings' in David Seed, *Cinematic Fictions: The Impact of the Cinema on the American Novel up to the Second World War*, Liverpool, 2012, pp. 7–25.

[73] Quoting George Simmel (1903) in Leo Charney and Vanessa R. Schwartz (eds), 'Introduction' to *Cinema and the Invention of Modern Life*, Berkeley and Los Angeles, CA and London, 1995, p. 10; Leo Charney, 'In a Moment: Film and the Philosophy of Modernity', in ibid., quoting 'The Metropolis and Mental Life', in Kurt H. Wolff (ed., trans.), *The Sociology of Georg Simmel* (1913), Glencoe, IL, 1950. See also, Walter Benjamin, 'The Work of Art in the Age of Mechanical Reproduction' (1935), in *Illuminations*, ed. Hannah Arendt, trans. Harry Zorn, London, 2015, pp. 211–44 (esp. pp. 226–30).

[74] Charney and Schwartz, 'Introduction', p. 10. See also Gor'kii's description of the first Lumière Brothers' screening at the Nizhnii Novgorod fair in 1896 in his 'Kingdom of Shadows' review in Leyda, *Kino*, pp. 407–09. The speed of early moving pictures tended to vary depending on the consistency of cameramen operating hand cranks, and also adjustments made by projectionists who were trying to reduce optical flicker. See James Card, *Seductive Cinema: The Art of Silent Film*, New York, 1994, pp. 52–55, and Kevin Brownlow, 'Silent Films — What Was the Right Speed?', in Thomas Elsaesser (ed.), *Early Cinema: Space, Frame, Narrative*, London, 1990, pp. 282–89.

[75] Vladimir Nabokov, *Lectures on Russian Literature*, Orlando, FL, 1981, pp. 24–25.

[76] Ibid., p. 141.

While Nabokov is commenting here on the evolution of literary description, this ability to accurately capture the tiniest nuance of detail — essentially conjuring the mechanistic quality of the camera lens — can also be aligned with a developing form of narrative perspective in nineteenth-century literature that is identifiably proto-cinematic. Eizenshtein was the first film-maker to recognize the ways in which literature anticipated cinema — 'this apparently unprecedented art' — especially in the 'nearness' of Dickens's fiction 'to the characteristics of cinema in method, style, and especially in viewpoint and exposition'.[77] Critics have identified other literary precedents, particularly in the work of Flaubert, Henry James and Joseph Conrad.[78] In his examination of *Madame Bovary*, Alan Spiegel argues that Flaubert adopts a 'reified narrative' that 'replaces the voice of an omniscient novelist with the seeing eye of a man and introduces visual perspective into the novel'. Thus a scene is 'limited by the way [a character's] eyes choose to see it; that truth itself now depends as much upon the angle of vision as upon the object of vision'.[79] Hugh Epstein has argued that the work of Thomas Hardy and Joseph Conrad is predicated on such experiences of 'encounter', whereby their protagonists are 'drawn to sensation, to surfaces, to the meeting point of self and the surrounding world', particularly through vision.[80] Conrad, for example, declared his central artistic aim to be 'by the power of the written word, to make you hear, to make you feel', and 'before all, to make you *see*'.[81] Epstein's study demonstrates the extent to which

[77] Sergei Eisenstein, 'Dickens, Griffith, and the Film Today', in *Film Form: Essays in Film Theory*, edited and translated by Jay Leyda, San Diego, CA, New York and London, 1977, pp. 195–255 (p. 206).

[78] See, for example, Alan Spiegel, 'Flaubert to Joyce: Evolution of a Cinematographic Form', *NOVEL: A Forum on Fiction*, 6, 3, 1973, pp. 229–243; Susan M. Griffin, *The Historical Eye: The Texture of the Visual in Late James*, Boston, MA, 1991; Kendall Johnson, *Henry James and the Visual*, Cambridge and New York, 2007, and Daniel Dufournaud, '"Queer as Fiction": Seeing and Being Seen in Henry James's *The Ambassadors*', *Studies in the Novel*, 54, 1, 2022, pp. 80–99; Hugh Epstein, *Hardy, Conrad and the Senses*, Edinburgh, 2021, and '*The Rescue*: The Physiology of Sensation and Literary Style', *Conradiana*, 43, 2/3, 2011, pp. 25–50. By his teens, 'besides hundreds of other books', Nabokov claimed to have 'read or re-read all Tolstoy in Russian, all Shakespeare in English, and all Flaubert in French'. Nabokov, *Strong Opinions*, p. 46. For an overview of Nabokov's cultural influences during this time, see Barbara Wyllie, 'Childhood', in David M. Bethea and Siggy Frank (eds), *Nabokov in Context*, Cambridge and New York, 2018, pp. 28–34.

[79] Spiegel, 'Flaubert to Joyce', pp. 231 and 232.

[80] Epstein, *Hardy, Conrad and the Senses*, p. 4. Nabokov identified, similarly, a 'close association of the visible and the heard, of shadow light and shadow sound, of ear and eye' in Tolstoi and Proust. See Vladimir Nabokov, *Lectures on Literature*, San Diego, CA, 1980, pp. 220–21.

[81] Joseph Conrad, 'Preface' (1897) to *The Nigger of the 'Narcissus'*, London, 1988, p. xlix. Emphasis in the original. Nabokov mentions Conrad and James in interviews

'Hardy's and Conrad's investigations of how the external world is felt to
be "in us", essentially, how we *see*', was informed by related contemporary
investigations into 'epistemological sensationism'.[82] These ideas could well
have reached the young Nabokov via his father, who had two of the key
works by one of the leading sensationist thinkers of the time, Alexander
Bain, in his library in St Petersburg.[83] Nabokov's early years in Russia,
therefore, which were so guided by his mother's instruction to remember
— '*Vot zapomni*'[84] — and her emphasis on the importance of visual
attention, need to be set against not only the emergence of a hypersensory
trend at the turn of the twentieth century, but also the shifts in philosophy
and scientific understanding that underpinned it, all of which coincided
simultaneously with the advent of moving pictures.

In 1908, Tolstoi commented on the challenges this new art form posed
to traditional literary conventions:

> But I rather like it. This swift change of scene, this blending of emotion
> and experience [...]. It is closer to life. In life, too, changes and transitions
> flash by before our eyes, and emotions of the soul are like a hurricane. The
> cinema has divined the mystery of motion. And that is greatness.[85]

(see *Strong Opinions*, pp. 42, 43, 57, 64, 103, 127, 139 and 147). Joyce became a favourite in
emigration (ibid., p. 46) — Nabokov met him in Paris in 1939 (Boyd, *The Russian Years*,
p. 504). Hardy's *Return of the Native* (1878) and *Jude the Obscure* (1895) were also in his
father's library. See *Sistematicheskii katalog biblioteki Vladimira Dmitrievicha Nabokova*,
St Petersburg, 1904, entry no. 592, p. 25, and 1911, entry no. 2658, p. 14 (with thanks to
Tat´iana Ponomareva, former director of the Nabokov Museum in St Petersburg).

[82] Epstein, *Hardy, Conrad and the Senses*, p. 85. Emphasis in the original. Epstein's
book features extensive discussion of Bain's philosophy set against that of his peers,
including Karl Pearson and William James, whom Nabokov also read as a boy (see Boyd,
The Russian Years, pp. 90–91). See also, M. Gail Hamner, 'Alexander Bain', in *American
Pragmatism: A Religious Genealogy*, Oxford and New York, 2003, pp. 73–88, and Cairns
Craig, 'Alexander Bain, Associationism, and Scottish Philosophy', in Gordon Graham
(ed.), *Scottish Philosophy in the Nineteenth and Twentieth Centuries*, Oxford and New
York, 2015, pp. 95–117.

[83] Entry numbers 2194: 'Bain, Alexander. *Education as a Science*, London, 1896',
and 2264: 'Bain, Alexander. *Les émotions de la volonté*, Paris, 1885', in *Sistematicheskii
katalog*, 1904, pp. 104 and 109. Bain argued 'against any sort of innate, a priori, intuitive,
or underived common-sense cognition'. Rather, he saw sensation 'as the beginning of
conscious life, both intellectual and emotional, and as the foundation of our knowledge,
both of the world and of ourselves'. W. J. Mander, quoting *The Senses and the Intellect*,
in *The Unknowable: A Study in Nineteenth-Century British Metaphysics*, Oxford, 2020,
p. 133. *The Five Senses in Nabokov's Works* (Cham, 2020), a collected volume edited by
Marie Bouchet, Julie Loison-Charles and Isabelle Poulin, provides extensive coverage
of Nabokov's treatment of sensory experience, but makes no mention of sensationist
thought.

[84] Nabokov, *Speak, Memory*, p. 25.

[85] 'Conversation with Tolstoy', p. 410.

Following his concession that same year to the young film-maker, Aleksandr Drankov, who was given exclusive access to film him on his estate, Tolstoi deemed cinema to be 'a good thing'. In 1910 he gave the industry its most meaningful endorsement by announcing that he had 'decided to write for the cinema'.[86] Developments in film techniques and production quality were by then attracting a number of prominent writers to the industry, including Maksim Gor'kii, whose initial reaction to moving pictures had been categorically negative.[87] Others, like Tolstoi, whose *Anna Karenina* 'was soaked in the burgeoning camera culture', were consistently positive. Aleksandr Blok and Andrei Belyi were 'incorporating jagged film syntax into their writing' and 'delighting in the earthiness of cinema culture',[88] while Leonid Andreev who, along with Vladimir Maiakovskii, had begun writing for film, claimed to 'really love the cinema and believe in its future (not greatly, but colossally)'.[89]

Nabokov's position, though, remained ambivalent, balanced between his first-hand experience of the industry in emigration, the ways in which he interacted with the medium in his work, and the delight he took in singling out 'an inept American film' — 'the more casually stupid it was, the more he would choke and literally shake with laughter, to the point where on occasion he had to leave the hall.'[90] The distinction that has to be made here, however, is between a bad film and a good film. Those that Nabokov listed as his favourites, for example, fell into the latter category.[91] Not only this, they featured a selection of classic American slapstick comedies. As we will see in the following section, this genre was to inform

---

[86] See Margarita Vaysman, 'Tolstoy as the Subject of Art, Painting, Film, Theater', in Anna A. Berman (ed.), *Tolstoy in Context*, Cambridge and New York, 2022, pp. 323–35 (p. 330); Youngblood, *The Magic Mirror*, p. 65, and Jay Leyda, *Kino*, p. 44.

[87] In his 'Kingdom of Shadows' review. By 1916 Gor'kii was developing plans for 'an entire film production unit attached to the [Moscow] Art Theatre'. Ibid., p. 77. His initial reaction was shared by many other spectators, who found the early cinema experience 'deeply alienating', although also, like Tolstoi, simultaneously 'exciting and strange'. The 'mute, two-dimensional world' of these moving pictures, in their 'bleak black and white made all this seem slightly ghostly and uncanny, animate and inanimate at the same time. All was familiar, yet it was "made strange" by the new "cinema machine"'. Annie van den Oever, 'Ostranenie, "The Montage of Attractions" and Early Cinema's "Properly Irreducible Alien Quality"', in eadem (ed.), *Ostrannenie: On 'Strangeness' and the Moving Image*, pp. 33–58 (p. 35).

[88] Stephen Hutchings, *Russian Literary Culture in the Camera Age: The Word as Image*, Abingdon and New York, 2004, pp. 39 and 58. Hutchings discusses the influence of photography on nineteenth-century Russian writing, from Gogol' to Turgenev, Tolstoi, Dostoevskii and Chekhov.

[89] Youngblood, *The Magic Mirror*, pp. 65 and 67. Andreev was commenting in 1915.

[90] Boyd, *The Russian Years*, p. 363.

[91] See *Strong Opinions*, pp. 163–64.

the themes and motifs of *The Defense*, along with a contemporary Soviet comedy whose influence has so far been only the subject of conjecture.

'The Defense' and contemporary cinema

One of the key film influences that has been generally assumed by Nabokov scholars is Vsevolod Pudovkin and Nikolai Shpikovskii's 1925 silent comedy, *Chess Fever*.[92] In its visual style it closely parallels *The Defense*, with its chess-obsessed hero surrounded by objects that mirror the black and white squares of a chessboard. These range from patterns on socks and handkerchiefs, hats and cigarette boxes, to the floor tiles in the lobby of his fiancée's apartment block, reminiscent of the final image in Nabokov's novel as Luzhin stares down into the 'chasm' from his fifth-floor bathroom window that obligingly 'divides' beneath him 'into dark and pale squares' (p. 256). Nabokov would no doubt have been curious to see *Chess Fever*'s real-life footage of the First International Chess Championship, held in Moscow between 10 November and 8 December 1925, which was reported on daily in the Berlin émigré press, as well as Capablanca's cameo appearances, in which he plays with a miniature chessboard identical to Luzhin's,[93] but cinema historians have so far concluded that the short film was not amongst the raft of Soviet exports distributed during the late 1920s, and was not shown abroad until it was acquired by New York's Museum of Modern Art Film Library in 1937.[94]

More recent scholarship, however, has changed this picture. Rather than concentrating their exports in the period following the Berlin premiere of Eizenshtein's *Bronenosets Potemkin* (*Battleship Potemkin*) in June 1926, and contrary to the contention that German import restrictions and censorship regulations obstructed the distribution of Soviet films,[95] Russian film

[92] See, for example, Charles Nicol, 'Did Luzhin Have Chess Fever?', *The Nabokovian*, 27, 1991, pp. 40–42; Ol'ga Skonechnaia in *Sobranie sochinenii russkogo perioda*, p. 716 n. 440, and Don Barton Johnson on *NABOKV-L*, 24 October 1997 and 31 July 2000 (<https://thenabokovian.org/node/32549>; <https://thenabokovian.org/node/29477>). In his 'Filming Nabokov', Yuri Leving argues that *Chess Fever* influenced *The Defense* (pp. 9–10), but provides no evidence to support this contention.

[93] Valentinov, Luzhin's chess mentor-cum-movie producer, wants him to make a similar cameo appearance in his new film that will feature a '"real tournament, where real chess players would play with my hero. Turati has already agreed, so has Moser. Now we need Grandmaster Luzhin…"'. *The Defense*, p. 248. For commentary on Nabokov's modelling of Valentinov on the 'regal corpse' of the American film idol, Rudolph Valentino, who died in 1926, and Valentinov's role in the movie business, see Parker, *Nabokov Noir*, pp. 90 and 93–98.

[94] See Leyda, *Kino*, p. 157.

[95] See Denise Hartsough, 'Soviet Film Distribution and Exhibition in Germany, 1921–1933', *Historical Journal of Film, Radio and Television*, 5, 2, 1985, pp. 131–48.

exports began in earnest from April 1922 following the Treaty of Rapallo.[96] Indeed, the initial survival of the Soviet industry was essentially dependent at that time on its trading relationship with Germany.[97] *Chess Fever* was produced by Mezhrapbom-Rus', a joint German-Russian film company set up in 1924, which worked primarily with Lloyd-Film (Lloyd-Kinofilms G.m.b.H), a Berlin-based company that acted as an agent, purchasing export licences and handling distribution. Establishing whether *Chess Fever* was ever shown in Berlin is difficult, however, primarily because of the scant attention short films were paid in the German film press and the Russian émigré papers, which consigned them to the *raznoe* (miscellaneous) columns in favour of reviews of longer, feature-length releases.[98] Compounding this was the tendency to 'consistently ignore everything in Soviet film art that could be understood as "real" cinema', a contention supported by a contemporary German journalist who bemoaned the silent vanishing of new Russian films from German press reviews.[99] Reports in German trade papers, however, indicate that there was an interest in Pudovkin and Shpikovskii's comedy, particularly because of its coverage of the Moscow International Chess Tournament. It was first mentioned in the Berlin-based *Film-Kurier* two days before its Russian release,[100] and at the beginning of 1926, *Kinematograph* announced that 'the little comedy' would be coming to Germany with a number of other new Soviet productions.[101] Although it was indeed one of thirteen films

[96] See Kristin Thompson, 'Government Policies and Practical Necessities in the Soviet Cinema of the 1920s', in Anna Lawton (ed.), *The Red Screen: Politics, Society, Art in Soviet Cinema*, London and New York, 1992, pp. 19–41.

[97] See Nataliya Puchenkina, 'What is so (Un)Exceptional About Soviet Cinema? The Pragmatics of Soviet Film Exports to Germany and France in the 1920s', *Images*, 32, 41, 2022, pp. 45–63.

[98] Luke Parker's listing of the reviews in *Rul'* confirm this: 'Appendix', *Nabokov Noir*, pp. 187–94. See also, Oksana Bulgakova, 'Russische Film-Emigration in Deutschland: Schicksale und Filme', in Karl Schlögel (ed.), *Russische Film-Emigration in Deutschland 1918 bis 1941: Leben im europäischen Bürgerkrieg*, Berlin, 1995, pp. 379–98 (p. 380). For an overview of the machinery of the German film press, see Thomas J. Saunders, 'The Setting: Weimar Germany and the Motion Picture', in *Hollywood in Berlin: American Cinema and Weimar Germany*, Berkeley and Los Angeles, CA, 1994, pp. 34–47.

[99] Rainer Rother, 'In Deutschland entschiedener Erfolg: Die Rezeption sowjetischer Filme in der Weimarer Republik', in Günter Agde and Alexander Schwarz (eds), *Die rote Traumfabrik: Meschrabpom-Film und Prometheus 1921–1926*, Berlin, 2012, pp. 22 and 21, and Bernard von Brentano, *Wo in Europa ist Berlin? Bilder aus den zwanziger Jahren*, Berlin, 1981, p. 220.

[100] '"Das Moskauer Schachturnier im Film": Von der Mejrabpom-Ruß wurde im Rahmen eines Grotesk-Lustspiels das Moskauer Schach-Turnier und alle an im beteiligten Meister aufgenommen.' *Film-Kurier*, 298, 19 December 1925, p. 6.

[101] 'Von den neueren Filmen des Meshrapbom Ruß sind noch zu erwähnen [...]

sold by Mezhrapbom-Rus' to Lloyd-Film in 1925,[102] it seems that *Chess Fever* was not released nationally, but had only a limited screening in Berlin.[103] This accumulation of new information does, however, make it seem more likely that Nabokov could have seen the film, or at least heard about it, as it would have found a ready audience in the city's large and culturally dynamic Russian émigré community.

The film genre with which *Chess Fever* is most closely aligned is contemporary American slapstick comedy. It is a feature noted by a Russian critic writing in January 1926, who compares the film's style of humour to that of Charlie Chaplin, commenting that *Chess Fever* borrows from the 'infinite continuity' of gags from 'a whole raft of comic films', producing 'almost as many of them as Ford cars: 8 per minute'.[104] In Nabokov's novel slapstick both underpins and serves as a release from the darkness of Luzhin's experience.[105] Its presence is explicitly signalled by a still of Harold Lloyd in *Safety Last* (1923), which Luzhin spots on Valentinov's desk — the 'white-faced man with lifeless features and big American glasses, hanging by his hands from the ledge of a skyscraper' (p. 247) — an image that not only anticipates, but even possibly 'suggests' to Luzhin his potential 'means of suicide'.[106] Elsewhere, incidental descriptions point to specific films. For example, when Luzhin's fiancée imagines introducing him to her parents, she visualizes him 'with a clumsy motion of his shoulder [knocking] the house down like a shaky piece of scenery that emitted a sigh of dust' (pp. 103–04), an image that recalls the house that collapses around Buster Keaton in *Steamboat Bill Jr.* (1928). Luzhin's tumble from the tram at the end of the novel is reminiscent of the perilous stunts of both Keaton and Charlie Chaplin. Luzhin, like Chaplin's tramp, who falls, drunk, from a moving tram in a sequence from the 1922 short, *Pay Day*, displays the same death-defying nonchalance:

das kleine Lustspiel "Schachfieber"'. 'Aus der russischen Filmindustrie: Von unserum Moskaues Korrespondenten', *Kinematograph*, 993, 28 February 1926, p. 7.

[102] Oksana Bulgakowa, 'Russische Filme in Berlin', in Oksana Bulgakowa (ed.), *Die ungewöhnlichen Abenteuer des Dr. Mabuse im Lande der Bolschewiki. Das Buch zur Filmreihe 'Moskau – Berlin'*, Berlin, 1995, pp. 81–94 (p. 84). See also listings in ibid, p. 209, and Agde and Schwarz (eds), *Die rote Traumfabrik*, p. 215.

[103] See Rainer Rother, 'In Deutschland entschiedener Erfolg: Die Rezeption sowjetischer Filme in der Weimarer Republik', in ibid., pp. 10–23 (p. 22).

[104] V. Pertsov, 'Smekh skvoz' smekh', *Kino*, no. 2 (122), 12 January 1926, p. 3.

[105] Although Nabokov's humour tended to be dark. See his comments about sharing Alfred Hitchcock's *'humour noir'* in Appel, *Nabokov's Dark Cinema*, p. 129. Nabokov was in correspondence with Hitchcock in 1964 and 1970. See ibid., and *Selected Letters*, pp. 361–66.

[106] Appel, *Nabokov's Dark Cinema*, p. 161.

when suddenly the car filled up with a horde of schoolboys, a dozen old ladies and fifty fat men, Luzhin continued to move about, treading on people's feet, and finally pushing his way onto the platform. Catching sight of his house, he left the car on the move; the asphalt swept by beneath his left heel, then turned and struck him in the back, and his cane, after getting tangled in his legs, suddenly leapt out like a released spring, flew through the air and landed beside him. Two women came running toward him and helped him to rise. He began to knock the dust from his coat with his palm, donned his hat, and without looking back walked toward the house.[107]

In Chaplin's films, the comedy often turns 'on the fact that people and objects share the same condition of physicality, and that the dominance of one over the other is not automatically assured'. Chaplin will be seen 'vying with doors, tables, rugs and beds, each of which refuse to submit to his ascendancy'.[108] Luzhin demonstrates a similar difficulty when faced with strangely animated everyday objects, for example, when he first arrives at his fiancée's parents' flat:

To a faceless taxi driver he read aloud the address on the postcard [...] and having imperceptibly surmounted the dim accidental distance, he cautiously tried to pull the ring out of the lion's jaws. The bell leapt into action immediately: the door flew open. [He] suddenly noticed that his left hand, already extended to one side, held an unnecessary cane and his right his billfold [...]. His cane dived safely into a vaselike receptacle; his billfold, at the second thrust, found the right pocket; and his hat was hung on a hook. (pp. 118–19)

Nabokov's use of personification in this passage communicates Luzhin's sense of disconnection from both the unfamiliar and familiar — his cane and his billfold — as he nervously contends with this new environment. These objects take on a force of their own, as if conspiring against him to comically subvert what would otherwise be a mundane ritual of arrival.

Slapstick comedy is also produced by mistakes and misapprehension. The two drunks who pick Luzhin up off the street during his breakdown think he is one of them, and this qualifies the rest of the episode as a piece of slapstick, with Luzhin bundled into a taxi, then bundled up the stairs to

---

[107] Nabokov, *The Defense*, pp. 249–50. Page numbers will be given in all subsequent passages quoted from this edition.

[108] Alex Clayton, *The Body in Hollywood Slapstick*, Jefferson, NC, 2007, p. 33.

his fiancée's parents' flat, with everyone falling over everybody, in a kind
of choreographed comic chaos. Meanwhile the two 'strangers' (the drunks
Kurt and Karl) who along with Luzhin end up in a heap in the back of
their taxi, so that 'when the driver opened the door he was unable at first
to make out how many people were inside' (p. 147), again seem to multiply
across the apartment:[109]

> In the darkness everything swung, there was a knocking and a shuffling
> and a puffing, someone took a step backwards and invoked God's name
> in German, and when the light came on again one of the strangers was
> sitting on a stair and the other was being crushed by Luzhin's body [...].
> The young strangers [...] were seen at once in all the rooms. [...] They were
> found on all the divans, in the bathroom and on the trunk in the hallway,
> and there was no way of getting rid of them. Their number was unclear —
> a fluctuating, blurred number. (p. 148)

The distortions of the strangers' alcohol-impaired vision are projected
into the surrounding space, magnifying the scene's surreal absurdity.
Visual misapprehension is generated across the novel by both internal
and external actors, from the psychological and emotional to the play
of light and shade on glass-fronted picture frames and doors, mirrors
and windows. As they do across Nabokov's fiction, and especially in *The
Defense*, these reflective surfaces also function as apertures, revealing
the spaces that exist beneath or behind them. Buster Keaton explored the
potential of this motif in *Sherlock Jr.* (1924), in which he plays a movie
theatre projectionist who falls asleep in his booth and dreams that he
sees his sweetheart in the film he is showing. He runs to her aid, jumping
through the screen's fantastical transparent meniscus and into the action
of the film.[110] Here Keaton extends the motif of the camera's aperture
from the visual framing of the projectionist in his booth and the window
through which he sees the screen, to the framed action on the screen
itself, while the world beyond the cinema screen mirrors the aperture of

---

[109] Andrew Field described these scenes as 'pure Keystone comedy'. *Nabokov: His Life
in Art*, Boston, MA and Toronto, 1967, p. 176.

[110] The trope of jumping through the screen (this time in righteous indignation)
was famously used by Władysław Starewicz in his 1912 animated film, *Mest'
kinematograficheskogo operatora* (The Camera Operator's Revenge), which Nabokov may
have seen as a boy. The film would perhaps have interested him both as an early parody of
the cinematic melodrama and because the animated protagonists are insects. With thanks
to Julian Graffy for bringing this to my attention.

the camera lens and the realms contained within it.[111] In this way Keaton exploits the dynamics that are unique to the cinematic experience, the notion of 'cinema as window and frame' that 'offers *special, ocular access* to an event', and 'the (real) two-dimensional screen' that 'transforms in the act of looking into an (imaginary) three-dimensional space which seems to open up beyond the screen'.[112] Meanwhile, the film's abstract quality 'corresponds to Buster's somewhat alien perspective, to his greater interest in physical properties than in the nuance of social interaction. To see the world as an intricate configuration of shape and movement', as Keaton and Luzhin do, 'is to see it at one remove'.[113]

As a major star of the genre, Keaton was unusual in that he was both a 'peerless physical comedian and a pioneering cineaste'. Over and above the extraordinary stunts he performed, his films often depicted 'deceptive landscape[s] of surrealistic transformations, misunderstandings, and implacable tricks of Fate':[114]

> Buster Keaton s'invente mille manières de pousser toute expérience jusqu'à l'absurde sans que son 'visage de pierre' traduise la moindre appréhension. L'impassibilité réelle ou simulée au contact d'un monde qui se désarticule, caractérise ce burlesque […]. Empêtré dans la machine et l'environnement, Keaton survit néanmoins, même s'il ne montre pas qu'il est heureux.[115]

Dubbed the 'Great Stone Face', Keaton's attempts to navigate a baffling, elusive and often sabotaging material environment, whilst showing barely any reaction, are reflected in Luzhin's faltering and precarious interactions with 'the incompletely intelligible world' that surrounds him, almost always in 'sullen' and 'bowed' silence.[116]

Ultimately, however, the key aspect of the slapstick comedian is their ability to defy mortality — 'the comedy hero cannot die, these deaths have

---

[111]   It is a conceit that Nabokov was subsequently to deploy in *Glory* with the painting of the path into the woods which Martin dreams of climbing into, and which alludes to a similar painting that hung over Nabokov's bed as a boy. Gavriel Shapiro has linked Keaton's movie to a 1924 story, 'La Veneziana' (*The Sublime Artist's Studio: Nabokov and Painting*, Evanston, IL, 2009, p. 73), although the film was not reviewed in *Rul'* until the following year. See Parker, *Nabokov Noir*, p. 188.

[112]   Thomas Elsaesser and Malte Hagener, *Film Theory: An Introduction through the Senses*, 2nd edn, London, 2015, p. 15 (emphasis in the original).

[113]   Clayton, *The Body in Hollywood Slapstick*, p. 52.

[114]   David Kalat, *Too Funny for Words: A Contrarian History of American Screen Comedy from Silent Slapstick to Screwball*, Jefferson, NC, 2019, p. 64.

[115]   Daniel Royot, *L'humour et la culture américaine*, Paris, 1996, pp. 168–69.

[116]   Nabokov, *The Defense*, pp. 134 and 234.

to remain in the realm of fantasy and their reality is denied by a narrative twist: suicides are narrowly averted, hanging fails because of an elastic rope, murders and accidental deaths turn out to have been only dreams.'[117] At the end of *The Defense* there is a suggestion that Luzhin, like his slapstick counterparts, does not in fact die, but is instead presented with a vision of his 'eternity' as he readies himself to jump (p. 256). The darkness of the yard below is reminiscent of 'the bottomless space' which, as Nabokov describes, lies 'beyond the chessboard',[118] indicating that he might be about to enter 'the same world he touched during the peak moments of his games'. As Vladimir Alexandrov notes, 'Nabokov once implied this possibility himself when he said: "As I approached the conclusion of the novel I suddenly realized that the book doesn't end."'[119]

'Kinematograf': Film as illusion
There is a sense, in Nabokov's portrayal of movie-going in his 1928 poem, 'Kinematograf', that the cinematic world it describes also exists like a 'bottomless space', set apart from real life, in an infinite void filled with ever-repeating scenarios that somehow continue even after the music stops, the house lights go up, and the 'melted fiction' of the on-screen world is replaced by the noise and cold of the street outside. Although 'nothing there trembles with life',[120] the world of 'Kinematograf' and its depiction of generic silent film melodrama nevertheless reveals a fascination with the improbability of its 'luxurious' but 'vulgar' storylines.[121] As Tatyana Gershkovich argues, Nabokov 'confesses to "love the spectacles of light" ("liubliu ia svetovye balagany"), and describes cinema's outlandish tricks — eavesdropping devices, captivating car chases — with a mix of irony and

[117] Muriel Andrin quoting Jean-Pierre Coursodon in 'Back to the "Slap": Slapstick's Hyperbolic Gesture and the Rhetoric of Violence', in Tom Paulus and Rob King (eds), *Slapstick Comedy*, New York and Abingdon, 2010, p. 233.
[118] See Nabokov's interview with Pierre Dommergues for *Les Langues Modernes*, 62, 1, January–February 1968, pp. 92–102 ('Entretien avec Nabokov'): 'Il n'y a pas de temps sur l'échiquier. Le temps remplacé par un espace sans fond... [...] J'ai pensé moi-même à des thèmes d'échecs, à des problèmes qui comprennent cette possibilité du cavalier qui s'envole; et puis qui revient d'un espace' (p. 99).
[119] Alexandrov, *Nabokov's Otherworld*, pp. 82 and 83, citing a comment Nabokov made to his biographer, Andrew Field, in *VN: The Life and Art of Vladimir Nabokov*, New York, 1986, p. 132. Boyd and Voronina also describe Luzhin's suicide, his 'sui-mate', as 'virtual', essentially unfulfilled. See Vladimir Nabokov, *Letters to Véra*, edited and translated by Olga Voronina and Brian Boyd, London, 2014, p. 699 — note to a letter dated 6 June 1939.
[120] 'Kinematograf', in Nabokov, *Sobranie sochinenii russkogo perioda*, p. 595 (hereafter, 'Kinematograf', translation mine).
[121] 'speshit roskoshnoe voobrazhen'e / samouverennogo poshliaka.' Ibid., p. 595.

admiration'.[122] While he 'always acknowledged the potency of the artistic devices Hollywood had mastered and the implacability of the appetites it fulfilled', she continues, Nabokov 'neither wanted nor expected readers to transcend such delights altogether [...]. But by making readers respond more selfconsciously to them, he hoped that they might enjoy these devices without being entirely in their grip'.[123]

There is, however, a key element to Nabokov's poem that critics have missed, something which Walter Benjamin identifies as the 'illusionary' quality that is unique to film. The 'equipment-free aspect of reality' that only film can project, essentially its ability, unlike theatre, to hide the machinery of its production — from cameras and lighting equipment to the processes of editing — brings it to the 'height of artifice', rendering it 'a work of art'.[124] It is the same artifice that Nabokov so celebrated, a form of 'magic', a 'game of intricate enchantment and deception'[125] that, he argued, 'characterize[d] all worthwhile art':[126]

> deception [...] in art, is only part of the game; it's part of the combination, part of the delightful possibilities, illusions, vistas of thought, which can be false vistas [...] a good combination should always contain a certain element of deception.[127]

In 'Kinematograf', as he sits beneath the film projector's 'twirl of mirror darkness' ('vrashchenie zerkal'noi temnoty'),[128] Nabokov briefly exposes this very artifice by granting his audience a privileged, behind-the-scenes glimpse of the action taking place on the other side of the screen, whilst revealing his insider's knowledge by reference, in a kind of industry

---

[122] Gershkovich, 'Self-Translation and the Transformation of Nabokov's Aesthetics', p. 217. So far, none of the available English translations agree, although Diment, Gershkovich, Grishakova and Leving render the Russian in its closest sense. Only Luke Parker has translated the poem in full, and in more than one version. See Grishakova, *The Models of Space, Time and Vision*, p. 187; Leving, 'Filming Nabokov', pp. 7–8; Parker, *Nabokov Noir*, pp. 56–57, and Luke Parker, '"This Fairground Farce of Light": Vladimir Nabokov's "The Cinema" (1928)', *Los Angeles Review of Books*, 19 December 2022 <https://lareviewofbooks.org/short-takes/this-fairground-farce-of-light-vladimir-nabokovs-the-cinema-1928>.

[123] Gershkovich, 'Self-Translation and the Transformation of Nabokov's Aesthetics', p. 217.

[124] Benjamin, 'The Work of Art in the Age of Mechanical Reproduction', pp. 226, 227.

[125] Nabokov, *Speak, Memory*, p. 95.

[126] Nabokov, *Strong Opinions*, pp. 160–61.

[127] Ibid., pp. 11–12.

[128] Grishakova, *The Models of Space, Time and Vision*, p. 187; 'Kinematograf', p. 595.

shorthand, to a specific piece of studio equipment — the 'Jupiter' lamp:[129]
'Vot spal´naia ozarennaia... Smotrite, / kak eta shal´ upala na kover. / Ne
viden oslepitel´nyi iupiter, / ne slyshen razdrazhennyi rezhisser (Here is a lit
bedroom... / Look how that shawl has fallen onto the rug. / The dazzling
Jupiter is invisible / the irritated director inaudible).[130] The brightness of the
light and the shouts of the director contrast starkly with the quiet stillness
of the scene being filmed, the camera focusing simply on the shawl, with
the viewer/reader left to wonder on the possible sequence that has played
out in the empty room. These four lines epitomise the 'equipment-free
aspect of reality' that only film can depict, qualifying Nabokov's cinema
as another form of artistic deception, functioning implicitly, like the
commotion behind the camera, such that the viewer is utterly beguiled by
its 'illusionary' surface.

In his foreword to the English translation of The Defense, Nabokov
reveals, in a rare move, much of the novel's 'combination' by detailing its
'fatal pattern' of themes that accumulate in a conspiracy of destruction.[131]
Nabokov's unusually explicit mapping of the novel's 'nerves'[132] offers the
reader a seemingly ready-made solution to what they are encouraged
to believe is a straightforward story constructed along the lines of
two chess strategies — the 'sui-mate' and 'retrograde analysis'.[133] It is,
however, misleading. As Don Barton Johnson points out, 'neither of the
problem types specifically discussed by Nabokov [in his 'booby-trapped'
Foreword] seems to fit the events of the novel',[134] thus presenting the
first elements of Nabokov's creative deception. It could be said therefore,
that the Foreword's purpose is to divert the reader's attention away from

---

[129] Jupiter was a well-known brand name of studio lighting manufactured in Berlin
from the 1920s to the 1970s. Nabokov would have been familiar with it from his work as
an extra in Berlin's film studios during the 1920s. So far, however, published translations
of the poem have missed the significance of this detail. Luke Parker, for example,
translates 'iupiter' as 'blinding projectors' (Nabokov Noir, p. 56) or 'klieg projector' ('"This
Fairground Farce of Light"'). The American-made 'Klieg' light was a floor-mounted
spotlight used in both theatre and film, whereas the Kliegl Light Projector was designed to
illuminate specific subjects at various pitches in confined spaces, such as shops, galleries
and laboratories. See 'Kliegl Picture Lighting Projectors', Marcel Breuer Digital Archive
<https://breuer.syr.edu/xtf/view?docId=mets/24898.mets.xml;query=;brand=default>
[accessed 16 January 2023]. These 'dazzling' Jupiters (slepitel´nye zherla iupiterov) had
already featured in Ganin's description of the film set in Mashen´ka. See Nabokov,
Sobranie sochinenii russkogo perioda, p. 60. In Michael Glenny's 1970 English translation
they are replaced with Kliegs. See Vladimir Nabokov, Mary, London, 1973, p. 30.
[130] 'Kinematograf', p. 595. See also, Leving, 'Filming Nabokov', p. 7.
[131] Nabokov, The Defense, pp. 8–10.
[132] Nabokov, The Annotated Lolita, p. 316.
[133] Nabokov, The Defense, pp. 8 and 10.
[134] Barton Johnson, Worlds in Regression, pp. 87 and 88.

the novel's 'secret points' and 'subliminal co-ordinates', which, it can be argued, are 'plotted'[135] also in terms of an abiding tension between the perspectives of Luzhin and the narrator. At the same time, the 'splendid insincerity' that lies at the heart of Nabokov's fictive and chess strategies[136] echoes the 'melted fiction' of film in 'Kinematograf', establishing a direct link between the artifice of cinema and the artifice inherent in the 'fatal patterns' of Nabokov's chess novel.

Nabokov's film strategy in 'The Defense'

In *The Defense*, Nabokov's hero is given an acute sensory ability to engage with the world, an ability that has a powerful mnemonic function but which, rather than granting artistic transcendence, ensnares him in an endlessly repeating vortex that threatens ultimate oblivion. The primacy of sensory experience in Luzhin's world is established in the novel's opening pages, in which 'Nabokov quickly engages, and pegs for future back-reference, all our senses, one after the other, appealing above all to our ability to recognize an image as both familiar and yet never registered before'.[137] Not only this, but Nabokov also establishes the novel's dual-aspect narrative perspective that constantly shifts between an over-arching authorial point of view — i.e. Nabokov's — and a very defined and narrow field of vision that is Luzhin's. This marks a departure from the more conventional narrative stance in *Mary* and *King, Queen, Knave*, which gave Nabokov universal access to the thoughts and feelings of his protagonists. The emphasis on vision in *The Defense* establishes a kind of sympathetic optical conspiracy between author/narrator and character, in which the narrator assumes Luzhin's point of view at critical moments (for example in the lead up to and during his play against Turati, after which he suffers a complete mental breakdown). Not only does this reinforce Luzhin's silence — his inability to articulate his experience verbally — but also Nabokov's deliberate choice to deploy the visual as a means of dramatizing Luzhin's emotional and psychological state. We see this in operation as early as chapter one, in the episode where Luzhin attempts to escape being taken back to school.

After climbing in through an open window, Luzhin takes refuge in the attic amongst various discarded objects, including 'a cracked chessboard'

---

[135] Nabokov, *The Annotated Lolita*, p. 316.

[136] See Nabokov, *Strong Opinions*, pp. 160–61.

[137] Gennady Barabtarlo, 'Nabokov's Trinity (On the Movement of Nabokov's Themes)', in Julian W. Connolly (ed.), *Nabokov and His Fiction: New Perspectives*, Cambridge and New York, 1999, pp. 109–38 (p. 120).

(p. 23).[138] Luzhin is alerted by the sound of people searching for him, but as he peers down through the aperture of the attic window the visual aspect takes over, the sounds are silenced, and we see the scene exclusively through Luzhin's eyes:

> Taking a cautious look through the little window he saw below his father, who like a young boy ran up the stairs and then, before reaching the landing, descended swiftly again, throwing his knees out on either side. [...] Finally, after another minute had passed, they all went up in a posse — his father's bald head glistened, the bird on mother's hat swayed like a duck on a troubled pond, and the butler's gray crew cut bobbed up and down; at the rear, leaning at every moment over the balustrade, came the coachman, the watchman, and for some reason the milkmaid Akulina, and finally a black-bearded peasant from the water mill. (p. 24)

Luzhin's perspective emulates a high-angled shot from his vantage point at the top of the stairs that depicts a comically surreal, disembodied parade of elbows, knees, hats and the tops of people's heads. These are faceless figures, identifiable only by their particular features — his father's baldness, the butler's grey hair and the peasant's black beard — their depersonalization revealing the alienation and dissociation that will characterize almost all his future interactions.

This scene is repeated later in the novel, when Luzhin returns to his fiancée's parents' flat, in a state of collapse. Again the angle of vision is extreme, this time from a low vantage point looking up at a window from the street below, and then up rather than down, from the bottom rather than the top, of a staircase:

> The window emptied, but a moment later the darkness behind the front door disintegrated and through the glass appeared an illuminated staircase, marble as far as the first landing, and this newborn staircase had not had time to congeal completely before swift feminine legs appeared on the stairs. [...]
>
> Meanwhile the staircase continued to spawn people... A gentleman appeared wearing bedroom slippers, black trousers and a collarless starched shirt, and behind him came a pale, stocky maid with scuffers on her bare feet. (pp. 148–49)

---

[138] The crack in the chessboard becomes indicative of Luzhin's damaged relationship with the game.

As before, the figures are oddly disembodied, reduced to legs and feet and slippers. This time, however, the perspective is not Luzhin's, but that of the two drunks — Kurt and Karl — who have brought him home. Nabokov indicates this by the way the staircase comes into view — it appears, 'newborn', like something never seen before as the lights are turned on inside the apartment building, the lighting assisting the men's inebriated vision to pull focus. The deployment of this low-angled perspective enhances the chaos of the scene, and the impaired vision of Kurt and Karl. Luzhin's perspective is meanwhile completely disengaged, as he sits outside on the steps with his back to everyone. It can be argued that this episode functions as the comic interlude in a Shakespearian tragedy, releasing the tension of Luzhin's crisis. Yet the tragedy of the situation is amplified both by the comedy duo's 'unawareness and irrelevance',[139] and by the fact that everyone else assumes, as they do, that Luzhin is just another drunk.

In these episodes, Nabokov consciously and deliberately emulates camera eye perspective to further enhance Luzhin's detachment, deploying this mechanical mode of vision to 'distance and finally alienate the seer from his field of vision by viewing the seen object through eyes that focus like a camera':[140]

> camera-like vision [indicates] that whatever the special circumstances, and however the participating observer, and however intimate this observer may become with whatever the field of vision may contain, the seen object itself will always remain slightly other than and slightly apart from the life of the observer. To see in the matter of the camera is to see without engagement, participation, or any hint of mental, moral, or spiritual assumption of the seen object.[141]

Whilst Luzhin's camera eye communicates the degree of his dissociation, it is also inextricably linked to his relationship with chess. Marina Grishakova comments that 'film as a combination of light and darkness [...] is the key metaphor of *The Defense*', and that the theme of retrograde analysis is played out as if Luzhin 'is watching a film of his life until a retake starts'.[142] This link between cinema and chess is established when Luzhin is first introduced to the game. Grishakova has noticed how the

---

[139] See Susan Snyder, *The Comic Matrix of Shakespeare's Tragedies*, Princeton, NJ, 1979, p. 5.
[140] Spiegel, 'Flaubert to Joyce', p. 241.
[141] Ibid., p. 242.
[142] Grishakova, *The Models of Space, Time and Vision*, p. 123.

scene 'unfolds as a movie in full darkness with the "lit island" of the table with chess pieces as an equivalent of the screen',[143] but there is much more to the way Nabokov constructs its cinematic elements, as closer analysis reveals.

Luzhin sneaks into the darkness of his father's study to get away from a party, 'settling on a divan in the corner' from where he listens to the 'tender wail of a violin', coming from several rooms away:

> He listened sleepily, clasping his knees and looking at a chink of lacy light between the loosely closed curtains, through which a gas-lamp from the street shone lilac-tinged white. From time to time a faint glimmer sped over the ceiling in a mysterious arc and a gleaming dot showed on the desk [...]. He had almost dozed off when suddenly he started at the ringing of a telephone on the desk, and it became immediately clear that the gleaming dot was on the telephone support. The butler came in from the dining room, turned on in passing a light which illumined only the desk [...]. A minute later he returned accompanying a gentleman [the violinist] who as soon as he entered the circle of light picked up the receiver from the desk and with his other hand groped for the back of the desk chair. (pp. 40–41)

Nabokov engages Luzhin's camera eye perspective, focusing it, initially, on the lilac light of the streetlamp which reaches into the room and lands as a 'gleaming dot' on the desk. The cinematic cast of the scene is established by this 'arc' of light — this 'twirl of mirror darkness' — that emulates the beam of a movie projector. It is an image which recurs the following day, when Luzhin's aunt takes him back to the study to teach him the game — 'they entered the study where a band of sunbeams, in which spun tiny particles of dust, was focused on an overstuffed armchair. She lit a cigarette and folds of smoke started to sway, soft and transparent, in the sunbeams' (p. 45). The quality of the daylight has the same lilac tinge — 'mauve, indigo and pale blue' — with the 'wooden street pavements' cast in a 'violet sheen' (p. 43), affirming a sense of continuation from the night before. It is also no coincidence that Nabokov chooses this particular colour, denoting, as it does across his fiction, not only 'the very colour of time',[144] suggestive of transcendence and immortality, but also his presence in the text.[145]

---

[143] Ibid., p. 119.

[144] See Nabokov, *Lectures on Literature*, p. 241.

[145] As James Joyce 'set[s] his face in a dark corner of this canvas' via *Ulysses*'s Man in the Brown Macintosh (Nabokov, *Lectures on Literature*, p. 320), here Nabokov establishes his presence through colour and light. On Nabokov's self-reference through colour, see

As in the attic episode, the sounds around Luzhin suddenly stop, the silence, until it is broken by the ringing telephone, magnifying the visual aspect of the scene. In the pitch black of his father's study, similar to the darkness of a cinema auditorium, Luzhin's attention is caught initially by the beam of the streetlight that guides his eye to the telephone, which acts as the scene's dramatic catalyst,[146] and then by the lamp which, like a spotlight, illuminates only one side of the violinist's face, and then his floating hands. The reified, disembodied description identifies him only by his 'ivory nose, black hair', and a single, 'bushy eyebrow' (p. 41). Luzhin's vision also exhibits a form of photographic 'depthlessness', whereby his eye 'flatten[s] out the depth of field', 'foreground[ing] and equaliz[ing] everything [...] on the same flat, two-dimensional plane', while through 'anatomization', his cinematic perspective 'places a new and concentrated attentiveness upon the infinite number of phases that constitute the shape of any single action' — here the violinist arriving to answer the telephone — able to follow and apprehend his every movement.[147]

As part of the novel's many repetitions and recurrences, this key cinematic episode anticipates a scene in which Luzhin goes to the cinema for the first time. His wife takes him to see an unnamed, generic, sentimental drama, at which he cries. One could say that the film is a success, in that it provokes the designed emotional response from its audience, but what is unusual here is that this is one of the rare occasions when Luzhin shows any form of emotional release. There are only four other times when he actually sheds tears — when he tries to escape being taken back to St Petersburg and to school; when he proposes to his wife; when Valentinov leaves him (he implies); and during his breakdown, as he runs through what he thinks are the woods that surround his family's Russian country estate but which are only the trees in a Berlin park.

Gerard de Vries and D. Barton Johnson, *Nabokov and the Art of Painting*, Amsterdam, 2006, pp. 39–41. In Nabokov's synaesthetic alphabet, the first letter of his pen-name, Sirin, takes on a 'curious mixture of azure and mother-of-pearl', essentially lilac (in Russian, *siren'*). Nabokov, *Speak, Memory*, p. 21. See also, Gavriel Shapiro, 'Setting His Myriad Faces in His Text: Nabokov's Authorial Presence Revisited', in Connolly (ed.), *Nabokov and His Fiction*, pp. 15–35. Nabokov made the first of such 'visits of inspection' in *King, Queen, Knave*. Vladimir Nabokov, 'Foreword' to *King, Queen, Knave*, London, 1993, p. vi. A similar 'inclined beam of pale light' appears at the end of *Bend Sinister* (1947), along which Nabokov travels to save Krug, his incarcerated protagonist, 'from the senseless agony of his logical fate'. See Vladimir Nabokov, *Bend Sinister*, New York, 1990, p. 233.

[146] Anticipating its function in *Lolita*, for example, as Humbert Humbert remarks: 'With people in movies I seem to share the services of the machina telephonica and its sudden god.' Nabokov, *The Annotated Lolita*, p. 205.

[147] Alan Spiegel, *Fiction and the Camera Eye: Visual Consciousness in Film and the Modern Novel*, Charlottesville, VA, 1976, p. 88.

These are all significant, life-changing events which could legitimately be expected to have an extreme emotional impact, yet this film — this highly manipulative, artificial, two-dimensional construct — also makes him cry.

Luzhin turns out to be a gullible subject, and conforms readily to the very particular environment of the cinematic space:

> In the cinema, the specific set-up of projection, screen, and audience, together with the centring effect of optical perspective and the focalising strategies of narration, all ensure or conspire to transfix but also to transpose the spectator into a trancelike state in which it becomes difficult to distinguish between the 'out-there' and the 'in-here'.[148]

Luzhin initially shows no interest in engaging with what is happening on the screen in front of him, although there is a sense that he has entered a trancelike state — 'the picture ran on in a white glow' (p. 191) — until his attention is finally caught by the vision of the father and doctor playing chess: 'In the darkness came the sound of Luzhin laughing abruptly. "An absolutely impossible position for the pieces," he said.' Luzhin adopts a position of objective irony in an attempt to detach himself from the drama being played out before him, a move which is reinforced by a sudden shift in perspective from Luzhin to his wife. The image of the father's face moving into an extreme, 'choker' close-up[149] is described from her point of view:

> but at this point, to his wife's relief, everything changed and the father, growing in size, walked toward the spectators and acted his part for all he was worth; his eyes widened, then came a slight trembling, his lashes flapped, there was another bit of trembling, and slowly his wrinkles softened, grew kinder, and a slow smile of infinite tenderness appeared on his face, which continued to tremble... (p. 191)

A change from past to present tense signals a return to Luzhin's point of view, which communicates both the intensity of this vision, and the intensity of his response to it: 'And the father, continuing the trembling, slowly opens his arms, and suddenly she kneels before him. Luzhin began to blow his nose.'

---

[148] Thomas Elsaesser and Malte Hagener, *Film Theory: An Introduction Through the Senses*, 2nd edn, New York and London, 2015, p. 77.

[149] 'A tight close-up that fills the frame with the subject's head, generally from the neck up.' Ira Konigsberg, *The Complete Film Dictionary*, 2nd edn, London, 1997, p. 54.

In a 1949 essay, the film theorist Hugo Mauerhofer describes a particular phenomenon which he calls the 'Cinema Situation', something which Luzhin, in this scene, submits to totally, and which also explains his response to the film. Luzhin exhibits the three main traits of Mauerhofer's cinema spectator — 'voluntary passivity', 'imminent boredom' and an amplified imaginative power — generated by the enclosed atmosphere of the cinema auditorium. These traits, combined with film's ability to alter our sense of time, 'cause[s] the unconscious to begin to communicate with the consciousness to a higher degree than in the normal state'.[150] As he sits in the still, hushed darkness of the cinema auditorium Luzhin relinquishes himself to the 'diffused mass' of the anonymous cinema audience. This sense of anonymity heightens his subjective response to the action and characters on the screen, such that he ultimately finds himself identifying with them 'uncritically',[151] thus allowing the drama playing out before his eyes to affect him, profoundly.

There are a number of ways to interpret Luzhin's response to this scene. Nabokov has already shown how Luzhin is susceptible to sentimentality when he is easily beguiled by the phoney nostalgia of the 'gaudy Russia boldly on display' (p. 120) at his parents-in-law's flat. It could be that it recalls the pivotal evening in his father's study, or more potently, Luzhin burying his father's 'precious box of chessmen' (p. 66) in an attempt to stop him trying to teach him how to play. Instead his father invites their doctor to play against him — he turns out to be 'first-rate' (p. 67) — their nightly matches marking the beginning of Luzhin's path towards open competition. Or it could simply be that this fleeting vision of a chess game serves as a potent and painful reminder of an existence that is now closed to him. Equally, though, this could also be an instance where Luzhin is simply overcome by the combined visual power of the images playing out before him — the close-up depicted, for example, as actual movement, as if the father is 'walking' out of the screen 'toward the spectators' (p. 191) — and the new environment that he finds himself in, which together intensify his emotional connection to the on-screen drama.

The close-up is perhaps '*the* most recognizable unit of cinematic discourse',[152] commented on, initially, by Béla Balázs in 1924, in a way that

---

[150] Hugo Mauerhofer, 'Psychology of Film Experience', *The Penguin Film Review*, 8, 1, January 1949, pp. 103–09 (p. 106).
[151] Ibid., p. 108.
[152] Mary Ann Doane, 'The Close-Up: Scale and Detail in the Cinema', *Differences: A Journal of Feminist Cultural Studies*, 14, 3, 2003, pp. 89–111 (p. 90). Emphasis in the original.

echoes the 'precise and silent beauty' which Nabokov saw in the magic lantern slides. The 'magnifying glass of the cinematograph brings us closer to the individual cells of life', Balázs argues, 'allow[ing] us to feel the texture and substance of life in its concrete detail':

> [The close-up lifts] the single image out of the whole. This enables us not only to see the minute atoms of life more clearly than anything on stage, but in addition the director uses them to guide our gaze [...] The close-up is the deeper gaze, the director's sensibility. The close-up is the poetry of cinema.[153]

Whereas many early cinema audiences found the close-up deeply unsettling, inspiring a mixture of 'fascination, love, horror, empathy, pain' and 'unease',[154] Balázs's response is unequivocally positive. Nabokov, via Luzhin's fiancée, also shows no sign of flinching at the growing image of the actor's trembling face. The emphasis here is on its melodramatic effect, as it is in an earlier story, in which 'the huge face of a girl with gray, shimmering eyes and black lips traversed vertically by glistening cracks, approaches from the screen'. The face 'keeps growing as it gazes into the dark hall, and a wonderful, long, shining tear runs down one cheek'.[155] Here, in the English translation, Nabokov has replaced 'glycerin' with 'shining'.[156] Glycerin, the term he originally used, reveals, as Jupiter does in 'Kinematograf', his inside knowledge of the industry, it being the substance used by film-makers to simulate tears. The image is also reminiscent of the 'female stars with low foreheads, magnificent eyebrows' and 'lavishly shaded eyes' that feature in the films he recalls from his St Petersburg movie-going.

Tom Gunning has described cinema as both 'an art of light [and] of darkness, not simply in the darkened room necessary for the light image to become visible, but in its actual process: the rhythm and pulse of the flickering light on the screen'.[157] The play of light and dark is a constant element of *The Defense*, and is part of the novel's patterning of motifs —

[153] Béla Balázs, 'Visible Man', in *Early Film Theory: Visible Man and The Spirit of Film*, trans. Rodney Livingstone, New York and Oxford, 2010, pp. 38 and 41.
[154] Doane, 'The Close-Up', p. 90.
[155] Vladimir Nabokov, 'A Letter that Never Reached Russia' (1925), in *Collected Stories*, p. 138.
[156] See Parker, *Nabokov Noir*, p. 39.
[157] Tom Gunning, 'Flicker and Shutter: Exploring Cinema's Shuddering Shadow', in Martine Beugnet, Allan Cameron and Arild Fetveit (eds), *Indefinite Visions: Cinema and the Attractions of Uncertainty*, Edinburgh, 2022, pp. 53–69 (p. 62).

windows, boxes, bridges, telephones — that operates alongside its chess imagery.[158] In film, this patterning would be described as an 'image system', which functions as 'an intrinsic part of the visual language of movies [that] can add layers of meaning, nuance and depth'.[159] Its success relies on a process of 'visual recalling and comparison' that is 'inherent in the way audiences extract meaning from images to understand a story, constantly making connections not only within, but also between shots'.[160] In *The Defense*, Luzhin is conscious of this system, which he responds to as both a participant and an objective viewer, believing, mistakenly, that he can accurately interpret and ultimately control it. Pekka Tammi has argued that because the novel's 'system of hidden correlations' is formulated by both Nabokov and Luzhin, it is 'important to distinguish between those instances in the text that are accessible to Luzhin's point of view and those that are not'. There is a sustained tension throughout the novel, therefore, between these parallel points of view, but despite the complexity of Luzhin's image system, it cannot compete with the sophistication of Nabokov's 'imaginative structure':[161]

> Glass surfaces, rectangular openings, doors and windows function everywhere in the novel as covert prefigurations of the concluding scene [...]. At the same time, the recurrences serve to confirm that Luzhin's final attempt to break out of the [narrator]-generated design has also been anticipated on the plane of his own reality.[162]

Dramatic irony is generated by the system of repeated images that Nabokov constructs to which Luzhin remains blind, yet this system is 'specifically manipulated to point beyond [Luzhin's] comprehension'.[163] Indeed, the novel's image system operates in such a way that it can can only be apprehended by the ideal Nabokovian 'rereader',[164] a reader who, like the film viewer, is capable of 'visual recalling and comparison'. As Aleksandr

[158] See Dolinin, 'Istinnaia zhizn´ pisatelia Sirina: pervye romany', pp. 31–32.
[159] Gustavo Mercado, *The Filmmaker's Eye: The Language of the Lens. The Power of Lenses and the Expressive Cinematic Image*, Abingdon and New York, 2019, p. 13. See also, Robert McKee, *Story: Substance, Structure, Style, and the Principles of Screenwriting*, York, 2014, pp. 400–08.
[160] Gustavo Mercado, *The Filmmaker's Eye: Learning (and Breaking) the Rules of Cinematic Composition*, Abingdon and New York, 2017, p. 21.
[161] Pekka Tammi, *Problems of Nabokov's Poetics: A Narratological Analysis*, Helsinki, 1985, p. 143.
[162] Ibid., p. 142.
[163] Ibid.
[164] Nabokov, *Lectures on Literature*, p. 3.

Dolinin details, Luzhin's impulse "to free himself, climb somewhere, even into oblivion'" after his game with Turati is adjourned, directly prefigures his death, while the vision of the yard 'into which he "is about to break loose" [has] already [been] seen through the eyes of his wife on her failed wedding night'.[165]

Whilst Nabokov and Luzhin overtly manipulate camera eye perspective, Nabokov deploys a range of devices that amplify the cinematic quality of Luzhin's experience. The most explicit of these is the jump cut[166] that occurs at the end of chapter four, which Nabokov announces, in the form of an 'unexpected' chess move, in his Foreword (p. 9). He also describes the tactic, however, as a distinctive process of pulling focus:[167]

> We switch back to the Kurhaus in Chapter Six and find Luzhin still fiddling with the handbag and still addressing his blurry companion whereupon she unblurs [...] and becomes a distinct part of the design. (pp. 9–10)

In other places, the manipulation is more subtle, combining several key cinematic devices in a seemingly incidental way. In his description of the arrival of the taxi that picks up Kurt, Karl and Luzhin, for example, angle of vision, lighting and visual motif combine not only to magnify the cinematic quality of the narrative, but also reinforce the novel's image system. The arrival of the taxi is signalled by the image of its headlamps 'glid[ing] over the asphalt', the angle of vision pitched downwards, so that only their light is registered. The scene is also silent, the taxi 'softly pull[ing] in alongside the sidewalk' (p. 146 — my emphasis). The perspective then shifts to the body of the taxi, this time lit by a different source — a streetlamp — which focuses like a spotlight on the 'large chess squares' on the door — 'the blazon of Berlin taxis' (p. 147) — in yet another recurrence of the novel's dominant chess motif.

Luzhin, meanwhile, demonstrates how he uses his camera eye to alter the composition of a scene, taking advantage of the angle and aspect of light and shade to engage its mechanism, here deliberately pulling focus to produce a specific vision:

---

[165] Dolinin, 'Istinnaia zhizn' pisatelia Sirina: pervye romany', p. 39 (translation mine). In the English version of the novel, 'oblivion' is translated as 'nonexistence' (see p. 140).

[166] 'A cut between two shots that seems abrupt and calls attention to itself because of some obvious jump in time or space'. Konigsberg, *The Complete Film Dictionary*, pp. 200–01.

[167] 'Changing the focus plane during a take. The focus plane goes soft while another part of the scene becomes the primary focus', essentially a process of blurring and unblurring the focal subject. Ibid., p. 152.

The avenue was paved with sunflecks, and these spots, if you slitted your eyes, took on the aspect of regular light and dark squares. An intense latticelike shadow lay flat beneath a garden bench. The urns that stood on stone pedestals at the four corners of the terrace threatened one another across their diagonals. (p. 59)

In the novel's final scene, Luzhin's camera eye perspective engages in such a way that he registers the details of the bathroom in a series of defamiliarized, reified images — the 'gleaming' white bathtub, the pencil drawing on the wall, the small chest and the window next to it with its two different panes of glass, black and frosted 'sparkly blue' (p. 253). The bathroom light functions as a source of 'high key' lighting that brings all these details onto the same focal plane,[168] presenting, in depthless equalization, a culmination of the principal elements of the novel's image system. Luzhin's drawing, of a cube casting a shadow, for example, recalls the shadow in a square of moonlight that he casts as he steps from his hotel balcony in chapter seven, while the 'sparkly blue' of the frosted glass recalls the 'shining blue window' at the hospital (p. 159) which he had interpreted nostalgically, but mistakenly, as the 'blue gleam of a Russian autumn' (p. 160). Meanwhile, the effect of the 'key' light serves to magnify the whiteness of the box-like bathroom, setting it against the pitch black of the night sky which is also presented as a contained space, confined, for the moment, to the upper pane of the window.

There is a sense, however, that Luzhin is aware that he is existing in a cinematic simulacrum. The scene in the yard below him that 'divides' before his eyes 'into dark and pale squares' (p. 256), dramatizes the 'special, ocular access' of the cinematic experience, whereby the mere 'act of looking' has the power to open up 'an (imaginary) three-dimensional space', here beyond the deep chasm of the night that confronts him.[169] Luzhin experiences similar moments of 'special ocular access' throughout the novel — the 'limpid sounds [that] strangely transformed in his reverie and assumed the shape of bright intricate patterns on a dark background' (p. 60) — but until this final scene they remain tantalizingly incomplete, only at the last moment coming fully into focus.

The dream-like quality of these visions correlates with the 'illusionary' nature of Nabokov's text and Luzhin's emblematic role within it — the

---

[168] Key light is 'the major source of illumination for a subject or scene'. Placed high it 'minimize[s]' shadows' and 'create[s] the widest and most intense area of illumination', Ibid., p. 203.

[169] Elsaesser and Hagener, *Film Theory*, p. 15.

'man of a different dimension, with a particular form and coloring that
was compatible with nothing and no one' (p. 103) — the 'invented creature'
whose 'name rhymes with "illusion"' (p. 7). Nabokov's deliberate focus,
in the opening lines of his Foreword, on the sound of Luzhin's name —
'pronounced thickly enough', it is possible 'to deepen the "u" into "oo"'
(p. 7) — seems initially to be a matter of emphasizing its Russianness for
the benefit of his new English readers. Yet the specific attention he pays to
it also points to the close affinity of its rhyme with its Russian equivalent,
иллюзион (*illiuzion*).[170] Nabokov had already established the centrality of
illusion to the cinematic experience in 'Kinematograf', but here the term
recalls its popular use by movie-goers in pre-revolutionary Russia. While
Western audiences referred to cinema as 'the pictures', early Russian film
audiences called it 'the illusions'.[171] Indeed, many of Russia's first movie
theatres were named 'Illiuzion', including the cinema at 74 Zagorodnyi
prospekt in St Petersburg which ran from 1908 to 1917.[172] Thus, by alluding
to the Russian reverberations of Luzhin's name, Nabokov directs his
readers to the fundamental importance of cinema to his protagonist's very
identity.

Alan Spiegel has argued that the 'literary cultivation of a passive and
affectless oval of vision [distinguishes] the cinematographic form of the
twentieth century from the concretized form of the late nineteenth. [...]
This manner of vision tells us that the modern novelist', from Conrad
and Joyce to Nabokov and Robbe-Grillet, 'has brought us further away
from the seen object' and 'closer to the eye of the subject'.[173] For Luzhin,
therefore, it is not a matter of the way he sees the world but the manner
in which he sees it. Under stress, it is his vision that is first to become
impaired, signalling the disintegration of his primary means of spiritual
defence. He experiences unnerving, 'intricate, optical metamorphoses'
when under threat of bullying at school (p. 29), the blurring of his vision
anticipating the same darkening that occurs after his last match with
Turati, where he finds himself surrounded by shadows and fog, taunted
by ghosts (pp. 140–43). His growing panic at the German resort as he tries

[170] Thomas Karshan argues that Luzhin's defence is one of illusion, denoted by the very
word - '*illiuziia*' - embedded in his name. Karshan, *Vladimir Nabokov and the Art of Play*,
p. 101.
[171] Prototype cinemas were also known as 'illusion-halls'. See Kovalova, 'The Film
Palaces of Nevsky Prospect', pp. 32, 42.
[172] Kovalova, *Kinematograf v Peterburge 1907–1917*, p. 353. Moscow has a famous
repertory cinema of the same name. With thanks to Julian Graffy for these further
Russian film history details.
[173] Spiegel, 'Flaubert to Joyce', p. 242.

to find the room where he had competed as a boy is also communicated as a set of reified images that register the scene in increasingly surreal and disjointed, abstract visions:

> a tower of plates ran past on human legs. 'No, farther,' said Luzhin and walked along the corridor. He opened another door and almost fell: steps going down, and some shrubs at the bottom, and a pile of rubbish, and an apprehensive hen, jerkily walking away. [...] Corridor. Window giving on garden. Gadget on wall, with numbered pigeonholes. (pp. 100–01)

Finally, as he watches his pocket chessboard 'dissolve in a pink and cream haze', Luzhin's eyes are forced to pull focus on the position of the 'tiny, insertable' celluloid chess pieces that transform into something 'complex, pungent, charged with extraordinary possibilities' (p. 218), the visual metamorphosis only serving to confirm the futility of his defence.

The disintegration of Luzhin's visual capacity as his illness takes hold magnifies its mechanical cast, laying bare his 'unconscious optics'.[174] This is introduced during the match with Turati by an image of film running through a projector. The 'boundary between chess and his fiancée's home' melts away, 'as if movement had been speeded up, and what at first had seemed an alternation of strips was now a flicker' (p. 125). Luzhin becomes increasingly aware of his vision as a form of apparatus such that, at the Russian ball, he 'half closes his eyes' so that his old schoolmate 'would not notice him' (p. 200), believing that by reducing his vision in this way and denying Petrishchev visual contact he can render himself invisible. It is as if he is finally fully manifesting the cinematic resonances that his name — Luzhin/*Illiuzion* — indeed his very identity, generates. Alan Spiegel's discussion of the Joycean observer's 'characteristic coldness of vision' can also apply to Luzhin here. Spiegel identifies a 'spiritual separateness that begins with a passive, affectless eye' which 'will never permit the observer total rapport with his visual field', resulting in 'a kind of ocular loneliness'.[175] The episode at the ball reveals the degree not only of Luzhin's visual estrangement, his 'ocular loneliness', but also his dependency on the empirical nature of vision — he exists in the realm of sight in the same way as the world only exists as far as he can see it, and as far as the tools of vision allow.

Yet Luzhin's camera eye perspective fails to provide him with the advantage he so desperately needs in his battle against the forces of chess,

---

[174] Benjamin, 'The Work of Art in the Age of Mechanical Reproduction', p. 230.
[175] Spiegel, *Fiction and the Camera Eye*, p. 67.

even though it allows him to believe that he can command, like a movie director, the constantly shifting light and darkness, the 'symmetries and combinations' that manoeuvre silently around him. Compounding this is his failure to realize what they actually signify, for, rather than having any real control over his own destiny, he is in fact nothing more than another piece on the board, to be played by intractable forces that lie beyond his reach or understanding. Ultimately the shaft of light that enabled his entry into the game becomes a light that confines him within it, irrevocably:

> the moon emerged from behind the angular black twigs, a round, full-bodied moon [...] and when finally Luzhin left the balcony and stepped back into his room, there on the floor lay an enormous square of moonlight, and in that light — his own shadow. (p. 117)

Conclusion

The cinematic cast of Luzhin's name, combined with the deployment of cinematic motifs and techniques in *The Defense*, demonstrates a clear development in Nabokov's experimentation with the medium, while the operation of camera eye perspective anticipates its distillation and concentration in the portrayal of his next protagonist, Smurov, in *The Eye*. Smurov's manipulation of the camera eye echoes both Dziga Vertov's privileging of mechanical cinematic vision[176] and Walter Benjamin's detailing of fluid camera movement, which 'intervenes with the resources of its lowerings and liftings, its interruptions and isolations, its extensions and accelerations, its enlargements and reductions':[177]

> Whenever I wish, I can accelerate or retard to ridiculous slowness the motions of all these people, or distribute them in different groups, or arrange them in various patterns, lighting them now from below, now from the side... For me their entire existence has been merely a shimmer on a screen.[178]

Whereas in *The Defense* the camera eye is deployed by Nabokov to express the extent of Luzhin's estrangement, and by Luzhin himself as a means of, albeit futile, control, Smurov assumes and is subsumed, utterly, by the mechanics of the movie camera.

---

[176] See Michelson (ed.), *Kino-Eye*, pp. 11–21. For commentary, see Wyllie, *Nabokov at the Movies*, pp. 18–29.

[177] Walter Benjamin, 'The Work of Art in the Age of Mechanical Reproduction', p. 230.

[178] Vladimir Nabokov, *The Eye*, London, 1981, p. 91.

Rather than serving as mere commentaries on film, however, these works demonstrate Nabokov's keen interest in the industry, and the extent to which he embraced cinema as an art form, as a medium which offered new ways of both seeing and interacting with the modern world. Unlike many contemporary writers and critics who condemned cinema, in its mass appeal and reach, as 'the most clearly expressed form of anti-art',[179] even seeing it as a threat to their very existence,[180] Nabokov's response to film was not to dismiss it, but to take away the elements that could be incorporated into his fiction, essentially to produce the 'new form of writing' that Tolstoi predicted in 1908.

[179] Parker, *Nabokov Noir*, p. 72, quoting Pavel Muratov in his 1925 article, 'Kinematograf'.
[180] For commentary, see Colin McCabe, 'On Impurity: The Dialectics of Cinema and Literature', in Julian Murphet and Lydia Rainford (eds), *Literature and Visual Technologies: Writing After Cinema*, Basingstoke, 2003, pp. 15–28.

Svalbard in Polish Documentaries (1930s–2020s): A Conceptualized Inventory

ANDREI ROGATCHEVSKI and JACEK SZYMALA

Introduction
Scientists need media to explain to a broad audience the purpose, meaning and possible impact of their research in order to secure public awareness, support and funding. The role of popular science documentaries in this process has always been significant, given that the documentary film in general 'seeks to portray the world [...] as a means to impart new knowledge and information'.[1] As visual media gain greater currency than print media, film has become more important than ever. Films about polar research are especially relevant in this respect, as they deal with hard-to-reach locations and investment-intensive science that benefits from (and to some extent depends on) wider understanding and appreciation.

Measuring the influence of cinematic representations of polar research, in particular countries, on research funders and on society at large is important. The process would naturally take into consideration the number and the content of film reviews, viewing figures and results of tailored opinion polls, when and if available. However, before doing this it

Andrei Rogatchevski is Professor of Russian Literature and Culture at UiT The Arctic University of Norway, and Jacek Szymala is a visual historian and part-time lecturer at the DSW University of Lower Silesia.

We would like to express our profound gratitude to Jakub Krakowiak and Marek Pelski (WFO), as well as Dagmara Bożek, Agata Lubowicka, Szymon Kostka, Ryszard Kruk, Ivar Stokkeland and Michał Szcześniak for generously sharing with us various films and publications to help us write this article. Special thanks are also due to Ilia Rogatchevski for his invaluable technical assistance, and to the anonymous peer reviewers for the final touches.

[1] Lilya Kaganovsky, Scott MacKenzie and Anna Westerståhl Stenport, 'Introduction: The Documentary Ethos and the Arctic', in L. Kaganovsky, S. MacKenzie and A. Westerståhl Stenport (eds), *Arctic Cinemas and the Documentary Ethos*, Bloomington, IN, 2019, pp. 1–28 (p. 2).

is essential to catalogue all the documentaries that are known to have been made on the subject, as well as to watch, analyse and classify those of them that are currently accessible in one format or another.

This article focuses on Poland, as a case study, because it is a non-polar country that has achieved remarkable success in polar research over the past century. Poland's polar achievements have been showcased for the benefit of the general public partly thanks to memorable documentaries about Polish polar research that have been historically linked to Svalbard, an archipelago in one of the world's most northern inhabited territories, lying under Norwegian jurisdiction.[2] It is a region that Poland has been exploring and researching since the 1930s.

The special role of films in attracting Polish scientists to polar research has been recently demonstrated by Professor Jan Marcin Węsławski. His 2020 article shows that in 2018, over 80 per cent of Polish polar researchers with a PhD degree, engaged full-time in the field of environmental and earth sciences and aged between thirty and sixty-five, have answered 'movies' to the question of what inspired them to undertake polar research in the first place.[3] Needless to say, not all such 'movies' are necessarily Polish in origin or are documentaries by genre. Therefore, in addition to compiling an analytical inventory of Polish documentaries about Svalbard and about Polish scientists on Svalbard, our task includes placing, to the best of our knowledge and ability, the inventorized films in the wider context of films made by other countries, especially documentaries and features with a focus on Svalbard.

Apart from inventorization and contextualization, a longitudinal conceptualization has been carried out on the most important changes in subject and style that Polish documentaries about Svalbard have exhibited in the ninety-odd-years of their existence. Space constraints preclude us from concentrating on more than a maximum of three films that are each particularly representative of several specific major shifts in the filmmakers' approach to their material. We have identified four such shifts over a ninety-year period, from the mid 1930s up to the present.' We have identified four such shifts over a ninety-year period, from the mid 1930s up to the present. Curiously enough, these shifts do not appear to cancel each other out, since some recent films contain elements typical of much earlier

---

[2] In this article, the term Svalbard is used when speaking about the archipelago as a whole. The term Spitsbergen is applied only to a specific island, i.e. one part of the archipelago.

[3] See Jan Marcin Węsławski, 'Polar Research in Public Discourse: Setting the Stage', *Oceanologia*, 62, 4, part B, 2020, pp. 634–36.

Svalbard-related documentaries, while sharing their time period with films that display a somewhat more modern stance. Tentative recommendations concerning the future of Polish documentary filmmaking on and about Svalbard will also be made.

It has to be stressed that Polish films about Svalbard vary in length and quality. They are mostly notable for leaving a substantial visual record of the explorers at work, rather than for their innovative approach to documentary filmmaking. This does not make the films in question less remarkable. The lasting value of the composite body of work consists primarily in chronicling Polish explorations on Svalbard as they were evolving, and in their focus on polar logistics, research priorities and the human impact upon nature. The fact that many films under discussion here have rarely been seen outside Poland has also necessitated a certain degree of descriptiveness.

Methods

Even though most of the films mentioned in this article have been screened, either in cinemas or on television or streaming platforms, it has not always been easy to retrieve them. A considerable amount of archival research, especially on films made before 1989, in repositories such as Wytwórnia Filmów Oświatowych (WFO) in Łódz and the Archive of Telewizja Polska (TVP) in Warsaw, has therefore been imperative. As for post-1989 films, in a number of cases, getting in touch with filmmakers personally has proved to be instrumental in obtaining access to both a particular film and background information on how and why it was shot. Communication with filmmakers has been complemented by correspondence with some of the scientists who have been avid viewers of, as well as participants in, science documentaries (not only about Svalbard). This has enabled us to secure a selection of informed opinions from both sides of the camera.[4] Where possible, these opinions have been supplemented by sources from news portals and online newspaper databases. Selected films have been analysed in depth following conventional approaches to determine how various means of expression were translated into specific messages. Overall, our research has been undertaken in the spirit of consilience, advocating an integrated body of knowledge, jointly formed by the sciences, the humanities and the arts, and involving, in particular, a 'full

---

[4] We are particularly grateful to Professor Jan Marcin Węsławski, a marine biologist, and Ms Iwona Bartólewska, a film director, both veteran Svalbardians, for sharing their insights with us, which shall be quoted as and when appropriate.

employment of [...] art and fiction as the best means for developing and expressing science'.[5]

Films about Svalbard in the context of Arctic cinemas and science documentaries

Most films about Svalbard, whether made in Poland or anywhere else, are in the documentary genre. The logistics and costs of bringing an extensive cast and crew necessary to make a feature film to the treacherous conditions of the extreme North have for many proved prohibitive. Occasionally Svalbard has been used as a stand-in for Greenland in feature films such as *Na białym szlaku* (On the White Trail, 1962, Poland, dir. Andrzej Wróbel and Jarosław Brzozowski)[6] and *Kjærlighetens kjøtere* (Zero Kelvin, 1995, Norway, dir. Hans Petter Moland),[7] but a non-Svalbard location as a stand-in for Svalbard has featured more often. For example, in *Krasnaia palatka* (The Red Tent, 1969, USSR/Italy, dir. Mikhail Kalatozov) and *Arkhipelag* (Archipelago, 2021, Russia, dir. Aleksei Tel'nov and Mikhail Malakhov Jr), the Gulf of Finland is meant to represent Svalbard fjords.[8] *Orion's Belt* (1985, Norway, dir. Ola Solum and Tristan de Vere Cole), however, is an exception in its combination of a thrilling fictional plot with actual Svalbard visuals that complement each other to produce a breath-taking effect. More often than not, however, purely factual accounts of going to and/or being on Svalbard are exciting enough in themselves, without the need for an attention-grabbing dramatic boost. This article will therefore concentrate primarily on documentaries.

Documentaries about Svalbard belong to the category of so-called 'Arctic cinemas', i.e. 'films portraying or documenting distant Arctic people and geographies',[9] which initially served as a 'blank canvas onto which

[5]   E. O. Wilson, *Consilience: The Unity of Knowledge*, New York, 1998, p. 29.

[6]   We shall deal with this film in more detail later in this article.

[7]   For more on this film, see A. Rogatchevski, 'Screen-testing Arctic Governance: *Zero Kelvin* (1995) and *How I Ended This Summer* (2010)', in Kari Aga Myklebost and Stian Bones (eds), *In the North, the East and West Meet: Festschrift for Jens Petter Nielsen*, Stramsund, 2019, pp. 249–66.

[8]   For details, see A. Rogatchevski, 'Svalbard on the (Post-)Soviet Screen', *Nordlit*, 45, 2020, pp. 150–74, as well as his review of *Arkhipelag* in *Kinokultura*, 76, 2022 <http://www.kinokultura.com/2022/76r-archipelago.shtml> [accessed 19 June 2023]. Setting the action in one location while filming it in quite another is known as 'location substitution'. See Scott MacKenzie and Anna Westerståhl Stenport, 'What Are Arctic Cinemas?', in S. MacKenzie and A. Westerståhl Stenport (eds), *Films on Ice: Cinemas of the Arctic*, Edinburgh, 2015, pp. 1–28 (p. 6).

[9]   Eva La Cour, 'Opening Insights: Presenting, Producing and Living Arctic Cinemas', in K.-P. R. Hart (ed.), *Arctic Cinemas: Essays on Polar Spaces and the Popular Imagination*.

imagery of a [...] supralocational wondrous sublime can be conjured' — 'otherworldly and at the end of the earth', 'the seedbed of life [...] and [...] the place of destruction' — but more recently also as a region increasingly 'endangered, volatile and in need of protection'.[10] The international nature of Arctic endeavour (which on Svalbard was enshrined by the Svalbard Treaty of 1920, enforced since 1925) has resulted in many common themes running through different national versions of Arctic cinemas, whether they have focused specifically on Svalbard or not. Among such common themes, the attractive yet forbidding landscapes, the vagaries of polar exploration, the variety of Arctic wildlife and the lifestyle of the indigenes (if any) feature prominently.

In Svalbard's case, the earliest documentary on record about the archipelago, *Au pays du soleil de minuit* (1909, France, dir. Jean Nédelec), depicted — judging by its catalogue entry[11] — 'a glacier bathing by the sea' and 'the midnight sun' while using only 140 metres of film. Some twenty years later, a much longer documentary, *Podvig vo l´dakh* (A Feat on the Ice) by the Soviet directors Sergei and Georgii Vasil´ev, revealed to audience how dangerous it was to attempt to reach spectacular Arctic sites, as the film detailed the search for and rescue of Umberto Nobile's 1928 expedition to the North Pole — Nobile's airship, the *Italia*, crashed north of Svalbard. As for wildlife, the film shows a polar bear being killed by a single rifle shot from on board a Soviet ship (polar bears reportedly outnumber Svalbard's human population even today).

With respect to the last of the potential topics, filming the indigenes' customs and mores, this is not applicable to Svalbard, as it has never had an indigenous population. Instead, films devoted to Svalbard tend to pay more attention to coal mining, adventure tourism and polar research, in keeping with what has defined Svalbard since the late nineteenth century. A fine early example of Norwegian coal mining on screen features tracking shots and panoramic views of the partly abandoned and partly active mining equipment at Tunheim and Austervåg on Bjørnøya, as well as in and around Longyearbyen on the Spitsbergen island, in an unattributed 1930 Norwegian documentary from the vaults of Nasjonalbiblioteket in Oslo.[12] A fairly recent specimen illustrating aspects of Svalbard adventure

Jefferson, NC, 2021, pp. 9–22 (p. 10).

[10] MacKenzie and Westerståhl Stenport, 'What Are Arctic Cinemas?', pp. 12, 13, 14, 16.

[11] See <https://www.fondation-jeromeseydoux-pathe.com/document/au-pays-du-soleil-de-minuit/5fdd2ac3af99ca9e7f27eec8?pageId=60cb01f76fb6ab1f3a2a5382&filtrerParRalisateur%5B0%5D=Nédelec,%20Jean&q=jean%20nedelec&pos=1> [accessed 20 June 2023].

[12] See <https://www.nb.no/items/7d2ef9684c2ee9eee0c08d8bee523d74> [accessed 20 June 2023].

tourism is the 2002 Czech documentary *Špicberky – Za půlnočním sluncem* (Svalbard: To See the Midnight Sun), made by Tomáš Sniegoň for the Cestománie TV show, which includes scenes of dog sledding and reindeer hunting.[13] However, only the last of the topics, polar research, is fully relevant to Polish films about Svalbard, because it is with precisely this, as well as Poland's presence on the archipelago, that these films have been mostly associated. Polish documentaries about Svalbard are therefore, to all intents and purposes, a subset of science documentaries and should be analysed in the context of the science documentary tradition. A science documentary (a term that also encompasses nature and natural history documentaries) is a 'film that portrays science to the public in a way that is engaging, entertaining and educational'.[14]

Christopher Michael Kustusch identifies three principal types of science documentaries as they had crystallized by the early 2000s: 1) 'animals in Eden', i.e. wildlife scenes narrated without much on-screen human presence and exemplified by the BBC's *Blue Planet* series (2001 and 2017), presented by Sir David Attenborough; 2) an 'illustrated lecture', such as *An Inconvenient Truth* about global warming, by Al Gore and Davis Guggenheim (USA, 2006); and 3) 'scientist as explorer', the format made popular by *Le Monde du silence* (1956, France, dir. Jacques-Yves Cousteau and Louis Malle).[15] This matrix, with its chief constituent parts, which overlap and cross-pollinate each other from time to time, can be usefully supplemented by a classification of science documentaries that is steeped in national cinematic traditions. The four leading national schools of science documentary making are:

1. British (developed to perfection by the BBC and David Attenborough): a competent presenter makes comments to the unique camerawork of excellent quality, achieved by recourse to the latest technology;
2. French (e.g. Jacques Cluzaud and Jacques Perrin, Yann Arthus-Bertrand): no presenter, minimal commentary, excellent photography relying first and foremost on the beauty of the shot, plenty of work and great technique involved in the films' accomplishment;

---

[13] See <https://www.ceskatelevize.cz/porady/1095875447-cestomanie/203562260100012/> [accessed 20 June 2023].

[14] Jared Lipworth, an Emmy-winning producer of science programmes at the Thirteen/WNET and National Geographic channels, as quoted in D. Pineda, 'Editing a Science Documentary: More Than Words (Literally!)', *Science Editor*, 27, 2, 2004, p. 47.

[15] See Christopher Michael Kustusch, *A Paradigm Shift for the Science Documentary: A Thesis Submitted in Partial Fulfillment of the Requirements for the Degree of Master of Fine Arts in Science and Natural History Filmmaking*, Bozeman, MT, 2007, pp. 34–36.

3. Entertaining Australian and American productions (e.g. *The Crocodile Hunter*, five seasons, 1996–2007, the Animal Planet channel): based on a distinct character and direct contact with animals/nature; catching snakes or crocodiles and swimming among walruses or seals; often low-budget films with a minimal didactic value; and

4. Classical — often German (some of which were prepared for the school curriculum at the request of the Ministry of Education) — scientific narratives: more like recorded lectures than a nature film; usually very thorough in terms of content, with animated inserts, infographics and explanations of complex phenomena; mostly not intended for a wider audience and often sponsored by scientific programmes or research institutes.[16]

We must ask, though, how Polish documentaries about Svalbard fit into these classifications. An answer can be obtained if we survey the totality of currently available documentaries, from the first extant Polish film about Polish explorers on Svalbard, *Do ziemi Torella* (To Torell Land, 1936, dir. Witold Biernawski), to the present day almost sixty items overall (see Appendix), most of them documentary shorts, made to account for the diverse activities of Polish (and other) scientists on the archipelago, with the research station in Hornsund as a principal (but not exclusive) focal centre. A rough preliminary periodization of these films reveals four chronological clusters: 1) the 1930s (heroic, exemplified by *Do ziemi Torella*); 2) the 1950s–70s (exotic, best represented by Włodzimierz Puchalski's *Wśród gór i dolin Arktyki* (Among the Mountains and Valleys of the Arctic, 1958); 3) the 1970s–90s (routine, typified by Ryszard Wyrzykowski's Svalbard trilogy); and 4) the 1990s–2020s (ethical, marked in particular by the input from women directors, such as Iwona Bartólewska, Katarzyna Dąbkowska, Dorota Adamkiewicz and Joanna Łęska). The following will consider each of these clusters in turn.

Films of the 1930s: 'Do ziemi Torella' and the heroic period
The heroism of this section was largely generated by its cinematic mode of representation, since Poland, having regained independence in 1918, turned its attention to the polar regions only after the 'golden' age of polar exploration was already over. Nevertheless, even at this stage, Polish involvement in things polar was seen by the Polish state and society as a

---

[16] Professor Węsławski, in correspondence with the authors as of 30 November 2020. All translations into English are ours.

shortcut to international respectability. The exploration itself was usually carried out by a handful of enthusiasts with a background in skiing and mountaineering. Government funding for their expeditions was often complemented by private and public donations.[17]

Poland acceded to the Svalbard Treaty on 2 September 1931. Less than a year later the country sent its first ever dedicated polar research team to Svalbard (more precisely, to Bjørnøya, or Bear Island) to set up a meteorological station there, as part of the Second International Polar Year (IPY, 1932–33). This IPY focused on collecting data in the polar regions, related to meteorology, magnetism and atmospheric science, in order to try and improve weather forecasting and the safety of sea and air travel. Over forty countries joined in and some thirty observation stations were established across the Arctic.

Of the five-strong Polish team, initially led by the then head of the Polish Meteorological Institute Jean Lugeon (1898–1976, a Swiss national), three individuals stayed for the full thirteen-month duration of the assignment that began in August 1932. Two of them — Czesław Centkiewicz (1904–96) and Stanisław Siedlecki (1912–2002), tasked with radiometeorological and meteorological observation respectively — subsequently became synonymous with pioneering Polish undertakings in the Arctic and will be mentioned repeatedly in this article. Both wrote books about their Bjørnøya experiences[18] but apparently left no film footage in the enterprise's immediate wake.

This omission was remedied during the second Polish Arctic venture, the summer expedition of 1934 to map the central part of Torell Land in the south-eastern part of the island of Spitsbergen that lies between the fjords of Van Keulen and Hornsund. The topographical mission (chiefly carried out by, and under the supervision of, two officers from the Polish Military Geographical Institute) was complemented by geological, glaciological, botanical, zoological and meteorological assignments. The expedition team, led by the mechanical engineer Stefan Bernadzikiewicz (1902–39), consisted of seven men (Siedlecki included), most of whom had prior mountaineering experience. The radiotelegraph operator Witold

---

[17] See, for example, Piotr Köhler, 'Polska wyprawa na Spitsbergen w 1934 roku', *Kwartalnik Historii Nauki i Techniki*, 60, 2, 2015, pp. 117–40 (p. 124).

[18] See Czesław Centkiewicz, *Wyspa mgieł i wichrów*, Warsaw, 1934, and Stanisław Siedlecki, *Wśród polarnych pustyń Svalbardu*, Warsaw, 1935. For more on the 1932–33 stay at Bjørnøya, see also Piotr Köhler, 'Pierwsza polska wyprawa polarna', *Kwartalnik Historii Nauki i Techniki*, 58, 4, 2013, pp. 43–59, and Jan Szupryczyński, 'Pierwsza polska wyprawa polarna', *Przegląd Geograficzny*, 85, 1, 2013, pp. 123–30.

Biernawski (1898–1957) was put in charge of filming the expedition to promote its achievements in both Poland and abroad.[19]

It was expected that the film would stimulate in Polish society a 'desire to learn about issues that other nations have already been keenly interested in' and serve as 'proof of national vigor, putting Poland on an equal footing with the already established researchers of Svalbard — the Norwegians, the Germans and the Brits'.[20] About 3,000 metres of film was shot, some 900 of which was later edited, with the help of the Warsaw-based company Panta Film, under the artistic supervision of the prominent Polish author Ferdynand Goetel (1890–1960),[21] into a documentary called *Do ziemi Torella* (To Torell Land).[22] It was released in 1936. According to two unsigned articles,[23] a second documentary from Biernawski's footage was made — *Ku wiecznym lodom Spitsbergenu* (Towards Svalbard's Eternal Ice) — of which we have unfortunately found no trace. Luckily, the first nine minutes and twenty-two seconds of *Do ziemi Torella* have survived, rediscovered by Jacek Szymala at the WFO with the help of its staff.

What remains of *Do ziemi Torella*, begins — after the opening credits which run against a background of stylized images of snowy peaks, the Northern Lights, a sailboat, a mountaineer, two skiers and four birds — with a revolving globe that stops to reveal Svalbard's and Torell Land's exact geographical location. This pictorial introduction is followed by narration by Professor Antoni Dobrowolski (1872–1954), who was a participant in the Belgian Antarctic expedition of 1897–99, and also sometime director of the Polish Meteorological Institute, an expert on the crystallography of ice and snow and head of the organizing committee of the 1934 Polish expedition to Spitsbergen. In his almost two-minute-long preamble, delivered next to a wall-mounted map of Svalbard, Dobrowolski describes the 1932 establishment of the Polish meteorological station on Bjørnøya and the 1934 exploratory visit to Torell Land as historic events, in which 'Poland stood for the first time among civilized states fighting together against a

---

[19] A map of the area was duly produced and other objectives reached. For more on the expedition, see Stanisław Siedlecki, *Wśród polarnych pustyń Svalbardu*, Warsaw, 1935; Stefan Zbigniew Różycki, *Wśród lodów i skal: Ze wspomnień uczestnika polskiej wyprawy polarnej na Ziemię Torella (Spitsbergen 1934 r.)*, Warsaw, 1959, and Jan Szupryczyński, 'Pierwsza polska wyprawa polarna na Spitsbergen', *Przegląd Geograficzny*, 87, 1, 2015, pp. 167–78.

[20] Piotr Köhler, 'Polska wyprawa na Spitsbergen w 1934 roku', p. 123.

[21] Known, among other publications, for a book about Iceland. See Ferdynand Goetel, *Wyspa na chmurnej północy*, Warsaw, 1928.

[22] See Köhler, 'Polska wyprawa na Spitsbergen w 1934 roku', p. 130.

[23] See 'Polska wyprawa polarna na Spitsberg sfilmowana', *Wiadomości Filmowe*, 24, 15 December 1935, p. 17, and 'Polska wyprawa polarna na Spitzberg', *Kurjer Warszawski: Wydanie wieczorne*, 352, 23 December, p. 14.

dangerous element — the great mystery of the North' (*Do ziemi Torella*, 02:39–2:53).

Dobrowolski's mini-lecture is followed by short video portraits of expedition members, beginning with Bernadzikiewicz and continuing with the triangulator Major Sylweriusz Zagrajski (1892–1940), the photogrammetry specialist Captain Antoni Zawadzki (1896–1974) and the geologist Stefan Zbigniew Różycki (1906–88). The portrait sequence (taking up a minute and a half in total) is concluded with Siedlecki and Biernawski, with the photographer and radiotelegraph operator Henryk Mogilnicki (1906–99) appearing between the two. On the one hand, the visual style of their introduction is reminiscent of a presentation of *dramatis personae* typical of a silent feature film. On the other, it may have been partially inspired by the more recent *All Quiet on the Western Front* (an Oscar-winning adaptation of Erich Maria Remarque's novel by Lewis Milestone, USA, 1930), which acquaints the audience with a company of future war heroes one after the other.

The centrepiece of the extant footage in *Do ziemi Torella* (almost three minutes altogether) is devoted to the expedition's journey from Tromsø to Van Keulen fjord on Spitsbergen, via Bjørnøya, on board the schooner *Husvika*, while successfully negotiating sizeable icebergs and ice floes. Afterwards, unloading the expedition's equipment is shown (three tons overall), to set up basecamp at the foot of Berzeliustinden, the highest peak in the neighbourhood. No sooner than the landing is completed, a Polish and a Norwegian flag are erected near the landing site, the former notably being larger in size and flying higher than the latter (07:13–07:29, see Fig. 1). According to *Kurjer Warszawski*, 'this was the first time when a flag with Polish national colours fluttered in the polar winds of Spitsbergen'.[24] The remaining footage (two more minutes or so) is preoccupied with equipment transfer up a steep craggy hill, putting up a tent, saying goodbye to the *Husvika* crew plus a few scenes featuring expedition members both inside and outside the tent, unpacking, gathering water, peeling potatoes and opening canned goods. The film ends abruptly with the characterization of Stanisław Siedlecki as an experienced polar explorer in whose presence all other team members (novices to the Arctic) feel right at home.

---

[24] 23 December 1935. A Polish national flag had actually been erected first on Bjørnøya on 3 May 1933, to celebrate the Polish Constitution Day. See Agata Lubowicka, 'Jak dołączyć do grona "państw kulturalnych": Historia wizualna pierwszej polskiej ekspedycji arktycznej w dwudziestoleciu międzywojennym', in D. Skotarczak and J. Szymala (eds), *Okno na przeszłość: Szkice z historii wizualnej*, vol. 2, Kraków, 2020, pp. 35–70 (pp. 52, 54, 64).

Fig. 1. *Do ziemi Torella* (1936) © WFO

What was in the part that has gone missing? The two unsigned articles cited above of December 1935 in *Wiadomości Filmowe* and *Kurjer Warszawski* (essentially the same text with minor variations) list 'the extremely fascinating adventure of discovery, work full of danger among the menacing peaks and glaciers of the polar mountains, camp life [...] full of specific humour [and] great cinematography on the same level as the best films of this kind'. It is hard to give full credence to this description, as both articles also mention 'polar nights', even though the expedition took place during the midnight sun season. This is either a Freudian error of some magnitude or the anonymous journalist had not really seen the film. The piece in *Kurjer Warszawski* promised that the film would be screened in Polish cinemas soon, but we have not been able to find any information about such screenings, let alone post-screening reviews.[25]

Meanwhile, the film was shown in Norway, at least once, on 17 September 1936, at the Victoria cinema on Karl Johans Street (no. 35), i.e. in the heart of Oslo, a short distance away from the Norwegian Parliament. This sole screening resulted in wider press coverage in Norway than has

---

[25] Enough of the film has survived, however, to classify it as a combination of the 'illustrated lecture' and 'scientist as explorer' subgenres, to use Kustusch's taxonomy.

been possible to detect for the film's Polish release. The Oslo event was reported next day in the central newspapers *Morgenbladet*, *Morgenposten*, *Nationen*, *Norsk Tidend* and *Tidens Tegn*; and on 22 September, in the provincial *Lofotposten*. Perhaps the high profile of several event attendees — high-ranking diplomats, researchers and industrialists — can explain such a concerted action. Two members of the most recent (July–September 1936) Polish expedition to Svalbard, Siedlecki and the physicist Konstanty Narkiewicz-Jodko (1901–63), were also at the event.[26]

The article in *Morgenposten* classified *Do ziemi Torella* as a *Kulturfilm*.[27] This notion was borrowed from Germany[28] and encompassed 'films made for cultivating and educating broad masses of primarily adult viewers, and presented as objective, universal, and truthful, [...] with the primary aim of shaping and ordering the audience's ideas about the world'.[29] Judging by what remains of *Do ziemi Torella*, it clearly belongs to the *Kulturfilm*'s subgenre of expedition film, and in that sense could be likened to Norway's early amateur films about Svalbard — *Vårtokt til Bjørnøya* (A Spring Trip to Bjørnøya) and *Svalbardtokt* (A Trip to Svalbard) — both from 1930, lasting about ten minutes each and edited from the footage by Thor Iversen (1873–1953), a fisheries official, who went to Svalbard to assess the commercial viability of its fish stocks and later toured Norway to screen the films he had shot on his travels in the North.[30]

However, on the basis of the surviving fragment of *Do ziemi Torella*, it is perhaps easier to draw conclusions about the debt it owes to a specific, rather than generic, origin, namely the 1930 eighty-two-minute-long American documentary, *With Byrd at the South Pole*, which was awarded an Oscar for cinematography (by Willard van der Veer and Joseph T. Rucker). The similarity between the two films was duly detected by the aforementioned

---

[26] The expedition team also included Bernadzikiewicz. During its course, the three explorers crossed the island of Spitsbergen on skis, without dogsledding. For more on the expedition, see Stanisław Siedlecki, 'Crossing West Spitsbergen from South to North', *Norsk Geografisk Tidsskrift*, 7, 2, 1938, pp. 79–91, and Piotr Köhler, 'Druga polska wyprawa na Spitsbergen w 1936 roku', *Kwartalnik Historii Nauki i Techniki*, 61, 4, 2016, pp. 135–43.

[27] See 'En polsk film om Svalbard', *Morgenposten*, 18 September 1936.

[28] See E. Beyfuss and A. Kossowsky (eds), *Das Kulturfilmbuch*, Berlin, 1924; W. Uricchio, 'The Kulturfilm: A Brief History of an Early Discursive Practice', in P. Cherchi Usai and L. Codelli (eds), *Before Caligari: German Cinema, 1895–1920*, Pordenone, 1990, pp. 356–78, and U. Döge, *Kulturfilm als Aufgabe: Hans Cürlis (1889–1982)*, Potsdam, 2005.

[29] Olga Sarkisova, 'The Adventures of the *Kulturfilm* in Soviet Russia', in Birgit Beumers (ed.), *A Companion to Russian Cinema*, Chichester, 2016, pp. 92–116 (p. 93).

[30] For more, see B. Sørenssen, 'Thor Iversen and Arctic Expedition Film on the Geographical and Documentary Fringe in the 1930s', in E. Frisvold Hanssen and M. Fosheim Lund (eds), *Small Country, Long Journeys: Norwegian Expedition Films*, Oslo, 2017, pp. 116–35.

pieces in *Wiadomości Filmowe* and *Kurjer Warsawski*, even though neither publication elaborated on the topic in any detail.

Byrd at the South Pole portrayed the American naval officer Richard E. Byrd's first mission to the South Pole and was a much more majestic affair than *Do ziemi Torella*. *Byrd* was distributed by Paramount Pictures and had a bigger budget, a larger crew and wider appeal. Still, it is *Byrd's* structure and tone that *Do ziemi Torella* is consciously trying to imitate, including its dramatic soundtrack, its live opening lecture (delivered by Byrd personally) and its *dramatis personae* introduction style, with personal appearances by the two above-named cameramen, as well as the subsequent occasional voiceover narrative and pictures of a perilous nautical journey through ice. Even the flag sequence in *Do ziemi Torella* is derived from *Byrd*, in which British, Norwegian and American flags are raised over Byrd's exploration camp in the Antarctic (48:51–49:30).

The flags' position is also unequal. The American one occupies the central space and is notably larger and taller than the Norwegian and British ones (erected to honour the previous South Pole visitors, Roald Amundsen and Captain Scott), which appear to be more or less equal in size and height. In *Do ziemi Torella*, the Polish flag is flying above the Norwegian, which is also smaller in size. This is symptomatic of the national pride of newly independent and reunited Poland, with its ability to punch above its weight and enhance its international profile thanks to the country's contribution to polar research.

The pioneering spirit that permeates the atmosphere of *Do ziemi Torella* (deriving from the excitement of charting the territories that no one has likely been to before) is nothing short of heroic. As the first intertitle in *Byrd* says, 'the Conqueror is still the Hero of Heroes. But War, once the Hero's only field, now gives place to a grander campaign — the conquest of the last mighty forces of Nature' (00:45–00:59) residing in the polar regions. Dozens of Poland-related placenames on Svalbard's geographical map — such as Bernadzikiewiczfjellet, Biernawskibreen and Siedleckibreen[31] — is proof of Poland's position in certain aspects of polar record (which, owing to global warming, may outlast on paper the actual existence of the glaciers that have been named after Polish explorers).

The rest of the Polish polar films that survived from what we have termed the heroic period are on a much more modest scale.[32] There are

[31] For a fuller list, see Köhler, 'Polska wyprawa na Spitsbergen w 1934 roku', pp. 132–34.
[32] For more on it see J. Szymala and A. Rogatchevski, 'Svalbard w filmach polskich z lat 30. XX wieku', *Kwartalnik filmowy*, 112, 2020, pp. 161–80.

in fact only two of them, made in the genre of actuality film, i.e. a (once popular) loosely structured moving-image documentation of real-life scenes, barely lasting for one or two minutes, for example, *Wyspa mgieł i wichrów* (An Island of Fog and Winds) and *Wśród mórz Arktyki* (On the Arctic Seas). Both were just over one minute long, released in 1937 via the Polish Telegraphic Agency (PAT) and linked to Centkiewicz, who most likely filmed them himself. The first one — part of PAT's *Tygodnik dzwiękowy* (Sound Weekly) — glances at the buildings on Bjørnøya where the Polish meteorological station used to be in 1932–33, as well as the multitudes of birds nesting in the island's cliffs, and an Icelandic horse that feeds on those birds. This actuality film must have been made during Centkiewicz's return visit to Bjørnøya in 1936.[33] The film shares its title with Centkiewicz's 1934 book, most likely in order to boost the sales of the second edition, which also came out in 1937.

The second film depicts hunting for seals and walruses from on board m/s *Isfjell*, which sailed from Tromsø to the White Sea towards Novaya Zemlya in late winter 1937, at times struggling with difficult ice conditions. From Centkiewicz's letter of 23 January 1937 to the director of the Svalbard and Arctic Ocean Research enterprise Adolf Hoel, it transpires that Centkiewicz (then an employee at the Polish Meteorological Institute) undertook this trip 'to make measurements of the permeability of sea water to light'. He also wished to acquaint himself 'with methods of winter travel through ice' and 'expose some of the scenes on a cinematographic film'.[34] We cannot therefore be sure how much of the film was shot near Svalbard, yet we include it in our inventory nevertheless, to err on the side of caution.

It is also known that during the last Polish interwar expedition to Svalbard in pursuit of glaciological, cartographic, botanical and meteorological research on Oscar II Land in June–September 1938,[35] Bernadzikiewicz (the expedition's technical leader) took some 1,000 metres of film 'documenting the activity and movement of glaciers in addition to the relevant field observations'.[36] Less than a year later, Bernadzikiewicz died in an avalanche in the Himalayas and the Second World War began.

[33] See Czesław Centkiewicz, *Znowu na Północy: Kartki z podróży na Wyspę Niedźwiedzią i Spitzbergen w roku 1936*, Warsaw, 1937.

[34] Statsarkivet in Tromsø, 'Norsk Polarinstitutt (med forløpere), 130, folder: Utenlandske ekspedisjoner Svalbard 1932–1933)'. See also the anonymous 'Wyprawa polskiego uczonego na ocean Lodowaty', *Wiarus*, 24, 1937, p. 584, and Czesław Centkiewicz, *Biała foka*, Warsaw, 1938, p. 15.

[35] For more on it, see, for example, Piotr Köhler, 'Polska wyprawa na Spitsbergen w 1938 roku', *Kwartalnik Historii Nauki i Techniki*, 63, 2, 2018, pp. 7–27.

[36] Köhler, 'Polska wyprawa na Spitsbergen w 1938 roku', p. 21.

As it is not clear what has happened since to the rough footage from Oscar II Land,[37] we do not include it in our inventory.

Films of the 1950s–1960s: 'Wśród gór i dolin Arktyki' and the exotic period
The Second World War, reconstruction costs and Stalinist purges are to blame for the almost two-decade-long hiatus in the Polish exploration of Svalbard. Poland's activities on the archipelago resumed in the run-up to, during, and in the immediate aftermath of the International Geophysical Year (IGY, 1957–58). Together with sixty-six other participating nations, Poland made a lasting contribution to the IGY's ambitiously comprehensive research programme. Head of the Polish IGY committee was Henryk Niewodniczański (1900–68), a prominent nuclear physicist. Another physicist, Stefan Manczarski (1899–1979), was appointed academic secretary to the committee. It was decided that the best person to lead Polish expeditions to Svalbard (as part of the Polish IGY input) would be Siedlecki, who by then had obtained a doctorate in geology and worked at the Department of Geology in the Polish Academy of Sciences.[38]

As Siedlecki later recalled in the film, *Polska stacja polarna w Hornsundzie* (The Polish Polar Station at Hornsund, 1993) by Ryszard Wyrzykowski (1946–2003), some colleagues suggested that the expedition could be done on the cheap: 'It's enough if two or three researchers are sent, let them overwinter there in some old trapper's house and we'll publicize it for you' (02:35–02:44). Siedlecki was vehemently against it: 'I'm not going to act in some advert in a dilapidated, rotting trapper's house and later claim we've accomplished a scientific feat. On the contrary: if we do a job, we do it in such a way that it is good enough to represent Poland on an international arena' (ibid., 02:51–03:13). To achieve this, Siedlecki proposed building a proper polar station on Svalbard: instead of 'camping in tents and spending thirteen or even fourteen months in very primitive conditions, [...] we will create a Polish research station similar to any research station existing in Europe' (ibid., 02:02–02:22). Siedlecki's view prevailed.[39]

Deciding where to locate the station was, however, problematic. A reconnaissance mission in August 1956 set its sights firmly on the Hornsund fjord, with a clear preference for Isbjørnhamna (or Polar

[37] Ibid., p. 23.
[38] For more on Siedlecki's *vita*, see Piotr Köhler, 'Stanisław Siedlecki (1912–2002) – polarnik, taternik, geolog: Stulecie urodzin', *Kwartalnik Historii Nauki i Techniki*, 58, 3, 2013, pp. 61–80.
[39] For more on the history of the station and expedition, see Stanisław Siedlecki, *Dom pod biegunem*, Warsaw, 1964.

Bears' Bay), partly for sentimental reasons (the Hornsund area had been familiar to Siedlecki since the mid 1930s),[40] and partly for photogenic reasons (Siedlecki believed that the bay had the most beautiful scenery on the archipelago).[41] The logistics of the location, however, left much to be desired, not least because of the regular calving of the nearby Hans glacier which could produce a significant commotion. The bay was too shallow and icy for a big boat to come close to the shore, which created difficulties whenever supplies and equipment had to be unloaded and transferred to the station. The challenge of delivering a tractor and a jeep from on board s/s *Bałtyk* in July 1957 can be seen, for example, in *W Zatoce białych niedźwiedzi* (At Polar Bears' Bay, 1961), a feature-length documentary by Jarosław Brzozowski (1911–69).[42]

Even so, those who know about Siedlecki's other career as a filmmaker would not be surprised that visual splendour played such a role in his choice of location for the base. In 1945–46, in parallel with his work at the Department of Geology at the Jagiellonian University, Siedlecki took part in the Film Workshop for the Youth (Filmowy Warsztat Młodych), organized in Kraków by the Polish Film Institute. Together with Brzozowski, he co-wrote the script for the prize-winning documentary short, *Wieliczka* (about the famous Polish salt mine), and co-directed another (commercially successful) documentary short, *Skroplone powietrze* (Liquefied Air, both 1946).[43] Moreover, Siedlecki was also an amateur cameraman (whose footage of the reconnaissance trip to Hornsund can be seen in *W Zatoce białych niedźwiedzi*, 03:09–04:35), as well as a consultant for, and a participant in, a number of popular science films about the Arctic.

Instead of 'two or three researchers', a total of ten were due to overwinter in Hornsund, and at least twice as many to stay for the two summer seasons. The winter group mostly engaged in astronomical, ionospheric, meteorological and glaciological research, while the summer group, in addition to the latter two branches of science, fulfilled tasks related to

[40] See Krzysztof Birkenmajer, '40-lecie polskiej stacji naukowej w Hornsundzie na Spitsbergenie (1957–1997)', *Biuletyn polarny*, 5, 1997, p. 57.

[41] Professor Węsławski's personal communication.

[42] For more on him, see M. Hendrykowski, 'Jarosław Brzozowski', in K. Mąka-Malatyńska and J. Lemann-Zajiček (eds), *(Nie)zapomniani dokumentaliści*, Łódź, 2020, pp. 9–25.

[43] For more on this, see Köhler, 'Stanisław Siedlecki (1912–2002)', pp. 64–65, and J. Szymala and A. Rogatchevski, 'Filmowe portrety Stanisława Siedleckiego (1912–2002) na tle Svalbardu: Fragmenty wizualnej historii nauki', *Kwartalnik historii nauki i techniki*, 66, 3, 2021, pp. 123–42 (pp. 127–29).

cartography, hydrology, geology, geomorphology, geophysics, botany and zoology. The pre-Second World War cohort of visitors to Svalbard, which included Centkiewicz and Różycki (now a professor), was joined by several scientists from the non-Svalbard Arctic experience, including the glaciologist Aleksander Kosiba (1901–81) and the geomorphologist Alfred Jahn (1915–99). A younger generation of Polish Svalbardians was represented by the architect Jerzy Piotrowski (1930–72), who designed and built the first (movable, prefabricated) Hornsund station, and the geologist Krzysztof Birkenmajer (1929–2019), who first came to Svalbard in 1956 and returned there a further twelve times. Among newcomers to Svalbard were the ornithologist Bronisław Ferens (1912–91), who came to Svalbard twice in 1957–58; the geodesist Jerzy Lech Jasnorzewski (1906–89), who went to the archipelago three times in 1957–58 and 1986;[44] and the photogrammetry specialist Colonel Cezary Lipert (1920–87), who visited Svalbard four more times in 1957–59 and 1982–83. Even Niewodniczański and Manczarski made a short trip to Hornsund, as did Lugeon (now President of the Swiss IGY committee), who was reunited with Siedlecki on Svalbard a quarter of a century after their first sojourn on Bjørnøya.

Needless to say, Polish scientific activities on Svalbard had to be chronicled for posterity. According to Siedlecki's ex-wife, Anna, Siedlecki

> was well aware of the value of film for popularizing knowledge and recording events [...]. During the years of constructing the Polish station in Isbjørnhamna and organizing summer and winter expeditions, he simply did not have time to film, so he entrusted this to other expedition participants, especially the experienced filmmakers.[45]

There were two film crews on Hornsund in 1957–58. The first was led by Siedlecki's old acquaintance and collaborator Brzozowski, and the second, by the renowned director of nature films, Włodzimierz Puchalski (1908–79).[46] Puchalski's job was to document the 'life of the Arctic flora and fauna',[47] while Brzozowski's responsibility seems to have been to film pretty much everything that was going on.

[44] See J. L. Jasnorzewski, *Spitsbergen bez retuszu*, Kraków, 2009.

[45] See Anna Wanda Grzymała Siedlecka's email to Jacek Szymala of 2 March 2021.

[46] On him, see, for instance, M. Łukowski, 'Włodzimierz Puchalski', in M. Łukowski (ed.), *Osobowość twórcza – film oświatowy*, Łódź, 1982, pp. 1–4, and J. Szymala and A. Rogatchevski, 'Svalbard w filmach polskich z lat 50. i 60. XX w: Perspektywa geografii wizualnej', *Prace i Studia Geograficzne*, 67, 1, 2022, pp. 45–60.

[47] Janusz Czecz, 'Spitsbergen', *Film*, 42, 515, 1958, p. 13.

Altogether, in the late 1950s and early 1960s, Brzozowski made six documentaries out of the black-and-white footage that he brought back from his journeys to and around Svalbard with members of Siedlecki's expedition. Two of these films, *Północna Norwegia* (Northern Norway; on the crossing of Øresund, passing through Lofoten and docking at Narvik and Tromsø) and *Notatki z rogatej ziemi* (Notes from a Horned Land, about a Sámi settlement), both from 1959, have nothing to do with Svalbard and will be neither considered here nor included in our inventory. The remaining four films — three shorts — *Mały reportaż spod bieguna* (A Short Report from Near the North Pole), *Na dalekiej północnej wyspie* (On a Faraway Northern Island) and *Szpicbergi* (Spitsbergen) — and the already mentioned *W Zatoce białych niedźwiedzi* — are remarkable in the way that they recycle the same or similar motifs and sequences. Brzozowski's four documentaries about Svalbard will therefore be examined as a kind of continuum (merging all three of Kustusch's subgenres, i.e. 'animals [and plants] in Eden', 'illustrated lecture' and 'scientist as explorer').

Almost the same can be said about the six documentary shorts, three black-and-white and three colour, filmed in Northern Norway and on Svalbard by Puchalski (except here we are only dealing with the summative 'animals and plants in Eden' variety). One of these shorts, *U brzegów Skandynawii* (On Scandinavian Shores), released in 1965 in conjunction with Puchalski's assistant and relative Janusz Czecz (1928–98), features the island of Risøya near Tromsø,[48] and so does not belong in our collection. In *Kwitnąca Arktyka* (The Blossoming Arctic), the first third of its nine minutes is devoted to plants that grow somewhere else in Northern Norway and not on Svalbard, yet we are still including this film in our selection. Of the remaining four films, all from 1958–59 — *Śpiewające góry* (The Singing Mountains), *Wyspa piór i puchu* (The Island of Feathers and Down), *W tundrach Arktyki* (In the Arctic Tundra) and *Wśród gór i dolin Arktyki* (Among the Mountains and Valleys of the Arctic) — the last one stands out, as it runs for nearly fourteen minutes (thus being the longest of Puchalski's Svalbard films), incorporates all the main themes related to Svalbard in Puchalski's *oeuvre* and also employs colour, which is arguably the best way to do Svalbard's scenery full justice, especially in the summer. In Puchalski's own words, the 'colourful green world of the Arctic [of moss and flowers], against the background of aquamarine waters of the ocean and ultramarine sky, makes it an irresistibly beautiful and vivid landscape'.[49]

---

[48] Ibid. See also R. Teyszerski, 'Maki kwitną na Spitzbergenie', *Ekran*, 1, 1959, p. 16.
[49] W. Puchalski, 'Tam, gdzie zwierzęta nie boją się ludzi', *Film*, 3, 476, 1958, pp. 8–9, 15 (p. 9).

Interested only in Svalbard's plants, birds and animals (and probably mindful of the fact that on Svalbard people have been incidental to nature), Puchalski shows himself only very rarely in the frame (as a kind of artist's signature), otherwise using camouflage and a telephoto lens to remove himself from the scene and allow his 'actors' to behave spontaneously and undisturbed. At this time, birds and animals in Hornsund were apparently so unused to human presence that they were not afraid at all and even posed willingly in front of the camera. Some expedition members, however, began firing guns for fun, frightening some of Puchalski's subjects away.[50] Bad weather provided another significant obstacle, since out of the hundred days spent by Puchalski on his first visit to Hornsund in July to September 1957, the midnight sun (which would have been ideal for filming around the clock) shone only for ten days in total. Also, at times, damp affected the film's emulsion and made shooting impossible.[51] By the time the expedition arrived at its final destination in July, quite a few plant and bird species had already blossomed, or bred and flown away. As a result, after using some 6,000 metres of film and intending to turn it into one black-and-white and two colour documentaries,[52] Puchalski decided he did not have enough footage, and returned to Hornsund the following June.[53]

Following the additional filming, some of Puchalski's footage was edited into two complementary shorts about birds. The first (*Śpiewające góry*, black-and-white) features, among others, black guillemots, black-legged kittiwakes and fulmars populating the Sofiekammen ridge in Hornsund. The second (*Wyspa piór i puchu*, colour) is dominated by common eiders, barnacle geese, terns and skuas, which bred on an unnamed small island (most likely one of Dunøyane), a few miles away from Spitsbergen's west coast, out of reach of Arctic foxes when the ice melts. Ivory gulls and snow buntings appear in both films. It is as if Puchalski was experimenting a little in an attempt to establish whether the same species would look better in colour or in black-and-white (for the period in question, colour film was a relative luxury in Poland, only rarely available to documentary filmmakers).

---

[50] See Puchalski, 'Tam, gdzie zwierzęta', p. 15. Dr Maciej Seweryn Zalewski (1932–2019), later head of the Department of Sea and Polar Research at the Institute of Geophysics at the Polish Academy of Sciences, admitted that he was the guilty party. See Wyrzykowski's 1986 film, *Polarne wyprawy Włodzimierza Puchalskiego* (Włodzimierz Puchalski's Polar Travels; 08:15–08:48).

[51] See Puchalski, 'Tam, gdzie zwierzęta', p. 9.

[52] See J. Hertel, 'Byłem na Spitzbergenie', *Ekran*, 1, 1958, p. 5.

[53] See 'To Polakker filmer og skriver bok om Svalbard: Kort opphold i Tromsø før reisen nordover', *Nordlys*, 6 June 1958, p. 1.

Kwitnąca Arktyka focuses almost exclusively on flora, with the sole exception of grazing reindeer — and here colour is an undisputed must, conveying multiple hues of yellow, brown and green as it pictures different kinds of vegetation growing on the stones. Viewers can observe cotton-grass, mountain avens, draba, campions, Arctic poppies and a wide variety of saxifrage (all obligingly identified for them by the voiceover). It is as if a herbarium — like those dutifully gathered by the Polish Svalbardians in the 1930s and lodged with scientific institutions on arrival home[54] — has suddenly come to life.

The black-and-white *W tundrach Arktyki* focuses on the archipelago's fauna. Arctic foxes (a visual leitmotif of at least three Svalbard films by Puchalski) and seals, as well as skuas, terns and barnacle geese, are depicted as rightful inhabitants of the seemingly serene Svalbard sea and landscape. In general, however, Puchalski avoids idealizing the animal kingdom around him. It is a bird-eat-bird world, as one may put it, when watching how a gull swallows eider eggs (*Wyspa piór i puchu*), or how the carcass of one bird is pecked at by another (*Śpiewające góry*, see Fig. 2). As the narrator in *Śpiewające góry* points out, 'Nature's law is the law of the strongest'.

Fig. 2. *Śpiewające góry* (1959): A bird-eat-bird world © WFO

[54] See Köhler, 'Polska wyprawa na Spitsbergen w 1938 roku', pp. 20–21, 23.

Finally, plants, birds and mammals share the limelight together in *Wśród gór i dolin Arktyki* as part of the same habitat. Specimens of Svalbard's flora take up the first third of the film, sometimes with a matchstick added for scale. Of those not already mentioned, we see rockfoils, snow-in-summers and alpine bistorts. Among the birds, a little auk makes an appearance in a kind of character role[55] (this species on its own will become the subject of a documentary by Dorota Adamkiewicz and Joanna Łęska, discussed in the section on the ethical period below). One Svalbard animal that is conspicuously absent in Puchalski's films, however, is the polar bear. In an article published after Puchalski's first stay on Svalbard, he admitted that he would have liked to film a polar bear but that year they all apparently 'wandered far into the icy North'.[56]

If there had ever been a rivalry between Puchalski's and Brzozowski's teams on Svalbard, Brzozowski shot ahead of his colleague by managing to catch several polar bears on camera (*Mały reportaż spod bieguna*), one of them even inside the glaciologists' tent camp (*Szpicbergi*) (see Fig. 3). *W Zatoce białych niedźwiedzi* also contains polar bears, which is lucky, as audiences would have been really disappointed if a film called *At Polar Bears' Bay* did not actually show any. But by following the scientists with his camera, Brzozowski ventured further than Puchalski inside Svalbard's territory, and had a greater chance of meeting the bears. Also, unlike Puchalski, Brzozowski captured some of the archipelago's dark season, as well as the Northern Lights.

The animal that Puchalski's and Brzozowski's footage shares is the Arctic fox. In Brzozowski's film one is shown playing with various items of his clothing. It is as if Brzozowski is sending a message to Puchalski, pointing out that while he could film wildlife just as well, instead of taking humans out of the picture he would rather concentrate on their interaction with nature. Another example of such an interaction can be seen in *Na dalekiej północnej wyspie*, in which a group of scientists is walking across the Svalbard terrain while spinning sticks above their heads to protect themselves from aggressive birds. Yet another, from *W Zatoce białych niedźwiedzi*, shows how an expedition member is feeding, from a milk bottle, an orphaned baby seal, brought to near the Hornsund station by storm.

---

[55] Repeatedly so, see also *Śpiewające góry*, *Szpicbergi*, *Na dalekiej północnej wyspie* and *W Zatoce białych niedźwiedzi*.

[56] Puchalski, 'Tam, gdzie zwierzęta', p. 15.

Fig. 3. *Szpicbergi* (1959): A polar bear in a science camp © WFO

It is not that scenes of human/animal interaction are completely non-existent in Puchalski's Svalbard documentaries, but they are very rare. One memorable sequence from *W tundrach Arktyki* includes Czecz's 'interview' with a newborn tern, while making a field sound recording. Brzozowski was equally interested in the interaction between humans (sometimes over vast distances), between humans and the elements (e.g. in *Mały reportaż* and *W Zatoce*, where the wind is stronger than several adult men who struggle to put up a tent), and between humans and man-made objects (such as scientific equipment). In *Szpicbergi* and *W Zatoce*, Professor Jahn and his team are measuring soil erosion with the help of a so-called soil movement gauge (or *gleboruchomierz*), devised by Stanisław Bac (1887–1970).[57] In the latter documentary, we see Svalbard's Governor Odd Birketvedt (1916–2009) on a visit to Hornsund by dog sled, and hear congratulatory radio messages from Manczarski and the overwinterers' families at Christmas.

W Zatoce provides a detailed account of exactly what each scientific team was doing and where (in the coastal areas of Treskelodden, Gåshamna and Van Keulen fjord, as well as on the Heclahuken mountain and the

[57] On *gleboruchomierz*, see J. Kołodziej, 'Wspomnienie o profesorze dr. hab. dr. h. c. inż. Stanisławie Bacu', *Woda-Środowisko-Obszary Wiejskie*, 12, 2, 2012, pp. 411–20 (p. 414).

Werenskiöld glacier, etc.), and could easily have served as a visual aid for the mission's final report. There is also a noticeable attempt to name as many expedition participants and visitors as possible. Yet there were so many of them that Brzozowski had to, on the one hand, respect the hierarchy and prioritize senior management (such as the expedition head and all the professors, who are jointly allocated most of the screen time, with Siedlecki in the lead), and on the other, pander to the need for watchability and specify the individuals who were involved in real-life dramatic events. Among them was the engineer Roman Trechciński (1923–2007), who fixed a problem with the Hornsund camp's electricity supply; the glaciologist Jarema Rdułtowski (1933–63), who fell off an icy cliff, injured himself and had to be carried on board the *Bałtyk* on a stretcher; and the physician Zbigniew Jaworowski (1927–2011), who suffered from stomach pains and, following a series of emergency radio messages, could only be rescued by a Soviet ice breaker (so isolated from the rest of the world Svalbard was at the time).

Overcoming such challenges as a hard-to-access location and danger to life can qualify human actions as heroic. Svalbard remains a remote and relatively risky place to be even today. Yet the way it is portrayed by Puchalski and Brzozowski should probably be defined as merely exotic. Being a pioneer is also a status that befits the concept of heroic achievement. However, when an exceptional deed is done repeatedly, its heroic lustre, if it had one, is bound to fade a little, no matter how demanding the deed is. In 1934, Siedlecki (although not a novice on Svalbard) was one of the very few first Poles on Torell Land. In 1936, and especially post-1956, he and those who came and went with him over and over again, became intermittent visitors on Svalbard. The Svalbard novelty would not, of course, wear off entirely, but the recurrent triumph is perhaps no longer felt as intensely — either by Polish Svalbardians or by the wider public.

The morphing of the heroic into the exotic can therefore be achieved with an admixture of habituation, familiarization and domestication. There is an obvious tendency to domesticate Svalbard a little in Brzozowski's and Puchalski's films, not only by featuring a Polish home on the Hornsund shores but also, for example, by pointing at the Svalbard plant species that can be found in the Tatra mountains (e.g. catchfly and alpine chickweed in *Wśród gór i dolin*, as well as Arctic buttercup and stitchwort in *Kwitnąca Arktyka*). Bringing Tatra shepherd dogs to the Hornsund station (including seven puppies, filmed in both *W Zatoce* and *Wśród gór i dolin* — in the latter, in and around a wooden crate marked 'Made in Poland') — can be treated as a minor act of domestication as well. A Polish flag in *Mały reportaż* (04:51–04:59), this time around displayed on its own, without a Norwegian or any other flag next to it on Svalbard's soil, speaks eloquently for itself.

A little domestication does not go amiss when it comes to promoting an exotic topic, because audiences may feel estranged if the subject matter is too unfamiliar. But exoticizing does not occur organically, so to speak. For example, the marketing strategy for Puchalski's films demonstrates a clear intention to exoticize. One of his working film titles, the matter-of-fact *Flora północi* (Flora of the North),[58] was turned into the more poetic, *Kwitnąca Arktyka*, thus sharpening its oxymoronic potential (as the Arctic is normally associated with ice, not flowers) and increasing its provocative appeal to Polish audiences, for whom the Arctic would first and foremost be associated with Russian/Soviet exile. The titles of some Svalbard films by Brzozowski also display the desire to exoticize by featuring polar bears and the North Pole.

It is hard to say if such a policy of exoticization succeeded in ensuring passable attendance figures in ordinary cinemas (Puchalski's films were released through Centrala Rozpowszechniania Filmów, or the Headquarters for Film Dissemination),[59] since they were unlikely to be screened on their own because of their format and so must have accompanied a main feature. We are unaware of any contemporary special screenings for Puchalski's Svalbard five. It was probably unwise to screen them all at the same time, considering how similar they were to each other. For its part, Brzozowski's full-length *W Zatoce białych niedźwiedzi* received several awards in 1961–62, including UNESCO's Kalinga prize for popularizing science.[60]

Brzozowski must have felt that such a great backdrop as Svalbard should not be limited to comparatively small documentary film audiences. The archipelago deserved to be seen by a much wider public, and usually attracted action adventures. A script by Centkiewicz and his wife Alina, *Na białym szlaku* (On the White Trail), about a Greenland weather station caught in Second World War crossfire (an adaptation of their own story), presented Brzozowski with an opportunity to showcase Svalbard (as a stand-in for Greenland), in a project financed by the filmmakers' association, Studio. Having little experience with feature films, Brzozowski teamed up with another director, Andrzej Wróbel (1933–99), who had

[58] See Czecz, 'Spitsbergen'.
[59] See Teyszerski, 'Maki kwitną'.
[60] See Köhler, 'Stanisław Siedlecki (1912–2002)', p. 76.

previously assisted Andrzej Munk and Andrzej Wajda. In June 1960, Brzozowski went to Svalbard once again to film a number of action scenes for *Na białym szlaku*. This visit was captured in a two-minute-long 1961 newsreel entitled *Biały szlak*, by Polska Kronika Filmowa (PKF). Both the newsreel and the feature film have been added to our inventory, yet the film will not be discussed here, since its plot has nothing to do with Svalbard.[61]

Films of the 1970s–1990s: Ryszard Wyrzykowski's Svalbard trilogy and the routine period

As the funding for large-scale international geophysical cooperation had run out, the Hornsund station was temporarily transferred into the care of the Governor of Svalbard and was not used for research purposes for most of the 1960s. Polish scientists returned to Hornsund in the 1970s, first for summer expeditions, and then after 1978 for research activities on a permanent (rotational) basis. This renewed presence (which also involved mountaineering, glaciospeleology[62] and boating), as well as the various anniversaries of earlier Polish journeys to the archipelago, prompted the appearance of yet another group of Polish documentaries about Svalbard. Most documentaries in this group, diverse as they are and usually combining a minimum of two if not all three of Kustusch's subgenres, share common features that came to dominate Polish filmmaking about Svalbard for over three decades. The shared trait of such features is perhaps best defined as routinizing the Arctic exploration.

We are not using the word 'routine' in any derogatory sense here. In the context of Polish documentaries about Svalbard made from the 1960s to 1990s, routine has more to do with the regularization, normalization and canonization of Arctic adventures, where appropriate, than with repetitiveness, boredom or fatigue. After all, it is probably fair to say,

---

[61] For more on *Na białym szlaku* and its reception, see M. Hendrykowski, 'Na białym szlaku: Zapomniany film o wojnie', *Images: The International Journal of European Film, Performing Arts and Audiovisual Communication*, 26, 35, 2019, pp. 103–15.

[62] For more on glaciospeleology as both science and leisure, see L. Piccini and A. Romeo, 'The Birth of Glaciospeleology', in G. Badino, A. De Vivo and L. Piccini (eds), *Caves of Sky: A Journey in the Heart of Glaciers*, Treviso, 2007, pp. 59–69, and Szymon Kostka's documentary, *Glaciospeleologia* (2012). An active glaciospeleologist himself, Kostka self-reflects on his progress from speleology to glaciospeleology thus: 'I am one of those typical speleologists who simply must get into a cave if they see one. [...] When you see an ice cave you fall in love with them and cannot get back to the ordinary caves anymore.' See Katarzyna Dąbkowska's *Gorączka polarna* (The Arctic Syndrome, 2009), 01:41–01:51, 01:53–02:02.

without diminishing anyone's endeavour, that the seventy-seventh human in space is not quite the same as the first human in space.[63] It is hard to suppress the 'yet again' feeling when watching cinematic representations of the Poles' 'fourteenth' overall voyage to Spitsbergen, or the Polish Institute of Geophysics' 'eighth' expedition there.[64] What is more, the stories of the pioneers of Polish polar exploration on Svalbard (and beyond) have been told over and over again, even entering primary school level.[65]

It is also no longer necessary for filmmakers producing Svalbard-related documentaries to even travel to Svalbard. Instead, someone else's original Svalbard footage (most often Biernawski's, Puchalski's and/or Brzozowski's) can be recycled.[66] Those filmmakers who do go to Svalbard still occasionally engage in paying homage to Puchalski and Brzozowski, either by quoting their images directly or by imitating their style and/or content.[67] Arctic flora, foxes and reindeer became staple features in a number of documentaries by different directors. However, polar bears, owing to the 1973 ban on their hunting, could turn danger-wrought yet highly sought-after photo-ops into a serious nuisance, as Zalewski testifies in Wyrzykowski's *Polska stacja polarna w Hornsundzie* (15:37–15:47): 'When polar bears became protected species on Svalbard and could not be shot, around two hundred of them would go through the Hornsund station annually.' This increased traffic could paralyse the station's work for days, making it too risky for scientists to venture outside to read their sensors' data.

However, if this was Svalbard's routine, it was still probably quite considerably further from most people's typical concept of it. In the opinion of Professor Jahn, voiced in Iwona Bartólewska's *Polonica arktyczne* (Poland in the Arctic, 1992; 10:30–10:40), 'if you take a person off the street and send them to Spitsbergen by plane, not everyone is going to like it there'.[68]

[63] Hundreds of Polish scientists have been trained at Hornsund over the years.

[64] See respectively the film *Spitsbergen* (1978), whose director is not named, and *Polarna Stacja Hornsund* (The Polar Station at Hornsund, 1988) by Bolesław Kapuściński (1949–2018).

[65] See, for example, *Alina i Czesław Centkiewiczowie* (1980) by Jadwiga Zajiček and *Jak tam jest* (What It's Like Over There, also 1980) by Andrzej Bednarek.

[66] See, for instance, Wanda Rollny's *Stanisław Siedlecki* (1988), which consists of an interview with the eponymous protagonist, interspersed with fragments from *Do ziemi Torella* and Brzozowski's material.

[67] See, for example, the aforementioned biopic by Wyrzykowski, *Polarne wyprawy Włodzimierza Puchalskiego*, illustrated by many Puchalski-filmed sequences, as well as the anonymous *Spitsbergen* (1978), in which a wedding ring (11:38–11:42) instead of Puchalski's matchstick (in *Wśród gór i dolin*) is put next to Svalbard's blossoming flowers to demonstrate their actual size.

[68] Since the opening of the Longyearbyen airport in the mid 1970s, it became

Another seasoned Svalbardian, Stanisław Siedlecki, actually welcomed the polar bears' visits to Hornsund as a kind of distraction from the monotony of everyday duties that made it difficult to motivate a small collective of people isolated from the rest of humanity, in challenging conditions, for many months (see *Stanisław Siedlecki* by Rollny, 16:40–16:57 and 17:45–17:53). The dangers of routine, understood as dullness, could therefore in fact be greater than those presented by wild beasts.

On the other hand, a well-established and observed routine could make it possible to organize life in a meaningful and responsible way, to ensure that the day's work is always done, no matter what, while timespans at the lab, the library and the field are alternated with periods of rest and recreation. From the outset, Siedlecki insisted that the Hornsund station should be bound by labour regulations and discipline, similar to any science lab in Poland, and should also be seen as a normal dwelling with its own conditions and conventions, just like any Polish family home (see *Zimny ląd*, or Cold Ice, by Kazimierz Błahij, 1984; 15:06–15:24). The best opportunity to get an insight into Hornsund's scientific and domestic traditions is to focus on Wyrzykowski's 1993 documentary, *Jak tam jest – rok w Hornsundzie* (What It's Like Over There: One Year in Hornsund) and its two companions, *Wyprawy z Hornsundu* (Travels from Hornsund, 1994), as well as the already-cited *Polska stacja polarna w Hornsundzie*, which were all filmed for TVP by WFO.[69]

Rok w Hornsundzie focuses not so much on what is exceptional but what is ordinary in polar researchers' lifestyle at the station: what motivates people to go there, how they get drinking water, when the dark season begins, how long it lasts, how cold it is. The station's tractor is shown making paths to observation sites through deep snow. Scientists venture out in pairs, accompanied by a dog, to protect them against polar bears (snow scooters are not really suited to escaping a bear attack, especially in

possible to travel to Svalbard by regular passenger aircraft. The airport received international flights from Moscow and Murmansk, while the local routes to and from the Soviet mining settlements of Barentsburg and Pyramiden had already been served by helicopters of their own, in operation since 1961. As citizens of the Soviet bloc, Polish scientists were permitted to avail themselves of the Moscow-Longyearbyen-Barentsburg-Hornsund flight itinerary. See, for example, W. E. Krawczyk, 'Najpiękniejsze miejsce na Spitsbergene', in K. Migała, J. Pereyma and J. Piasecki (eds), *Magiczne miejsce 'Baranówka': Zbiór wspomnień w 40-lecie stacji polarnej im. Stanisława Baranowskiego na Spitsbergene*, Wrocław, 2011, pp. 49–64 (pp. 53, 57), which consequently reduced the number of cinematic accounts of their arrivals to Hornsund by boat, and increased those by helicopter, providing some spectacular aerial shots.

[69] Just like Brzozowski and Puchalski, Wyrzykowski put together several films from the footage he had taken during his time on Svalbard.

polar night conditions). Daily observations and measurements are carried out regardless of the conditions, and should lead to MScs and PhDs, the narrator says, adding: 'Not much polar romanticism here' (07:20–07:23).

As far as the living quarters were concerned, each expedition member had a room of their own, decorated to their individual tastes. In winter, however, leisurely activities outside working hours tended to gravitate towards the common room. Here station occupants can be seen playing chess and doing jigsaw puzzles. There is even an opportunity for personal grooming — a hair trimming session is filmed. 'The times when polar explorers smelled of fur and cod-liver oil have passed', the narrator comments (18:06–18:11).

Even kitchen duties are described: everyone (presumably, among the overwinterers, up to ten in total) had to cook and wash up once every ten days. Canned food was very much a thing of the past: a pantry stuffed with fruit and vegetables is shown. When drinks are mentioned, an Amundsen quote is invoked (from chapter two of his 1912 book, *South Pole*): alcohol is 'a medicine in polar regions'. Who would argue against Amundsen's authority? Hornsund dwellers are said to celebrate not only their own birthdays but also those of their wives and their mothers-in-law.

Although there was regular contact with Poland via radio (connection quality varies) and postal services (depending on the weather, Norwegian helicopters tried to deliver and collect mail every ten days; it took less than a week for letters from Poland to arrive in Hornsund),[70] explorers missed their families badly, especially during Christmas and New Year. Christmas dinner leftovers are given to a polar bear that has dropped by. The arrival of 1993 (Wyrzykowski came to Hornsund in October 1992) is greeted by firing signal pistols and drinking champagne.

The station's international context and significance are foregrounded in another Wyrzykowski film, *Polska stacja polarna w Hornsundzie*. When interviewed in it, Siedlecki presents the station as a kind of cultural envoy that can demonstrate Polish values to the world, especially the West. After all, Poles have two fatherlands, he says: 'planet Earth and our own country' (05:55–06:02). In his interview in the same documentary, Zalewski illustrates Siedlecki's thought thus: Hornsund is part of Global Change, the international scientific programme which monitors alterations occurring

---

[70] The topic of postal communications between Poland and Hornsund is touched upon in *Pocztówka ze Spitsbergenu, czyli oczarowanie* (A Postcard from Spitsbergen, or Under the Spell, 1975), the tenth episode in a TV series called *Czterdziestolatek* (The Forty-Year Old). Even though Svalbard itself is not shown in the episode, we include it in our inventory because of its subject-matter.

across the planet by means of seismology, magnetism, climatology and permafrost studies. Later in the film, Zalewski specifically mentions Polish scientific cooperation with the Norwegian Polar Institute and University of Oslo (UiO). A Norwegian physicist from UiO is introduced as a regular visitor to Hornsund. He is shown installing a computer programme at the station, so that observations he needs can continue without him present.

As far as Norwegian visitors were concerned, not only tourists and scientists stopped by at, or passed through, or stayed near the Hornsund station. A young Norwegian miner called Lars Fasting (1938–2021) was hired by Siedlecki as a technician in spring 1958. Fasting worked at the Hornsund station for some months and learnt Polish well enough to subsequently study architecture in Warsaw.[71] The legendary Norwegian trapper Fredrik Rubach (1915–89) lived in Hyttevika, in the vicinity of Hornsund, for years. He can be seen in Czajkowski's *99 dni na Spitsbergenie* (Ninety-Nine Days on Svalbard; 21:41–23:30).[72] Also, Svalbard's Governors came to Hornsund. *99 dni na Spitsbergenie* shows Governor Frederick Beichmann (1924–2002) travelling to Hornsund by m/s *Nordsyssel* and bringing mail with him. Reciprocal visits took place as well. Wyrzykowski's last film in the trilogy, *Wyprawy z Hornsundu*, describes how he went to Governor Odd E. Blomdal (1927–2015) in Longyearbyen seeking permission to film birds in the archipelago's nature reserves, which were usually only accessible to scientists.

Soviet researchers, normally based at the Soviet/Russian mining town of Barentsburg, also frequented Hornsund. *Wyprawy z Hornsundu* mentions the Russian presence on board RV *Oceania*, a vessel in the service of Polish oceanographers that entered the Arctic fjords to take hydrobiological samples. However, before the collapse of the USSR, the Soviet/Russian desire to partner with Poles on Svalbard may well have had an ulterior motive, as Węsławski recalls:

> At that time, Russians still considered Svalbard their historical territory, and Norwegians, its administrators. [...] Sometimes Russians made this all too clear to the inhabitants of Norwegian settlements, as well as to

---

[71] Later he became a well-known architect in Trondheim. Fasting kept a diary of his Hornsund sojourn, and published accounts of his stay at the station in, for example, *Trønder-Avisa* of 19 September 1958 and 24 December 1960. Fasting can be seen in Wyrzykowski's *Polarne wyprawy Włodzimierza Puchalskiego*, reminiscing in fluent Polish about being Puchalski's *ad hoc* film assistant.

[72] Rubach is not named in the film but can be identified thanks to Dagmara Bożek-Andryszczak, *Ryszard Czajkowski: Podróżnik od zawsze*, Kraków, 2019, pp. 174–76.

scientists from various countries, that it was Russia that held the rights to the archipelago. This was particularly obvious with regard to the scientific staff of the Polish station in southern Spitsbergen, which, from a military point of view, was treated as a strategic outpost. The station was located in a place eminently suitable for targeting nuclear submarines. Russians have always been interested in what we've been doing. They also liked working with us because, under the pretext of scientific cooperation, they always controlled us. They wanted to emphasize that it was them who wielded real power.[73]

Nevertheless, during the Iron Curtain era, Svalbard was a major attraction for Polish scientists precisely because, thanks to the Svalbard Treaty, it was possible to enjoy contact with Westerners there without securing a visa.[74] Another Polish scientist remembers how in the late 1970s to early 1980s, at and near Hornsund, she met British, Belgian and French citizens.[75] In 1957–58, in the course of the IGY, the Hornsund station neighboured Swedish, Finnish, Swiss and Austrian research stations. As the narrator in Bartólewska's *Polonica arktyczne* points out (19:11–19:18): 'It was polar research that raised the Iron Curtain for Poland in science.' The Hornsund station remains an important hub for international scientific cooperation today.

Rok w Hornsundzie was not the first documentary solely devoted to the oldest Polish research station on Svalbard. Kapuściński's *Polarna Stacja Hornsund* (shot in 1985–86 and released in 1988 by Interpress-Film) preceded it by five years. Among other scenes, Kapuściński's documentary featured the painstaking unloading of many tons of supplies (brought over by m/s *Jantar*), by recourse to a winch, muscle power and multiple motorboat rides. Similar sequences had been included not only in *Do ziemi Torella* and Brzozowski's *W Zatoce* but also in Ryszard Czajkowski's *99 dni na Spitsbergenie* (1971), in the anonymous *Spitsbergen* (1978) and in the 1986 PKF actuality short, *Za Kołem Polarnym* (Beyond the Arctic Circle), and thus became something to expect in a Polish film about Svalbard rather than being a novelty.

The visual *motif* of a researcher doing something with a piece of scientific gear (a variation on the man-machine trope) was in constant use in Polish documentaries about Svalbard, ever since Brzozowski's *Mały*

[73] See 'Stan wojenny na Spitsbergenie', *Opoka.org.pl*, 14 December 2011 <https://opoka.org.pl/biblioteka/I/IH/niedziela201151-stan.html> [accessed 21 June 2023].
[74] Professor Węsławski's personal communication.
[75] See Krawczyk, 'Najpiękniejsze miejsce', pp. 52, 59.

reportaż demonstrated a hand-held anemometer. This *motif* is employed repeatedly by Kapuściński. Thus, the seismologist Wiesław Wierzbicki (17:00) can be seen studying the Northern Lights with the help of an all-sky camera mounted on the station's rooftop, taking pictures every other minute.

The tradition of depicting the past and present managers of Polish stations on Svalbard remained a feature. In Kapuściński's film, in addition to the renowned Siedlecki (Hornsund's guest of honour at that moment in time), it is possible to spot Węsławski, head of the outgoing expedition team, and the geophysicist Antoni Andrzej Szymański (1938–92), head of the incoming expedition team. Moreover, the legendary achievements of the first generation of Polish Svalbardians were purposefully re-enacted for commemorative reasons, which also contributed to routinization. It was not enough, for example, that in 1980 Norwegians reprised the 1936 feat by the three Poles (Siedlecki among them) who had crossed Spitsbergen from South to North on skis without the help of dogs. On the fiftieth anniversary of the original event (Kapuściński reports), Wojciech Moskal (of subsequent North Pole ski conquest fame), Tomasz Janicki, Zbigniew Pietroń and Jan Michał Zazula (1953–97) reconstructed the 1936 ski run once again.

Kapuściński is aware that his film reflects, to a considerable degree, fairly routine incidents (broadly speaking) at and around the Hornsund station. Unloading goods, replacing one overwintering group with another, personifying scientific research and management, and even reconstructing polar celebrities' old deeds appear on screen as conventional procedures, generated for and by an entity that has been in existence for a long time. Kapuściński actually uses the word 'routine', when the station's working schedule is disrupted by Norwegian tourists. Once they are gone, the narrator says, scientists are '[b]ack to customary, routine work' (23:17). Tourist visits happen sufficiently regularly to qualify as a kind of typical occurrence, too. Symptomatically, the film ends with the phrase, 'Farewell, Spitsbergen — or maybe see you again, Svalbard?' (26:50), indicating that yet another (i.e. most likely replicated) Polish journey to the archipelago is likely to take place soon.

Not everyone would want to return to Svalbard after a spell there, but there are those who caught the so-called 'Svalbard bug', or 'Arctic bug' (i.e. they suffer from an inexplicable urge to come back to Svalbard, something that will haunt them forever). Such individuals would like to revisit the place, thus effectively participating in a routinization of the Svalbard experience. Film-wise, the Svalbard bug phenomenon was first mentioned by Siedlecki in Rollny's biopic about him. In it, he ascribes the notion of the Svalbard bug to Norwegians, and says that he has been affected by the bug himself and is not ashamed of it (see 18:38–19:00). Wyrzykowski discusses the Svalbard bug too, for example in *Rok w Hornsundzie*, which uses a quote from Centkiewicz about the bug being 'contagious and dangerous'. Notwithstanding, Wyrzykowski claims that both he and his companions have caught the bug and shall miss the archipelago when they get home to Poland (25:02–25:14).

Wyrzykowski's *Rok w Hornsundzie* is preoccupied not so much with what happened at the station in a particular year, no matter how ordinary (as Kapuściński's *Polarna Stacja Hornsund* shows), but with what usually happens there, year in, year out (even though Wyrzykowski's experience at Svalbard in the film — and the trilogy as a whole — was limited to the 1992–93 season). It suddenly transpires that religious rituals at Hornsund (another routine) played an important role, for example. At its start, *Rok w Hornsundzie* portrays a gathering of the station dwellers to mark All Saints' Day, even though there are no Polish graves on the archipelago. Near the end of the film, a Catholic Easter service can be seen, conducted by Father Wojciech Egiert (who is based in mainland Northern Norway and came to Hornsund at least once a year, sometimes by the Governor's helicopter).

To the best of our knowledge, such scenes had not been part of any Polish documentary about Svalbard before, presumably because of Communist censorship. It is not clear when communal practices like these began at the station. Yet both episodes take place at a cross erected in 1982 in commemoration of the fiftieth anniversary of the Polish presence on Svalbard, and the twenty-fifth anniversary of the station's existence,[76] so at least the rituals' location of choice cannot pre-date 1982. In 1981–83, martial law was declared in Poland. According to Siedlecki, speaking in *Polonica arktyczne* (23:50–25:35), the cross was erected as an expression of the scientists' emotions that the law provoked. In particular, their religious feelings were hurt at a time when Polish Communist authorities took an especially negative view of Catholicism. The cross was chosen as a symbol of the Hornsund staff's unity with the Polish nation and the Catholic faith.

While the Hornsund station is the oldest and biggest Polish research outlet on Svalbard,[77] attracting mass media attention bordering on

[76] See 'Stan wojenny'.
[77] For more on its history, see, for example, Birkenmajer, '40-lecie polskiej stacji', 1997.

Horsundocentrism, it is not the only one. Ever since the early 1970s, the number of Polish institutions carrying out research on Svalbard has been on the increase.[78] Owned by the Institute of Geophysics, the Hornsund station could not accommodate everyone, so the range of Svalbard sites where it was possible to conduct research expanded. Some of these sites were located quite a distance away from Hornsund, and it made perfect sense for different Polish research units to establish stations of their own. In 1971, Werenhus (Værenhus; or Baranówka, after the name of its founder Stanisław Baranowski, 1935–78), on Wedel Jarlsberg Land, not too far from Hornsund, was built next to the Werenskiöld glacier at the behest of Wrocław University. Four years later, the Hahut station was opened by the Nicolaus Copernicus University in Toruń at the Kaffiøyra plain on Oscar II Land, in the vicinity of the Aavatsmarkbreen and Waldemarbreen glaciers. In 1986, a station set up by the Maria Curie-Skłodowska University (UMCS) in Lublin started functioning in the abandoned mining town of Calypsobyen in Bellsund, near Renardbreen and Scottbreen. In 2011, the Petuniabukta station in Billefjord was established by the Adam Mickiewicz University in Poznań (this is not even a complete list).

It is not surprising that these other stations, important as they are for the scientific community, have also been captured on film. Sometimes — as in the case of *Hahut* (by Ryszard Kruk, 2022) — they have even been accorded a documentary devoted solely to them and their inhabitants, following the example of the Hornsund station. While observing the chronological order of our account, and glimpsing occasionally into the twenty-first century, let us highlight briefly some key events in the stations' history, and the way they have been reflected in particular documentaries.

Czajkowski's *99 dni na Spitsbergenie* immortalizes the construction of Baranówka by Baranowski, the electrical engineer Jan Szymański, the meteorologist Bronisław Głowicki and others, in the form of a prefab house (designed by Baranowski's wife Krystyna), (see especially 24:23–25:07).[79] Błahij's *Zimny ląd* shows an ice pick erected at Baranówka in memory of the station's founder, who died in an accident in the Antarctic. In Szymon Kostka's *Ostatni raz* (The Last Adventure, 2011), Baranówka is filmed at the end of the 2010 summer season, while occupied by a Czech-Polish team of glaciospeleologists, led by Josef and Stanislav Řehák. The area immediately

---

[78] For details, see Przybylak et al, 'Polskie badania polarne z zakresu meteorologii i klimatologii', *Przegląd geofizyczny*, 64, 1–2, 2019, pp. 3–32.

[79] For more on Baranówka's history, see J. Pereyma, 'Stacja Polarna im. Stanisława Baranowskiego Uniwersytetu Wrocławskiego na Spitsbergenie', *Biuletyn polarny*, 15–16, 2010, pp. 71–76, and Migala, Pereyma and Piasecki, *Magiczne miejsce 'Baranówka'*.

outside the house is being cleaned up and strengthened by them to protect the building from an advancing moraine.

In 2015–16, at the fortieth anniversary of its foundation, Hahut became the subject of three documentaries, all of them enjoying significant input from the film director and cameraman Łukasz Kajetan Pochylski. Research was initially undertaken in Kaffiøyra in 1938 by, among others, the geomorphologist Mieczysław Klimaszewski (1908–95), who published his findings twenty-two years later.[80] The station was erected in 1975 to engage further in geological and glaciological research, as well as climate studies and soil science. A house for a team of twelve students and staff, led by Professor Szupryczyński, was brought to the site on board m/s *Włókniarz*. Over 150 scientists have since had a placement at Hahut.[81]

Unlike Hornsund, which is part of the South Spitsbergen National Park, Hahut is located outside its territory. This affords the Kaffiøyra station occupants extra freedom for research. The station functions only in the spring/summer season but remains open throughout the year, in case a traveller needs it as shelter. At first it was just a small house with two rooms (a bedroom and a kitchen) plus separate buildings for a warehouse and a workshop. By 2004, up to nine people could sleep in the living quarters. However, in 2007 the station expanded considerably and can now accommodate up to fifteen people with some comfort. The station even boasts the northernmost Polish sauna, built out of driftwood. However, there is still neither running water nor reliable internet on the station's premises, yet up to five satellite phones can be used for long distance communication, and several marine radios for roaming the adjacent area.

Pochylski's Hahut trilogy consists of the shorts *Colloquium – 40 lat Stacji Polarnej UMK* (Colloquium: The 40th Anniversary of the Toruń University's Polar Station), *Dom daleko od domu* (A Home Away from Home) and *'Najdłuższy dzień życia' na Spitsbergenie* (The Longest Day of Life on Svalbard). The first of these is an eighteen-minute-long interview with the glaciologist Ireneusz Sobota, who since 1996 had been a frequent visitor to Hahut and was now its director. The second includes brief interviews with the participants of Toruń University's 42nd expedition

---

[80] See Köhler, 'Polska wyprawa na Spitsbergen w 1938 roku', and M. Klimaszewski, 'Studia geomorfologiczne w zachodniej części Spitsbergenu między Kongs-Fjordem a Eidem-Bukta', *Zeszyty naukowe Uniwersytetu Jagiellońskiego, Prace geograficzne – Seria nowa*, 32, 1, 1960, pp. 1–167.

[81] For more on the station's history, see I. Sobota (ed.), *Dom daleko od domu: Stacja Polarna Uniwersytetu Mikołaja Kopernika na Spitsbergenie*, Toruń, 2015. Visuals from its early period are gathered in Roman Tondel's short *Pocztówki z przeszłości – Spitsbergen* (Postcards from the Past – Svalbard, 2019).

to Kaffiøyra, for example the geomorphologists Piotr Weckwerth and Katarzyna Greń; the meteorologist Patrycja Ulandowska-Monarcha; the hydrologist Marcin Nowak; and the student Michał Dziembowski (all of whom speak positively about their time on Svalbard). The third film charts the filmmakers' and scientists' journey from a scorching Poland to an invigorating Svalbard during the midnight sun season. In the trilogy, the archipelago's airplane and helicopter vistas are supplemented by particularly spectacular drone footage, featured probably for the first time ever in Polish films about Svalbard.

By contrast, Calypsobyen has so far not been popular with filmmakers. Only Wyrzykowski's *Wyprawy z Hornsundu*, Kostka's *Ostatni raz* and Wojciech Puchejda's *Polskie bazy polarne na Spitsbergenie* (Polish Polar Stations on Svalbard, 2020) contain modest sequences about it — as an abandoned coal mining site, formerly belonging to the Northern Exploration Company, since used by trappers — and now, with the Governor's permission, a UMCS research base. Petuniabukta is the youngest and photogenically unluckiest research station of them all, making a fleeting appearance only in a two-part 2017 travel vlog by Marcin Mossakowski (aka Mosak), *Spitsbergen* (Part I, 09:37–10:05).

Poles have been exploring the archipelago not only by building research bases there but also through sport, such as mountaineering. In 1934, Mogilnicki made a solo ascent to Raudfjellet (1016m) on Wedel Jarlsberg Land; Bernadzikiewicz, to the highest peak of Torell Land, Berzeliusfjellet (1204m); and Bernadzikiewicz and Siedlecki together, to Kopernikusfjellet (1055m).[82] The 'routine' decades kept this trend going. Thirty-seven years later, in *99 dni na Spitsbergenie*, Czajkowski informed viewers about scaling the summits of five peaks.[83] In Bartólewska's *Polonica arktyczne*, Professor Ryszard Schramm (1920–2007) — a biologist who went to Svalbard eight times, mostly as a mountaineer (on the final occasion, at the age of seventy-four) — jokes that Kopernikusfjellet is the most Polish mountain on Spitsbergen, not only because it was named after Nicolaus Copernicus but because its summit has been reached by Poles several times (09:40–09:50). Together with Jerzy Piotrowski and Brzozowski's assistant Andrzej Zawada, Schramm summited Hornsundtind, the highest peak in the southern part of Spitsbergen (1433m), in 1958. Schramm did not limit his athletic pursuits on Svalbard to mountain climbing alone. In 1980 and 1983, in two attempts,

---

[82] For more Polish ascents on Spitsbergen in 1934, see Köhler, 'Polska wyprawa na Spitsbergen w 1934 roku', p. 131.

[83] For exact details, see also, R. Czajkowski, 'Spitsbergen, lato 1971', *Taternik*, 3, 220, 1973, p. 132.

together with a few companions, he successfully undertook a small boat journey around Spitsbergen, which is briefly visualized in the same film by Bartólewska, thanks to amateur camera footage by none other than Siedlecki, who took part in the 1980 trip (23:15–23:50).[84]

Polish explorers have been examining Svalbard not only vertically and horizontally, as it were, but also subterraneously, by lowering themselves into ice caves beneath various glaciers in an attempt to find out how deep such caves go and what their shapes are; to chart waterways inside glaciers; and to try and establish if drainage systems of different glaciers are connected to each other (see Fig. 4). Glaciospeleology can be a useful supplement to geophysical methods, when data obtained from the surfaces of glaciers are not enough to come to a particular conclusion — but it is also an exciting if unsafe pastime[85] and an opportunity to film a picturesque space that has never been filmed before. *Zimny ląd* was a trailblazing film, in which the cameraman Kapuściński manages to take his camera deep into the glacier to produce pictures of unparalleled beauty.[86] As for the permanently looming danger, a scene from *Polarne lody* (Polar Ice, 1999) by Jerzy Zygmunt depicts a glaciospeleologist[87] emerging from a cave to say that the ice inside closed in on him but fortunately did not collapse.

Constructing bases on Svalbard and exploring it in every imaginable direction is one way for Poles to make the archipelago their own, and thus to routinize their Svalbard experience through domestication. The codification of the history of Poles on Svalbard and its canonization by widely accessible visual means, to impress it on audiences back home, is another way of Polonizing Svalbard and advancing routinization further.

---

[84] For more on the two boat trips, see, for example, Janusz Karkoszka, 'Łodziami do 81 równoleżnika', *Trybuna robotnicza*, 231, 30 September 1983, p. 5, and R. W. Schramm, *Dwa długie dni*, vols 1–2, Poznań, 1996. For more on Schramm as a polar explorer, see T. Schramm, 'Działalność polarna profesora Ryszarda Wiktora Schramma', *Biuletyn polarny*, 15–16, 2010, pp. 64–70.

[85] Unlike mountains, glaciers are in constant motion. The caves formed by them are strikingly beautiful but relatively short-lived and the risk of cave-in is huge.

[86] Seven years after its creation, *Zimny ląd* was routinized in Czajkowski's TV broadcast called *Przez lądy i morza: Spitsbergen* (Through Sea and Ice: Svalbard). Czajkowski alternated segments from *Zimny ląd* (totalling about a half of the film's overall length) and a live studio interview with the geophysicist Piotr Głowacki of the Silesian University in Katowice, who had taken part in Pulina's 1983 expedition and went inside the glacier, too. The interview, interesting as it was, lasted just a little longer than the film fragments. To those who had seen the entire film previously, these fragments must have looked like recycled footage.

[87] Adam Małachowski from the Katowice speleoclub. See S. Misztal, 'Jaskiniowcy czyli glacjospeleolodzy w Værenhusie', in Migala, Pereyma and Piasecki, *Magiczne miejsce 'Baranówka'*, pp. 89–90.

Fig. 4. *Glaciospeleologia* (2012): Exploring Svalbard's Blue Light Cave
© Szymon Kostka

Polonica arktyczne sets out to demonstrate that the breadth of Polish scientific achievements on Svalbard can be partly explained by the research tradition established by tsarism's involuntary political exiles to Siberia — such as Jan Czerski (1845–92), Aleksander Czekanowski (1833–76) and Benedykt Dybowski (1833–1930) — who had the strength of character and the presence of mind not only to survive in (sub)polar regions but also to produce ground-breaking discoveries related to Siberia's topography, geology and palaeontology. On Svalbard, this tradition was continued by the Polish scientists who joined the Russo-Swedish Arc-of-Meridian expedition (1898–1902), such as the biologist Aleksei Białynicki-Birula (1864–1937).[88] In other words, Polish Svalbard roots actually go back for at least a century and a quarter. It is therefore hardly surprising that, after all this time, and especially in the past thirty years or so (judging by the Polish documentaries about Svalbard), quite a number of Poles have emerged who care strongly about Svalbard's natural environment. This brings us to the latest, ethical period in Polish Svalbard documentary history.

[88] For more on the Arc-of-Meridian expedition, see, for example, Urban Wråkberg, 'The Russo-Swedish Arc of the Meridian Expeditions to Spitsbergen 1898–1902', in Evgeny Bouzney (ed.), *International Scientific Cooperation in the Arctic*, Moscow, 2002, pp. 15–52.

The 1990s to the present: Global warming, female polar researchers and the ethical period

The ethical treatment of Svalbard (and the Arctic at large) implies that it is not a place which threatens humans but is rather a place threatened by humans and is therefore in need of urgent protection.[89] Such a change of attitude has a great deal to do with the phenomenon of global warming, caused by human activity.

Recent studies indicate that the air temperature on Svalbard is rising six times faster than the global average.[90] Climate changes on the archipelago have been observed for a long time, manifesting themselves most visibly in the shrinking of glaciers, now believed to be irreversible. Ice measurements have regularly featured in Polish films about Svalbard ever since Brzozowski's 1959 *Mały reportaż*, which shows a group of glaciologists led by Professor Kosiba setting up an observation camp (consisting of several tents and crates with supplies and equipment) in the mountainous part of the Nordenskiöld glacier. Viewers are told that such measurements (also conducted at the Hans glacier) have been useful to explain climate changes.

Brzozowski's *W Zatoce* develops the topic further. 'For glaciologists, ice is a key to the secrets of the Earth' (32:20–32:23), the voice-of-God narrator states. Above the Van Keulen fjord, Różycki is pictured while 'retracing his old steps' (29:36) from twenty-five years ago (i.e. the 1934 expedition to Torell Land). He can compare the extent to which some of Spitsbergen's glaciers have since receded, owing to the global warming (29:31–29:38). The comparison is partly made with the help of Kosiba, as well as twenty-year-old photographs of a glacier terminus in Burgerbukta (01:05:40–01:05:46).[91]

---

[89] Not all the films made during the ethical period adhere to its dominant perception that Svalbard is at risk. Thus, the short feature *Spitsbergen* (2017) by Michał Szcześniak upholds the time-honoured view that Svalbard poses a risk. The film's action does not take place on Spitsbergen. The story focuses on a female paramedic who saves lives while suffering from a personal bereavement: her boyfriend committed suicide after losing his legs in an accident on Spitsbergen. The island is only shown on a photograph and serves as a sign of fascination with mortal danger. According to the film's scriptwriter Monika Sirojc (as interviewed by Andrei Rogatchevski on Messenger on 24 April 2023), Svalbard is 'a wild and strong place, a place of isolation, solitude, a place of escape, a place to prove yourself, a place to test yourself'. Sirojc has been fascinated with Svalbard for years and visited it.

[90] See J. Phelan, 'Svalbard: The Arctic Islands Where We Can See the Future of Global Heating', *The Observer*, 13 May 2023.

[91] Rephotographing Svalbard's glaciers to demonstrate their retreat has been done many times since (if not before), most recently in Sindre Kolbjørnsgard's documentary,

There is, however, no obvious ecological or apocalyptical angle in these scenes yet. In the 1950–80s, Svalbard glaciers were studied by Polish scientists primarily because three quarters of today's Poland had been covered by ice once and Spitsbergen was considered 'a key to the geographical past of the Polish terrain' (according to Professor Szupryczyński speaking in the anonymous 1978 documentary *Spitsbergen*, 09:32–09:40). Even though in *99 dni* (1971) Głowicki could already be seen measuring how variations in the solar activity and atmospheric conditions correlated with glacier movements, only in *Polarna Stacja Hornsund* (1988) was a warning about the dangers of the thinning ozone layer made. The centre of the 4.5 sq km-wide ozone hole near the North Pole was apparently located right above Spitsbergen, with direct consequences for its ice covers.

Of the Polish documentaries at our disposal, it was Bartólewska's *Ślad na lodzie* (A Mark on Ice, 1993) that first made explicit the connection between human activity and melting ice in the Arctic.[92] As a result of industrial emissions, which the film insisted should be stopped, a kind of 'gigantic greenhouse has surrounded Planet Earth' (02:56–03:00) and affected the Arctic regions particularly strongly. The film's two principal case studies are Svalbard and Franz Josef Land, with Svalbard serving as a prediction model. 'Spitsbergen today is Franz Josef Land tomorrow' (21:22–21:25), the voiceover claims. According to the narrative (13:56–14:08), since the start of the twentieth century the ice cover on Spitsbergen has decreased by 6 per cent, or 2,500 sq km, and the process keeps accelerating. Warmer waters around Svalbard have encouraged different species to come and settle where they have not been seen before. For example, grey shrimps now keep company with pink shrimps, while cod and redfish (usually found in the North Atlantic) are more frequently landed by trawlers' nets around Spitsbergen.

Also for the first time in Polish documentaries about Svalbard, underwater creatures (crabs, snails, brittle stars, catfish, ribbon worms) have been filmed up close. Bartólewska lavished praise on her cameramen, Andrzej Galiński and Wojciech Ostrowski:

> We filmed *Ślad na lodzie* on [celluloid] tape, which is not like now, when you press a button and after a while take turns with your colleagues to keep shooting for hours. Tape mostly means brief shots, you need to have

---

Voice of the Glaciers (2021).

[92] Her *Ekologia arktyczna* (Arctic Ecology), released one year before *Ślad*, has not been available for viewing to the authors of this article.

an amazing eye for what can be done really quickly, because tape is worth its weight in gold, there is not much of it and it is transported in cans containing five or ten minute spools.[93]

Another first for *Ślad na lodzie* was its depiction of representatives of Arctic fauna and flora as linked together into a communal ecosystem: birds eat the organisms that live in the water; birds' droppings contribute to the formation and richness of vegetation which the reindeer feed on; and so forth. An Arctic fox on the lookout for skua eggs is seen again, just like in the Polish films about Svalbard in the late 1950s–early 1960s. Yet now the skua and the fox are presented not simply as noteworthy species but as links in a food chain (22:36–22:53). The film asserts that even if just one species were to disappear in the wake of human-induced climate change, it can lead to an ecological disaster. In other words, during the ethical period, the 'animals in Eden' mode (as per Kustusch's classification) morphs into 'endangered species in fragile Eden'. As the archaeologist Marek Jasiński of the Norwegian University of Science and Technology in Trondheim explains on camera in *Ślad na lodzie*, in the past humans damaged the environment, too, but not as disproportionately as they do these days (00:49–01:10).

To the best of our knowledge, the intertwined themes of industrial pollution, melting ice and endangered ecosystems on Svalbard, important as they are, had not been developed in Polish cinematography further, in earnest, until twenty years later, in *Mały alczyk – wielka sprawa* (Little Auk – Big Deal, 2013) by Adamkiewicz and Łęska.[94] By then global warming had progressed from bad to worse. Little auks were a staple, albeit episodic, feature of several films by Puchalski and Brzozowski, partly thanks to the species' comical, penguin-like features. Half a century passed, and little auks suddenly took centre stage, for a very serious reason. According to the onscreen testimony of the professional auk watchers Professor Dariusz Jakubas and Dr Katarzyna Wojczulanis-Jakubas, the vanishing glaciers and cold-water streams will inevitably result in the disappearance of the plankton that little auks consume. There will not be enough food for the hundreds of thousands of auks that come to Svalbard to breed every spring. The auk numbers will dwindle, which will lead to a shortage of natural fertilizer for Svalbard's tundra. This will reduce the sustenance

[93] Bartólewska's telephone interview with Jacek Szymala on 1 December 2020.
[94] The co-directors' earlier Svalbard-related film, *Małe życie* (Small-size Life, 2012), has not been available for viewing to the authors of this article.

rations for reindeer, which already struggle to feed themselves, and so the chain reaction will continue, with devastating consequences on a wide scale.

Obviously, Arctic climate change concerns more than just plankton, little auks and reindeer. Another commentator in *Mały alczyk*, Professor Węsławski, reminds us that floating ice (when Svalbard had a great deal of it) hosted shellfish eaten by seals. Seals, in turn, were eaten by polar bears. This food chain is now under serious threat. With the disappearance of shellfish, polar bears (among other species) will disappear, too, unless they become omnivorous. Yet another expert, Professor Lech Stempniewicz, remarks in the film that polar bears have recently started eating auk and seagull eggs (quite literally leaving no stone unturned in the process, as the eggs are often hidden under stones) but this is an extreme measure which will not help the bear population long-term.[95]

Mały alczyk's narrator expresses hope that there will still be a place for auks on Svalbard, even if the ice melts away completely and there is no plankton left in the sea. What will happen to auks remains to be seen but the ice does not seem to have much of a chance. Węsławski explains why (15:20–15:41). The dominant colour scheme of the melting Arctic is changing from white to dark. The dark colour absorbs the rays of the sun instead of repelling them, accelerating the warming process.

Mały alczyk is a remarkable work not only because of its content. It also memorably portrays underwater micro-objects, such as plankton, thus going a few steps further than even Galiński and Ostrowski's sophisticated sub-aquatic camerawork in *Ślad na lodzie*. It lends credence to Marta Głuchowska's declaration (*Mały alczyk*, 35:43–36:07) that plankton may appear insignificant from a food chain's point of view but it is impossible not to fall in love with its elegant movements and varied colours. Furthermore, a stop-motion computer-enhanced technique is employed to highlight the real-life footage of a seagull attacking and killing a fledgling auk (the fact that *Mały alczyk*'s cameraman Tomasz Michałowski managed to capture a moment like this would likely have made Puchalski jealous). It is still a bird-eat-bird world out there, just as Puchalski recorded it in *Wyspa piór i puchu* and *Śpiewające góry*, only now it is visualized by partial recourse to advanced software.

---

[95] In 2018, the Norwegian filmmaker Asgeir Helgestad released a documentary called *Queen Without Land*, about the influence of global warming on a Svalbard-bound polar bear family. *Queen Without Land* sends a message similar to *Alczyk*'s, with the aid of a much grander protagonist.

Another film about climate change on Svalbard, Kuba Witek's *Ruch lodu* (Ice Motion, 2019),[96] utilizes footage normally unavailable to filmmakers, from a drop-camera and an underwater robot at the Polish research vessels *Oceania* and *Magnus Zaremba*, which scrutinize the fjord bottom to detect any organisms that may have entered areas left vacant by the withdrawing glaciers. A related topic of plastic waste is invoked here, too, as it is plastic that can transport organisms to Svalbard from warmer regions. According to the film, the melting Arctic is likely to produce shorter winters and dramatic weather phenomena, for example, more avalanches and landslides, torrential rains leading to floods and rising sea levels.

Among the future victims of climate change, *Ruch lodu* specifically names polar bears (which live not only on Svalbard, of course, but across the Arctic). Why are they especially important? The polar bear is a symbol of the Arctic (*arktos* meaning 'bear' in Greek). With the polar bears' demise, the region will lose a substantial part of its identity. The polar bears' current circumstances on Svalbard are discussed in *Hahut*, which is mostly set at the Polish research station on Kaffiøyra but also at Longyearbyen, during the COVID-19 pandemic.[97] The film demonstrates clearly that the hunger inflicted on polar bears by melting ice is making them more aggressive towards humans. An early scene shows how a helicopter tries to scare several polar bears away from Longyearbyen, where they are looking for food.[98] A little later it is reported that one of these bears has killed a man in a tent a mere mile away from where the Polish researchers have been quarantining in order to get permission to proceed to Hahut to conduct their annual observations.[99] In this context, two film sequences acquire a particularly ominous significance: 1) Professor Sobota teaching the new arrivals at Hahut how to fire a warning shot at a polar bear (aiming the signal pistol in front of the animal, not behind, so that it runs away from you when scared, not towards you); and 2) Sobota repeating a line by the Polish hip-hop band Molesta Ewenement: 'Does it really matter where death comes from?'

Death provides a continuous backdrop to *Hahut*. The sense of mortality in the film stems not only from the general atmosphere of COVID-19,

---

[96] Somewhat reminiscent of Jeff Orlowski's larger-scale and better-known documentary *Chasing Ice* (2012), unrelated to Svalbard.

[97] For a review of the film, see A. Jósefiak, 'HAHUT Ryszarda Kruka', *KlubFilmovy. com*, 10 November 2022 <https://klubfilmowy.com/hahut-ryszarda-kruka> [accessed 22 June 2023].

[98] Apparently, some of these bears featured previously in *Queen Without Land*.

[99] For details, see, for example, D. Nikel, 'Dutch Man Killed by Polar Bear on Svalbard Campsite', *Forbes*, 28 August 2020.

which necessitated strict isolation measures on the archipelago (thinly populated as it is), but also from a fatal accident when a reindeer's horns get stuck in a fishing net washed onto the shore and the animal dies of starvation.[100] Another example concerns the doomed glaciers. To make the viewer empathise with them (as part of a strategy to promote an ethical attitude towards the environment), *Hahut* anthropomorphizes them. This is achieved by adopting a perspective related to irretrievable loss: some glaciers last longer than others yet every single one of them will ultimately meet its end (44:00–44:14).[101] The film concludes with an apocalyptic animation sequence counterpointing several quotes from a poetry collection by Marcin Ostrychacz (2020), which contends that human action will bring about its own demise — through hunger and madness — by gradually destroying the natural world (44:30–47:10).[102]

We cannot help but notice that the rise in Polish scientists' awareness of the lethal dangers of climate change on Svalbard roughly coincides with the increase in the presence of Polish female scientists there. In 1956–57 (not to mention the 1930s), no women took part in the Polish expeditions to Spitsbergen. The men stationed at and near Hornsund must have missed women rather badly. This is evident from the silhouette of a female torso that expedition members assemble from scraps of food on the dinner table in Brzozowski's *W Zatoce* (01:10:33–01:10:38, see Fig. 5). In those days — and even much later, not only among polar explorers but also in mountaineering circles — the view prevailed that 'women's participation in expeditions is rather disruptive and widens the ground for possible conflicts'.[103]

Bartólewska, a graduate of the Faculty of Navigation at the Maritime University of Szczecin, wanted in the late 1980s to embark on a doctoral

---

[100] This is a glaring example of human-caused pollution at work. Quite beside himself, Sobota comments: 'It took me forty minutes to dig the fishnet out of sand. [...] This is the human race in all its fucking glory' (36:41–36:48).

[101] An earlier instance of anthropomorphizing glaciers takes place in *Gorączka polarna*, also in the context of mortal illness and decay. A boat passes by a glacier and the passengers are shouting at it (as a joke) to try and make it calve. The glacier does not calve but the echo brings the scream back. 'It's answering us', remarks one passenger. — 'Yes, but the answer is not very intelligible', says another. — 'Well, it's a very old glacier. It probably has Alzheimer's' (03:13–03:46).

[102] Poetic documentaries are extremely rare among Polish films about Svalbard, which are dominated by the three subgenres as defined by Kustusch. We can name only one more such documentary, Zygmunt's *Polarne lody*, in which a female voice recites Svalbard-inspired poetry by the biochemist Zbigniew Jóźwik, a UMCS employee who went to Spitsbergen in 1987, 1989, 1991, 1993, 1995 and 2000.

[103] A. Krawczyk, 'Syndrom Værenhusa', in Migała, Pereyma and Piasecki, *Magiczne miejsce 'Baranówka'*, pp. 73–78 (p. 74).

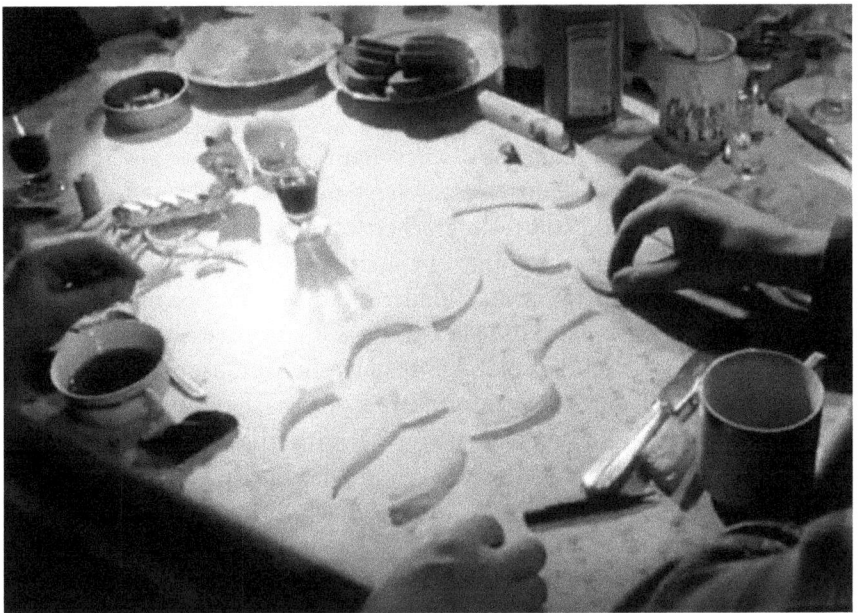

Fig. 5. *W Zatoce Białych Niedźwiedzi* (1961): Women, where are you?
© WFO

research project that would involve 'a year's stay at Hornsund, but was told that it was out of the question because women were not allowed to overwinter, as they were in general conflict-prone and no such option existed for them at all'.[104] The first female scientist to overwinter at Hornsund was a geologist, Danuta Bednarek, and this happened only in the 1995–96 season, during the eighteenth polar expedition of the Polish Academy of Sciences, under the leadership of Jacek Bednarek, Danuta's husband and also a geologist by training. By then, it must have been decided by the powers-that-be that 'it is not women's participation in a polar expedition but the level of culture of male participants that is a problem' (to quote Baranowski, who held such a view on the so-called 'women's issue' in the early 1970s if not before).[105] Needless to say, women began to come to Polish research stations for shorter periods (spring and summer expeditions) much earlier than the mid 1990s, including Różycki's supervisee Zofia Michalska (1927–2007; of Warsaw University) and Siedlecki's wife Anna (of the Mining Academy in Kraków), who went

[104] A telephone interview with Jacek Szymala on 1 December 2020.
[105] See Krawczyk, 'Syndrom Værenhusa', p. 75.

to Hornsund in 1958 and 1960 respectively.[106] A chronological list of Polish women conducting research on Svalbard from then onwards can be found at <https://polarniczki.pl> (the website lists over 370 individuals in total since 1958 if the expeditions to the Antarctic are included).[107]

Even in the early to mid 1980s, when many women had already done their work at different Polish research stations on Svalbard, received wisdom in Poland could still reassign their agency as polar researchers to men. *Zimny ląd* is a case in point. In the middle of the film (14:50–15:25) one can see Wiesława Krawczyk, a holder of an MSc degree in chemistry, on her third visit to Svalbard in 1983, testing water samples at a lab she had set up at Baranówka. Yet the voiceover read by the famous media presenter Jerzy Rosołowski (1930–2001) informs the viewer that this is 'magister Wiesław Krawczyk', at complete variance with the person's womanly appearance. 'While reading the text about the harsh polar conditions, frosts, snowstorms and polar bears, he must have concluded that a mistake had probably been made in adding letter "a" to the male name',[108] and took the initiative to drop the feminine ending. To avoid something similar ever happening again, Wiesława Krawczyk has started using her second name (Ewa) in addition to her first.

Curiously, the increased female presence at the Polish stations on Svalbard did not seem to alter much the traditional gender division of labour as far as housework was concerned. During her first sojourn on Spitsbergen in 1979, Krawczyk, in addition to her duties as a researcher, got more than her fair share of chores at Baranówka. For example, she had to roast a duck and sew curtains, because of the perception that women could do such things better than men.[109] This perception, however, was at odds with reality and must have occasionally served as an excuse for men to renege on their household obligations. When the Hornsund station was in its infancy and all the Polish researchers there were male, the following process was observed: while 'cooking their own meals, cleaning up their dwellings and doing the dishes, scientists learnt to appreciate the labours of their beloved female slaves [...] and became excellent housekeepers'.[110] Yet these housekeeping skills would not necessarily transfer automatically

---

[106] In 1958, Alina Centkiewicz (1907–93) went even to the Antarctic, the first Polish woman to do so.

[107] Some of these women's stories have been told in Dagmara Bożek, *Polarniczki: Zdobywczynie podbiegunowego świata*, Kraków, 2021.

[108] W. E. Krawczyk, 'Najpiękniejsze miejsce na Spitsbergene', p. 57.

[109] Ibid., pp. 49–50.

[110] Hertel, 'Byłem na Spitzbergenie'.

to subsequent generations of male expedition members, when expeditions became unisex. For example, in *Dom daleko od domu*, almost sixty years after Hertel's observation, Dziembowski described house rules at Hahut thus: 'everyone does what they can do best; typically, [men] are busy with resolving technical problems, while women mostly deal with household chores' (11:11–11:26).

In a parallel development, Polish female researchers on Svalbard paved the way for Polish female filmmakers, who have been coming to the archipelago since the early 1990s. It was only a matter of time until a film appeared devoted to distinguished Polish women, who have left a remarkable but insufficiently known legacy as polar researchers and sometimes even as heads of expeditions and research stations. Dagmara Bożek and Kuba Witek's *Polarnyczki* (Ant/Arctic Women, 2023) focuses, apart from Krawczyk, on the ecologist Anna Krzyszowska Waitkus, the hydrologist and poet Joanna Pociask-Karteczka, the biotechnologist Anna Kołakowska and the botanist Maria Agata Olech, all of whom had illustrious careers owing to time spent at the Polish polar research bases, either on Svalbard or in the Antarctic, or both.[111]

Conclusions

To complete our observations and categorization of the main trends detectable in the available Polish documentaries about Svalbard over approximately ninety years, two principal questions have to be discussed: 1) is there anything in Polish documentaries about Svalbard that makes them distinct from similar films made in other countries? and 2) what would be desirable to find in future Polish films about Svalbard?

It is obvious that the thematic evolution of Polish documentaries about Svalbard largely coincides with the general trajectory of many international films about the Arctic, from conquering and exploring an unfamiliar and hostile terrain to valuing and protecting a unique and vulnerable environment (both tendencies sometimes turn out to be complementary rather than mutually exclusive). In this context, Svalbard's specifics predominantly consist of ignoring the otherwise very important issues to do with an indigenous population, as there has never been one on the archipelago.

---

[111] One should not forget the glaciospeleologist Anna Haczek, who could be seen in Kostka's *Trzynasty raz na Spitsbergenie* (The Thirteenth Visit to Svalbard, 2007) and *Ostatni raz*.

Above and beyond this, it is possible to find purely Polish features in the documentaries under scrutiny, if we compare them first and foremost to Norwegian and Soviet/Russian documentaries about Svalbard, i.e. those filmed in the two countries with the longest history of continuous joint presence on the islands. For Russian documentaries, the question of the archipelago ownership has been essential, as some of them insisted that Pomors had discovered Svalbard before Barents and therefore Russia is somehow entitled to a special claim to this land.[112] Norwegian documentaries are as a rule relaxed about the ownership issue and often take it for granted, as international law is indisputably on Norway's side, thanks to the Svalbard Treaty of 1920. As for Poland, it duly asserts priority wherever Polish cartographers were the first to chart sections of Spitsbergen — but Polish names on its map have never amounted to a territorial claim. Also, in addition to polar research, both Norway and Russia/the USSR have engaged in mining coal on, or fishing near, Svalbard, or developing tourism there, and therefore inevitably treat Svalbard as an economic resource, in life and in cinematic representations. By contrast, Poland did little else but research on the archipelago, so Polish documentaries by and large do not deviate from this phenomenon.

As a sum of their constituent parts, Polish documentaries about Svalbard present a concise user-friendly history of Polish Arctic research, with the added value of highlighting women's role in it, as well as leaving behind a visual record of deceased scientists and disappearing species.[113] What is more, quite a few Polish filmmakers involved in documentaries about Svalbard — such as Czajkowski, Bartólewska, Sławomir Swerpel and Wiktor Niedzicki — obtained a science degree before moving into mass media, which gave them an advantageous insight into Svalbard-related matters.[114] It would be ideal if, despite the formidable copyright obstacles, this composite legacy is restored, digitized, subtitled in English and placed in a single online repository for unrestricted public use.

Polish documentaries about Svalbard have not been entirely devoid of deficiencies but even these deficiencies bear a specific national mark,

---

[112] For details, see Rogatchevski, 'Svalbard on the (Post-)Soviet Screen'.

[113] Professor Jahn noted in his diary that at the end of the 1970s, for lack of food, there were much fewer birds on Svalbard than in the late 1950s, when Puchalski had filmed them there. See Szymala and Rogatchevski, 'Svalbard w filmach polskich z lat 50. i 60. XX w.', p. 51.

[114] Unfortunately, neither Swerpel's nor Niedzicki's films have been available for viewing to the authors of this article. Niedzicki's films about Svalbard could not even be included in our inventory because there is no reliable information concerning when they were made and what their titles were. Niedzicki did not respond to our request for clarification and access.

as Professor Węsławski (a frequent participant in Svalbard-related film projects since at least the early 1990s) has communicated to us. According to him, Polish films about Svalbard are usually characterized by three features: 1) low budget; 2) lack of time; and 3) lack of a good story. As a result, such films are based on a fairly randomly selected narrative and average quality photography, made with rather mediocre technical equipment (although recently, good effects have been achieved thanks to the use of drones). With a budget of several thousand PLN or so for a twenty-minute film, a run-of-the-mill camera and one week at his or her disposal, a Polish filmmaker cannot produce a first-class nature documentary, even in a very attractive location.[115] Technical and financial deficiencies can be surmounted if the film concentrates on a coherent story that will interest the viewer. Most often, however, films are made 'about nature', that is, about everything and nothing in particular. The reason is rational, as the film crew (usually the cameraman and the director), upon their arrival in the Arctic, try to record everything they see, hoping that it will prove useful. *Mały alczyk* is an exception.

This may well be so, but it is also undeniable that, despite their budgetary limitations and temporal restrictions (which, however, are not fully applicable in the cases of the films by Puchalski, Brzozowski and Wyrzykowski), Polish documentaries about Svalbard have jointly managed to punch well above their weight. The daring spirit of the Polish polar explorers of the 1930s–50s lives on, in particular in the speleoglaciological pursuits of the 1980s–2010s, and would not have made the same impact without its onscreen depiction.

How might Polish films about Svalbard evolve in the near future, given more time and money? Could a comprehensive and systematic archival search be undertaken to try and locate more overlooked Polish films about Svalbard? Could a multipart series about the history of Polish polar research be attempted, with ample use of archival footage and the (yet unrecorded) reminiscences of the late Communist/early post-Communist generations of Polish scientists, with perhaps a special focus on science diplomacy during the Cold War?[116] Might it be possible to make a full-length

---

[115] On the subject of the comparative availability of resources, Węsławski recalls that once on Svalbard he witnessed how three filmmakers from the Discovery Channel were waiting for three weeks on a snow slope to shoot a two-minute sequence of a polar bear emerging from her den.

[116] For research on this topic (not involving Poland as yet), see, for instance, Stian Bones, 'Science In-Between: Norway, the European Arctic and the Soviet Union', in S. Sörlin (ed.), *Science, Geopolitics and Culture in the Polar Region: Norden beyond Borders*, London, 2013 (chapter 6).

thriller or two, shot in authentic Svalbard locations? It is hard to predict what will happen, but one thing is certain: Polish filming on and about Svalbard will continue for as long as there are Poles on the archipelago.

Appendix

A Chronological List of Svalbard-related Polish Films

The filmography below typically includes the information (if known) about the film's title, director, production company, year of release, length and availability (as of October 2023). The film genre is documentary, unless stated otherwise.

Abbreviations:
PKF – Polska Kronika Filmowa
PAT – Polska Agencja Telegraficzna
WFO – Wytwórnia Filmów Oświatowych (if a film has been made for WFO, it is more often than not kept in the WFO archive)
TVP – Telewizja Polska
UG – Uniwersytet Gdański
UMK – Uniwersytet Mikołaja Kopernika

1. *Do Ziemi Torella* (To Torell Land), W. Biernawski, Panta-film, 1936, 9'22, WFO
2. *Ku wiecznym lodom Spitsbergenu* (Towards Svalbard's Eternal Ice), W. Biernawski, 1936
3. *Wyspa mgieł i wichrów* (An Island of Fog and Winds), C. Centkiewicz?, PAT, 1937, 1'11 <http://www.repozytorium.fn.org.pl/?q=pl/node/9897>
4. *Wśród mórz Arktyki* (On the Arctic Seas), C. Centkiewicz, PAT, 1937, 1'11 <http://www.repozytorium.fn.org.pl/?q=pl/node/8333>
5. *Na Spitzbergen* (To Svalbard), PKF, 1957/28A, 0'43 min <http://www.repozytorium.fn.org.pl/?q=pl/node/6589>
6. *Kwitnąca Arktyka* (The Blossoming Arctic), W. Puchalski, WFO, 1958/1959, 8'56
7. *Śpiewające góry* (The Singing Mountains), W. Puchalski, WFO, 1958/1959, 9'21
8. *W tundrach Arktyki* (In the Arctic Tundra), W. Puchalski, WFO, 1958/1959, 8'35
9. *Wśród gór i dolin Arktyki* (Among the Mountains and Valleys of the Arctic), W. Puchalski, WFO, 1958/1959, 13'44
10. *Wyspa piór i puchu* (The Island of Feathers and Down), W. Puchalski, WFO, 1958/1959, 10'03
11. *Mały reportaż spod bieguna* (A Short Report from Near the North Pole), J. Brzozowski, WFO, 1959, 20'42

12. *Szpicbergi* (Svalbard), J. Brzozowski, WFO, 1959, 17'49

13. *Na dalekiej północnej wyspie* (On a Faraway Northern Island), J. Brzozowski, WFO, 1960, 10'19

14. *W Zatoce Białych Niedźwiedzi* (At Polar Bears' Bay), J. Brzozowski, WFO, 1961, 74'

15. *Biały szlak* (The White Trail), PKF?, 1961, 1'58 <https://www.britishpathe.com/video/VLVA59A9SSPNXHCLKM5LR49KDNTI2-POLAND-SPITSBERGEN/>

16. *Na białym szlaku* (On the White Trail),[1] J. Brzozowski and A. Wróbel, Zespół realizatorów filmowych 'Studio', 1962, 73'54, feature film <https://www.youtube.com/watch?v=R7e-YGRIHjs>

17. *99 dni na Spitsbergenie* (Ninety-nine Days on Svalbard), R. Czajkowski, TELE-AR, 1971, 31'44

18. *Lato na Spitsbergenie* (Summer on Svalbard), W. Zadrowski, Interpress-Film, 1975

19. *Pocztówka ze Spitzbergenu, czyli oczarowanie* (A Postcard from Svalbard, or A Magic Spell),[2] J. Gruza, TVP, 1975, 56'14, Part Ten of the *Czterdziestolatek* (The Forty-year Old) TV series <https://www.youtube.com/watch?v=OsSsUXTdVvo&list=PLjlsoKUwtAUJ6i49bSxes4cqPGdCeyz-j&index=10>

20. *Spitsbergen*, TVP?, 1978, 19'47

21. *Jak tam jest* (What It's Like Over There), A. Bednarek, WFO, 1980, 10'02

22. *Alina i Czesław Centkiewiczowie*, J. Zajiček, WFD, 1980

23. *Zimny ląd* (Cold Ice), K. Błahij, Interpress-Film, 1984, 27'55

24. *Za Kołem Polarnym* (Beyond the Arctic Circle), R. Biczyńska, PKF, 1986, 2'17 <http://repozytorium.fn.org.pl/?q=en/node/9385>

25. *Polarne wyprawy Włodzimierza Puchalskiego* (Włodzimierz Puchalski's Polar Travels), R. Wyrzykowski, WFO, 1986, 28'01

26. *Polarna Stacja Hornsund* (The Polar Station at Hornsund), B. Kapuściński, Interpress-Film, 1988, 27'53

27. *Stanisław Siedlecki*, W. Rollny, WFO, 1988, 21'36

28. *Stanisław – syn Michała* (Stanisław, Michał's Son), I. Bartólewska, OTV Gdańsk, 1989?

29. *Przez lądy i morza: Spitsbergen* (Through Sea and Ice: Svalbard), R. Czajkowski, TVP, 1991, 30'40, Archiwum TVP

---

[1] Even though the action in this film is said to be taking place in Greenland, the sequences were shot on Spitsbergen and in the Tatra Mountains.
[2] In this film, Spitsbergen is named but never shown, not even on the postcard of the title.

30. *Ekologia arktyczna* (Arctic Ecology), I. Bartólewska, TVP, 1992
31. *Polonica arktyczne* (Poland in the Arctic), I. Bartólewska, Video Studio Gdańsk, TVP, 1992, 27'52, Archiwum TVP
32. *Ślad na lodzie* (A Mark on Ice), I. Bartólewska, Video Studio Gdańsk, TVP, 1993, 27'03, Archiwum TVP
33. *Polska stacja polarna w Hornsundzie* (The Polish Polar Station at Hornsund), R. Wyrzykowski, WFO for TVP, 1993, 27'15
34. *Jak tam jest – rok w Hornsundzie* (What It's Like Over There: One Year at Hornsund), R. Wyrzykowski, WFO, 1993, 26'27
35. *Wyprawy z Hornsundu* (Travels from Hornsund), R. Wyrzykowski, WFO, 1994, 24'15
36. *Polarne lody* (Polar Ice), J. Zygmunt, EXON, 1999, 18'16 <https://www.youtube.com/watch?v=bokmbIoJznA>
37. *Eksploracja Cristal Cave* (Exploring the Crystal Cave), S. Kostka, SAYMONFILM, 2004, 20'48 <https://www.youtube.com/watch?v=4OmoOR7kP5s>
38. *Beneath the Arctic / Wyprawa do wnętrza Arktyki*, S. Kostka, SAYMONFILM & SPELEO Řehák, 2005, 12'54 <https://www.youtube.com/watch?v=2Mdy8DsoSY8>
39. *Klimaty Svalbardu* (Svalbard's Weather), S. Kostka, SAYMONFILM, 2007, 14'20 <https://www.youtube.com/watch?v=e6_CGX2vYPw>
40. *Trzynasty raz na Spitsbergenie* (The Thirteenth Visit to Svalbard), S. Kostka, SAYMONFILM & SPELEO Řehák, 2007, 13'17 <https://www.youtube.com/watch?v=-sm1IJo9Vmg>
41. *Rewolwer klimatu: Cykl odcinków* (The Climate Revolver: A Cycle of Fragments), S. Swerpel, Akademicka Telewizja Edukacyjna UG, 2008
42. *Gorączka polarna* (The Arctic Syndrome), K. Dąbkowska, Uniwersytet Śląski, 2009, 22' <https://www.youtube.com/watch?v=e-vpR-e5jK8>
43. *The Last Adventure / Ostatni raz…*, S. Kostka, SAYMONFILM & SPELEO Řehák, 2011, 29'21 <https://www.youtube.com/watch?v=ABFLrL1rByo>
44. *Glaciospeleologia*, S. Kostka, SAYMONFILM & SPELEO Řehák, 2012, 22'06 <https://www.youtube.com/watch?v=t5sWovKvz7A>
45. *Małe życie* (Small-size Life), D. Adamkiewicz and J. Łęska, Mirar and ForestFilm, 2012, 46'
46. *Alfred Jahn*, L. Kaletowa, TVP Wrocław, 2013, 12'
47. *Mały alczyk – wielka sprawa* (Little Auk – Big Deal), D. Adamkiewicz and J. Łęska, International Link and ForestFilm, 2013, 51'33
48. *Colloquium – 40 lat Stacji Polarnej UMK*, J. Janik and K. Pochylski, UMK TV, 2015, 18'48 <https://www.youtube.com/watch?v=ujvDaOSwUys>

49. *Dom daleko od domu* (A Home Away from Home), K. Pochylski, UMK TV, 2016, 19'48 <https://www.youtube.com/watch?v=mqabPE83uqo>

50. *'Najdłuższy dzień życia' na Spitsbergenie* (The Longest Day of Life on Svalbard), M. Pańka, R. Tondel and K. Pochylski, UMK TV, 2016, 9'40 <https://www.youtube.com/watch?v=Tfm_9K6qWcc>

51. *Spitsbergen* (parts 1 and 2), M. Mossakowski, www.livealife.pl, 2017, 12'35 + 12'22 <https://www.youtube.com/watch?v=L6obPBfFm2s> + <https://www.youtube.com/watch?v=_Gno8S29bxQ>

52. *Spitsbergen*, M. Szcześniak, Polski Instytut Sztuki Filmowej, Stowarzyszenie Filmowców Polskich, Studio Munka, Wajda Studio, 34 Film, 2017, 24'10, feature short <https://vimeo.com/183616677>

53. *Pocztówki z przeszłości – Spitsbergen* (Postcards from the Past – Svalbard), R. Tondel, UMK TV, 2019, 2'54 <https://www.youtube.com/watch?v=swJ8Eb3QoPY>

54. *Ruch lodu / Ice Motion*, K. Witek, Northcam Pictures and Instytut Oceanologii PAN, 2019, 21'50 <https://www.youtube.com/watch?v=jZf5hMDGOdo>

55. *Polskie bazy polarne na Spitsbergenie* (Polish Polar Stations on Svalbard), W. Puchejda, 2020, 38'29 <https://www.youtube.com/watch?v=i3YI7iQ1z4U>

56. *Hahut*, R. Kruk, Biały Kruk, 2022, 49'13 <https://www.youtube.com/watch?v=G1Ek403-VtE>

57. *Polarniczki* (Ant/Arctic Women), K. Witek, Northcam Pictures and WFO, 2023, 58'05

A European Entrancement: Animal Magnetism among the Russian Nobility in France and St Petersburg, 1784–1787

ROBERT COLLIS

ON 18 August 1784, Ivan Sergeevich Bariatinskii, the Russian ambassador to France, wrote a report to Empress Catherine II, on her orders, about Franz Anton Mesmer and animal magnetism.[1] The ambassador's despatch was written a mere seven days after the presentation of a report to King Louis XVI by a specially-appointed Royal Commission composed of five scientists of the French Academy of Sciences (Benjamin Franklin, Antoine Lavoisier, Joseph-Ignace Guillotin, Jean d'Arcet and Michel-Joseph Majault). These five eminent figures signed their names to a report that largely dismissed the purported curative powers touted by Mesmer.[2]

Bariatinskii's own report on Mesmer and his theory of animal magnetism is not revelatory. The ambassador himself passed no real judgement on animal magnetism but did indicate to the Russian monarch that the 'public

Robert Collis is Assistant Professor of History at Drake University, Des Moines.

[1] See Rossiiskii gosudarstvennyi istoricheskii arkhiv (hereafter, RGIA), St Petersburg, f. 1284, op. 2, kn. 23, no. 23, ll. 40–43, 'O zhivotnom magnetizme'.

[2] Two separate royal commissions began in March 1784. One by the five members of the French Academy of Sciences, which was submitted to Louis XVI on 11 August 1784. The second report was submitted on 16 August 1784 by five physicians of the French Royal Society of Medicine (Charles-Louis-François Andry, Claude-Antoine Caille, Antoine Laurent de Jussieu, Pierre Jean Claude Mauduyt de La Varenne and Pierre-Isaac Poissonnier). For each separate report, see *Rapport des commissaires chargés par le Roi de l'examen du magnétisme animal*, Paris, 1784; *Rapport des commissaires de la Société Royale de Médecine, nommés par le Roi pour faire l'examen du magnétisme animal*, Paris, 1784. The commissioners of the Royal Society of Medicine were also largely dismissive of the efficacy of animal magnetism. For two recent articles on the impact of the condemnation of animal magnetism by the two commissions, see Bruno Belhoste, 'La condemnation du mesmérisme revisitée', *Revue d'histoire des sciences humaines*, 39, 2021, pp. 187–214; Chloé Conickx, '(Re-)defining "Animal Magnetism": The Mesmerism Investigations of 1784', *Cahiers de l'Institut d'histoire de la Révolution française*, 24, 2023, pp. 1–22.

Slavonic and East European Review, 101, 4, 2023

are divided into two parts: one believes and the other does not'. Moreover, he added that 'several court ladies' were among Mesmer's patients.[3] The Russian ambassador's explicit reference to court ladies may well have been influenced by the widespread concerns among many in Parisian educated and noble circles about the potential for sexual abuse by male magnetizers on supposedly vulnerable female patients. Indeed, the royal commissioners themselves communicated to Louis XVI about 'how easy it would be to abuse a woman in such a state'.[4]

Bariatinskii also supplied the Russian Empress with a basic description of Mesmer's techniques, which he had been promoting in Paris since 1778, as well as highlighting that Mesmer himself had refused to demonstrate his technique before the Royal Commission. In his stead, as the ambassador noted, Charles Deslon sought to prove the efficacy of the medical treatment.[5] Initially, Mesmer treated patients individually, with the goal of restoring the equilibrium within the human organism of a universal 'fluid'. In other words, ailments within the human body stemmed from obstructions to this invisible fluid. Mesmer's goal was to restore a natural balance to his patient by banishing these obstacles via direct (and often prolonged) massaging of bodily poles. This physical procedure was intended to induce a 'crisis' — convulsions were common — that preceded the reestablishment of harmony within a patient.[6] By 1784, the popularity of Mesmer's method of magnetic healing in Paris led Mesmer to adapt his technique in order to accommodate the increased demand on his services: instead of one-on-one treatment, he devised a method of simultaneously treating groups around a wooden tub, or *baquet*. The tub contained iron filings and was filled with 'magnetized' water. Patients gathered around the *baquet* in a circle, holding hands, whilst also touching protruding iron rods in order to be healed.[7]

The publication of the Royal Commission's reports on animal magnetism dealt Mesmer and Deslon a blow from which they never truly recovered.[8] The flood of satirical prints that were published in France in

---

[3] 'O zhivotnom magnetizme', RGIA, f. 1284, op. 2, kn. 23, no. 23, ll. 44, 40.

[4] Ellen R. Cohn (ed.), *The Papers of Benjamin Franklin*, vol. 42, New Haven, CT, 2017, p. 479.

[5] 'O zhivotnom magnetizme', RGIA, f. 1284, op. 2, kn. 23, no. 23, l. 40.

[6] Robert Darnton, *Mesmerism and the End of the Enlightenment in France*, Cambridge, MA and London, 1968, pp. 3–4.

[7] Alan Gauld, *A History of Hypnotism*, Cambridge, 1995, p. 5.

[8] On the contemporary furore created by the Royal Commission reports, see Jean-Roch Laurence, '1784', *International Journal of Clinical and Experimental Hypnosis*, vol. 50, 2002, pp. 309–19.

the wake of the report, alongside plays such as *Les docteurs modernes* by Pierre-Yves Barré and Jean-Baptiste Radet,[9] is testament to the hostility felt among sections of French *ancien regime* society towards Mesmer and his theory: it was variously ridiculed as being a superstitious, occult-ridden remnant of an *unenlightened* age that promoted devilish manipulation, sexual depravity and was a threat to social cohesion and the status quo.[10]

The Russian Empress was surely encouraged when reading the reports of the French Royal Commission and her own ambassador in August 1784. As Rodolphe Baudin has recently noted, Catherine II at this time was already scathing of what she saw as the excitable tendency of the denizens of Paris to need 'a new *marotte*', that is a new folly or fad, 'every month to take the place of its puppets'.[11] She made these remarks on 8 May 1784 in a letter to Friedrich Melchior Grimm, after receiving regular reports on the exploits of the Montgolfier brothers and their hot air balloon from Bariatinskii since November 1783.[12] By the time that the Empress had penned her letter to Grimm she had already taken decisive action in her realm by banning so-called aerostations on 4 April 1784, shortly after a Frenchman named Mesnil made two attempts in a hot air balloon in Moscow in February and March.[13] Significantly, in this

---

[9] The play premiered on 16 November 1784. See Pierre-Yves Barré and Jean-Baptiste Radet, *Les Docteurs modernes*, Paris, 1784. On reaction to the so-called 'Franklin Report' in the United States, see Philipp Ziesche, 'Containing the Flow of Animal Magnetism: Benjamin Franklin, Thomas Jefferson, John Adams and the Mesmer Report', *Transactions of the American Philosophical Society*, 110, 2, 2022, pp. 295–311.

[10] This is epitomised in the contemporary engraving entitled 'Le Magnétisme Devoilé' (1784), which depicts Benjamin Franklin and the other commissioners holding up a copy of their report. Rays of light can be seen emanating from the report, which are depicted as having the power to ward off Mesmer and his adherents (depicted as superstitious charlatans). See also the frontispiece to Jean-Jacques Paulet, *L'Antimagnétisme*, London, 1784.

[11] Rodolphe Baudin, 'Aeromania and Enlightenment: The Politics of Hot Air Balloons in Karamzin's "Letters of a Russian Traveler"', *Вивлиофика: E-Journal of Eighteenth-Century Russian Studies*, 7, 2019, p. 6. For Catherine II's letter to F. M. Grimm, see *Pis'ma Imperatritsy Ekateriny II k Grimmu (1774–1796)*, ed. Ia. Grot, *Sbornik russkago imperatorskago istoricheskago obshchestva*, vol. 23, St Petersburg, 1878, p. 327.

[12] On Bariatinskii's reports from Paris to Catherine II on the furore surrounding hot air balloons between November 1783 and September 1784, see Nicolas Galitzyne, 'Les premières experiences de Montgolfier D'après des documents russes', *Annales Internationales d'Histoire Congrès de Paris 1900*, Paris, 1901, pp. 146–54. For the actual despatches, see Moscow, Arkhiv vneshnei politiki Rossiiskoi Imperii, f. 'Snosheniia Rossii s Frantsiei', op. 93/6, d. 394.

[13] On the early history of hot air balloons and their exponents in Russia between 1783 and 1785, see John T. Alexander. 'Aeromania, "Fire-Balloons," and Catherine the Great's Ban of 1784', *The Historian*, 58, 3, 1996, pp. 497–516; A. V. Chudinov, 'Polety nad Moskvoi

same letter she also tellingly compared the foolishness and fraudulence of
balloon adventurers to the work of 'the charlatan who cures vapours', or
in other words nervous disorders including hysteria. Here, Catherine II
was taking direct aim at the followers of Mesmer, who were particularly
associated with treating this common ailment among the noblewomen of
Paris.[14]

The swift action of the Russian Empress in April 1784 against aerostation
adventurers in her realm — ostensibly on the grounds of the risk of fire
posed by their gaseous inventions — was not necessary against so-called
'vapour charlatans', as none had yet sought to promote their purported
medicinal art. Indeed, in a letter written to Grimm in March 1785
Catherine II conveys a dismissive, yet relaxed, attitude to the controversial
medical theory: 'I have always said that this magnetism, which does not
cure anyone, cannot kill anyone either.'[15] Thus, in the spring of 1785, the
Russian monarch did not convey any sense that animal magnetism posed
a threat within her large empire to either the medical establishment or
the moral order of her nobility. The timely surveillance reports on hot air
balloons and animal magnetism supplied by Bariatinskii from Paris in 1783
and 1784 allowed the Russian Empress not only to monitor the negative
effects of such fads in the French capital, but also to remain vigilant against
any such follies attracting any modicum of éclat in her own realm.

By this time few among the Russian nobility would have remained
oblivious to the renown of Mesmer's controversial technique. Readers of
the *Sanktpeterburgskie vedomosti*, for example, first began to be informed
about the seemingly miraculous cures achieved by Mesmer on 31 March
1777, when the Swabian physician was still plying his trade in Vienna. On
this day, the capital city's principal newspaper featured a lengthy report
about how Mesmer had purportedly cured the blindness of Maria Theresia
von Paradis, a well-known eighteen-year-old pianist.[16] Irregular reports

---

(frantsuzy-guvernery i pervye opyty vozdukhoplavaniia v Rossii XVIII v.)', *Homo
Historicus*, Moscow, 2003, pp. 209–23; Elena Leonidovna Zheltova, 'Vozdukhoplavanie v
Rossii i Frantsii v 1783–1785 gg.: "Peresborka sotsial'nogo"', *Sotsiologiia nauki i tekhnologii*,
12, 2, 2021, pp. 7–25.

[14] For a contemporary pamphlet explicitly extolling the use of animal magnetism to
treat the nervous condition of vapours, see Claude Paumerelle, *La philosophie des vapeurs,
ou Correspondance d'une jolie femme. Augmentée d'un petit Traité des Crises magnétiques
à l'usage des Mesmériennes*, Paris, 1784. For a discussion of vapours as a nervous
condition, see Edward Hare, 'The History of "Nervous Disorders" from 1600 to 1840, and
a Comparison with Modern Views', *British Journal of Psychiatry*, 159, 1991, pp. 37–45.

[15] *Pis'ma Imperatritsy Ekateriny II k Grimmu (1774–1796)*, p. 327.

[16] See *Sanktpeterburgskie vedomosti*, no. 26 (31 March 1777).

about the cures rendered on patients by Mesmer continued to feature in both the *Sanktpeterburskie vedomosti* and the *Moskovskie vedomosti* into the early 1780s.[17]

Mesmer's possessive control over his secretive technique ensured that for many years he maintained a virtual monopoly on the promotion of and treatment by animal magnetism. Consequently, until 1784 Europe as a whole remained devoid of practitioners of animal magnetism, apart from a relatively small number of Mesmer's devotees in Paris. Thus, although many European wondermongers came to promote their miraculous cures in the Russian Empire in the early 1780s, none advertised themselves as animal magnetists. Most notably, for example, the Italian Giuseppe Maggi successfully promoted his use of electrical medicine as a wondrous cure of a host of ailments among the Russian nobility between 1773 and 1787.[18] Nonetheless, at no point during his relatively long career, based in Moscow, did Maggi advertise any form of animal magnetism.

Hence, with her gaze focused on the French capital and the negative ramifications heaped on Mesmer and his Parisian followers, Catherine II was not overly preoccupied with the possibility that the nobility within her realm would be swayed by what seemed to be a pseudo-medical theory widely mocked and held in disrepute. Yet, unbeknownst to either Bariatinskii or herself, a different form of animal magnetism, which came to be known as magnetic (or artificial) somnambulism, was being developed by Freemasons of a distinctly Illuminist hue in Lyon in the summer of 1784.[19] Christine Bergé has defined Illuminism at this time as a 'complex intellectual and spiritual movement', the practitioners of which 'were adventurers of thought'.[20] I would add that these 'adventurers of

---

[17] The *Sanktpeterburgskie vedomosti* also featured a further report in June 1777 regarding how Mesmer had cured the blindness of another young women. See ibid., no. 45 (6 June 1777). For a report on magnetic cures performed in France in 1780, see *Moskovskie vedomosti*, no. 42 (23 May 1780), pp. 335–36. On Mesmer's treatment of M. T. von Paradis, see Jane Madell, 'Rapport and Subversion: Mesmer's Treatment of Paradis and Its Influence on the Fiction of E. T. A. Hoffmann', unpublished PhD thesis, University of East Anglia, 2015, pp. 10–81.

[18] On Giuseppe Maggi as a practitioner of medical electricity in Russia, see Robert Collis, '"A Veritable Eldorado": European Wondermongers in Russia, 1755–1803', in Emmanuel Waegemans, Hans van Koningsbrugge, Marcus Levitt and Mikhail Ljustrov (eds), 'A Century Mad and Wise': Russia in the Age of the Enlightenment, Gröningen, 2015, pp. 489–517.

[19] For a historical overview of the development of magnetic somnambulism from 1784, see Tony James, 'Somnambulism, Natural and Magnetic', in James, *Dream, Creativity, and Madness in Nineteenth-Century France*, Oxford, 1995, pp. 14–26.

[20] Christine Bergé, 'Illuminism', in Wouter J. Hanegraaff (ed.), *Dictionary of Gnosis & Western Esotericism*, Leiden, 2005, p. 600. On Illuminism, see also, Andreas Önnerfors,

thought' often delved into occult philosophy, as it was known in the early modern period, or Western esotericism, as has become commonplace in academia since the 1970s.[21]

It was during the summer of 1784 that Alexandre Pierre Louis de Barberin du Bost developed a form of magnetic somnambulism in Lyon that differed considerably from the form of animal magnetism promoted by Franz Anton Mesmer in Paris since 1778. Unlike the Mesmerist version of animal magnetism, Barberin's magnetic somnambulism involved no physical contact with patients and entirely jettisoned the utilization of a *baquet*. Indeed, Barberin argued that it was possible to magnetize and cure a patient from afar.[22] His innovative theory was embraced by both the local Illuminist lodge of La Respectable Loge de la Bienfaisance and the affiliated Société de la Concorde, which were both led by Jean-Baptiste Willermoz. Furthermore, in the second half of 1784, Barberin and the Mason-magnetizers of Lyon, led by Willermoz, came to believe that those in a state of magnetic somnambulism, particularly women, were able to prophesize and could communicate with angelic entities.[23] This Barberinian strand of magnetic somnambulism was redolent of Emanuel Swedenborg's espousal of spirit communication that purported to offer prophetic potentiality. Indeed, it can be viewed as a distinctive branch of a broader fascination among Swedenborgians, and other like-minded illuminists in the late eighteenth century, in direct correspondence with paranormal entities that offered up (in their view) new revelatory insights into the divine secrets of God's universe.[24] Thus, Barberin's strand of

'Illuminism', in Christopher Partridge (ed.), *The Occult World*, Abingdon, 2015, pp. 173–81.

[21] For a concise explanation of the history of Western esotericism as an academic term and discipline, see Wouter J. Hanegraaff, *Western Esotericism: A Guide for the Perplexed*, London, 2013, pp. 1–18.

[22] For contemporary (sympathetic) descriptions of Barberin's theory of animal magnetism, see A. E. de Dampierre, *Réflexions impartiales sur le magnétisme animal*, Geneva, 1784, pp. 8–18; 'Méthode de M. de Barberin', in *Système Raisonné du Magnétisme Universel*, Ostend, 1786, pp. 55–63; Antoine-Joseph de Luetzelbourg, *Extrait des journaux d'un magnétiseur, attaché à la société des amis réunis de Strasbourg*, Strasbourg, 1786, pp. 141–45.

[23] On the influential role of Jean-Baptiste Willermoz, as well as the La Bienfaisance Lodge and the affiliated La Concorde society of animal magnetists, in promoting a distinctive form of somnambulistic animal magnetism, see Alice Joly, *Un Mystique lyonnais et les secrets de la Franc-Maçonnerie. Jean-Baptiste Willermoz, 1730–1824*, Paris, 1986, pp. 215–62; René Le Forestier, *La Franc-Maçonnerie Templière et Occultiste aux XVIIIᵉ siècles*, 2nd edn, Paris, 1987, pp. 792–812; Nicole Edelman, *Voyantes, guérisseuses et visionnaires en France, 1785–1914*, Paris, 1995, pp. 21–39.

[24] For more on spirit communication and the paranormal in late eighteenth-century Europe, see Clarke Garrett, 'Swedenborg and the Mystical Enlightenment in Late

magnetic somnambulism shared the original form of animal magnetism advocated by Mesmer vis-à-vis the ability to heal patients (although the methods were entirely different). However, in a radical departure from the materialist techniques avowed by the Swabian physician, Barberin embraced the spiritual potential of magnetic somnambulism to facilitate divine communication and insights from somnambules.

The principles of magnetic somnambulism developed by Barberin at this time followed rapidly on the heels of the ground-breaking use of somnambulism in May 1784 by Armand-Marie-Jacques de Chastenet, Marquis de Puységur on his country estate near Soissons in northern France. Puységur's form of magnetic somnambulism never ventured into the realms of spirit communication. Instead, he developed the notion of the power of suggestion and the ability of a patient to gain a heightened state of inner awareness or consciousness in a somnambulistic state. This method of magnetic somnambulism was soon enthusiastically embraced by his fellow Freemasons in Strasbourg and has been recognized by historians of behavioural science as a crucial moment in the history of modern psychology.[25]

Hence, by the summer of 1784, two distinct forms of magnetic somnambulism had emerged in Lyon and Strasbourg that, whilst owing their existence to Mesmer's doctrine of animal magnetism, had branched off into two completely different spheres: a spiritual realm in Lyon and a form of early suggestive hypnotism in Strasbourg (long before James Braid's adoption of the term hypnotism in 1842) as a harbinger of dynamic psychiatry.[26] Crucially, both these strands of animal magnetism relied neither on formal endorsement by the scientific establishment, nor on the

---

Eighteenth-Century England', *Journal of the History of Ideas*, 45, 1, 1984, pp. 67–81; Ritchie Robertson, '"Wir sind so klug und dennoch spukt's in Tegel": The Enlightenment and the Paranormal', *KulturPoetik*, 19, 1, 2019, pp. 29–44.

[25] On the particular form of somnambulistic magnetism propagated by Puységur and its importance in the history of the modern conception of dynamic psychiatry and the subconscious, see Henri F. Ellenberger, *The Discovery of the Unconscious: The History and Evolution of Dynamic Psychiatry*, London, 1994, pp. 53–83; Adam Crabtree, '1784: The Marquis de Puységur and the Psychological Turn in the West', *The History of the Behavioral Sciences*, 55, 3, 2019, pp. 199–215.

[26] As a twelve-year-old boy Pavel Aleksandrovich Stroganov described witnessing a demonstration of animal magnetism in Strasbourg on 9 August 1786 in which a female patient entered a state of somnambulism redolent of the techniques espoused by Puységur. Stroganov also adds that his tutor at the time, Gilbert Romme, had tried this form of animal magnetism. See Moscow, Rossiiskii gosudarstvennyi arkhiv drevnikh aktov (hereafter, RGADA), f. 1278, op. 1, d. 348. Also quoted in Rodolphe Baudin, *Nikolaï Karamzine à Strasbourg: Un écrivain-voyageur russe dans l'Alsace révolutionnaire (1789)*, Strasbourg, 2011, p. 197. On James Braid and hypnotism, see Gauld, *A History of Hypnotism*, pp. 279–87.

income generated by wealthy clients. Instead, they thrived in a Masonic milieu, largely devoid of scrutiny.

By the summer of 1784, the Mason-magnetizers of Lyon saw an opportunity to promote their pioneering form of magnetic somnambulism as an enticing means to attract eminent young noblemen from across Europe, including the Russian Empire, into their fold. With this in mind, this article will specifically focus on an examination of how three prominent Russian noblemen — Mikhail Andreevich Golitsyn, Aleksei Grigor'evich Bobrinskii (the illegitimate son of Catherine II) and Vasilii Nikolaevich Zinov'ev — were all drawn into the milieu of Lyon magnetists through a Masonic network promoted from the city by Jean-Baptiste Willermoz that stretched across the European continent. The second part will then focus on the notable importation of both Mesmerist and Barberinian forms of animal magnetism into St Petersburg in 1786, where it was briefly practised by Carl Friedrich Tieman and a certain Major Blanckennagel. However, the arrival of the much-maligned treatment in the Russian capital soon attracted the ire of the Russian Empress, who quickly nullified the perceived threat for the rest of her reign.

Very little has been written about the influence of animal magnetism on educated society in the Russian Empire in either its first period of relative popularity, between when it was first championed by Franz Anton Mesmer in Vienna in the mid 1770s and the French Revolution, or when it saw a revival throughout Europe after the final defeat of Napoleon in 1815. The sole English-language account amounts to a short summary written in 1968 by Ludmila Zielinski, which merely provides a simplistic and condescending overview.[27] According to Zielinski, the history of animal magnetism in the Russian Empire only began in 1815 owing to the fact that 'specific historical and geographical factors' meant that 'cultural developments in the West took a considerable time to reach' the country. Furthermore, she argues that animal magnetism in Russia was largely limited to a scientific approach after 1815, which was propounded by German academics.[28]

Limited correctives to this blinkered appraisal have been provided since the late 1980s by the Russian historians Sergei Mikhailovich Grombakh, Konstantin Anatol'evich Bogdanov and Iurii Evgen'evich Kondakov. All three historians briefly discuss evidence suggesting that animal magnetism was practised in the Russian Empire, albeit not in a widespread

---

[27] Ludmila Zielinski, 'Hypnotism in Russia', in Eric J. Dingwall (ed.), *Abnormal Hypnotic Phenomena: A Survey of Nineteenth-Century Cases*, vol. 3, New York, 1968, pp. 1–105.
[28] Ibid., pp. 3–4.

manner, before the French Revolution.[29] Most recently, Victoire Feuillebois and Laetitia Decourt, in their study of the subject of animal magnetism in Russian romantic short stories of the 1830s and 1840s, contextualize their work by providing a succinct overview of the introduction of the pseudo-scientific discipline into Russia in the 1780s and its subsequent resurgence after the conclusion of the Napoleonic Wars.[30]

While historical analysis of animal magnetism in the Russian Empire before the French Revolution is sparse, anyone wishing to know more about the historical significance of animal magnetism in French society during this era can draw on a wealth of excellent material. The reassessment of the importance of animal magnetism within French culture and society stems, in large measure, from the publication of Robert Darnton's seminal work, *Mesmerism and the End of the Enlightenment* in 1968.[31] This debt is acknowledged in a 2018 special edition of *Annales historiques de la Révolution française* devoted to animal magnetism, in which a variety of specialists assess the profound impact of animal magnetism in France in the decade before the French Revolution.[32]

Whilst we are spoilt for choice when seeking to know more about the complex phenomenon of animal magnetism within France in the 1780s, it was still the case until the end of the twentieth century, as Patricia Fara noted in 1995, that 'very few historians have described contemporary practices' in other European countries.[33] Since this statement, however, numerous scholars have drawn attention to the links between animal magnetism and various aspects of late eighteenth- and early nineteenth-century culture throughout Europe, including the Romantic movement in Germany, medicine in Spain and the Holy Office in Rome.[34]

---

[29] See S. M. Grombakh, *Pushkin i meditsina ego vremeni*, Moscow, 1989, pp. 132–51; K. A. Bogdanov, 'Magnetizm i cherep’slovie', in Bogdanov, *Vrachi, patsienty, chitateli: Patograficheskie teksty russkoi kul´tury*, Moscow, 2005, pp. 178–96; Iu. E. Kondakov, 'Zhivotnyi magnetizm v Rossii', in *Ezotericheskoe dvizhenie v Rossii kontsa XVIII – pervoi poloviny XIX vv.*, Moscow, 2018, pp. 161–200. For the earliest history of animal magnetism in the Russian Empire, see Aleksei Dolgorukii, *Organ zhivotnogo mesmerizma*, St Petersburg, 1860, pp. 266–86.

[30] Victoire Feuillebois and Laetitia Decourt, 'Introduction', in *Récits romantiques russes sur le magnétisme*, Paris, 2021, pp. 15–23. This introduction draws heavily on the work of Grombakh, Bogdanov and Kondakov.

[31] Darnton, *Mesmerism*, see note 6 above.

[32] 'Le mesmérisme et la Révolution française', *Annales Historiques de la Révolution Française*, 391, 1, 2018.

[33] Patricia Fara, 'An Attractive Therapy: Animal Magnetism in Eighteenth-Century England', *History of Science*, 33, 1995, pp. 127–77.

[34] See Matthew Bell, 'Romanticism and Animal Magnetism', in Bell, *The German Tradition of Psychology in Literature and Thought, 1700–1840*, Cambridge, 2005, pp.

The Russian nobility and magnetic somnambulism in France (1784–87)

By 1784, J.-B. Willermoz had succeeded in forging an extensive network of Illuminist Freemasons across Europe, who adhered to his highly esoteric form of Freemasonry, officially known as the Rectified Scottish Rite.[35] A more common name for this branch of esoteric and mystical Freemasonry was Martinism, after its founder Martinez de Pasqually and its foremost thinker, Louis Claude de Saint-Martin.[36] Among the highest-ranking Masons loyal to Willermoz at this time were José de Ribas, Jean Pierre Massenet and Carl Friedrich Tieman, all of whom were in Russian service and charged with overseeing the education of young Russian noblemen. Today Ribas is principally known for his military exploits on behalf of the Russian Empire, as well as being the founder of Odesa.[37] Less well-known is his role from 1776 as the educational supervisor of Aleksei Grigor′evich Bobrinskii.[38] Both Massenet and Tieman had been employed

167–207; Burkhart Brückner, 'Animal Magnetism, Psychiatry and Subjective Experience in Nineteenth-Century Germany: Friedrich Krauß and his *Nothschrei*', *Medical History*, 60, 2016, 1, pp. 19–36; Claire Gantet, 'The Dissemination of Mesmerism in Germany (1784–1815): Some Patterns of the Circulation of Knowledge', *Centaurus*, 63, 2021, pp. 762–78. On the reception of animal magnetism in Spanish medicine, see Angel González de Pablo, 'Animal Magnetism in Spanish Medicine (1786–1860)', *History of Psychiatry*, 17, 2006, pp. 279–98. On the attitude of the Holy Office in Rome to animal magnetism in the late eighteenth and early nineteenth century, see David Armando, 'Scienza, demonolatria o "imposture ereticale"? Il Sant' Uffizio romano e la questione del magnetismo animale', *Giornale di Storia*, 2009, pp. 1–13. On animal magnetism in Scandinavia in the eighteenth century, see Søren Bak-Jensen, 'Mesmerism in Denmark', in Henrik Bogdan and Olav Hammar (eds), *Western Esotericism in Scandinavia*, Leiden, 2016, pp. 264–68; Tonje Maria Mehren, 'Mesmerism in Norway', in Bogdan and Hammar (eds), *Western Esotericism*, 269–84; Olav Hammar, 'Mesmerism in Sweden', in Bogdan and Hammar (eds), *Western Esotericism*, pp. 285–91.

[35] On the Rectified Scottish Rite, see Arturo de Hoyos, 'Masonic Rites and Systems', in Henrik Bogdan and Jan A. M. Snoek (eds), *Handbook of Freemasonry*, Leiden, 2014, pp. 369–70. For an informative overview of the plethora of high-degree forms of Freemasonry and the use of the umbrella term of 'Illuminism' to describe the strands of Western esotericism present within these groups, see Nicholas Goodrick-Clarke, *The Western Esoteric Traditions: A Historical Introduction*, Oxford, 2008, pp. 131–53.

[36] For an overview of Martinism in eighteenth-century France, see Christian Giudice, 'Martinism in Eighteenth-Century France', in Christopher Partridge (ed.), *The Occult World*, Abingdon, 2015, pp. 182–87. For a study of Martinism in Russia, see M. N. Longinov, *Novikov i moskovskie martinisty*, Moscow, 1867.

[37] Surprisingly little has been written on Ribas given his prominent role in Russian military service, which included a principal role in the foundation of the city of Odesa in 1794. See Luigi Jaccarino, 'Giuseppe De-Ribas', in Jaccarino, *Vite e rittratti degli uomini celebri di tutti i tempi e di tutte le nazioni*, vol. 3, part 2, Naples, 1843, pp. 605–14; A. de-Ribas, *Staraia Odessa*, Odesa, 1913, pp. 12–25; P. M. Maikov, 'Ribas, de-, Iosif', *Russkii biograficheskii slovar′: Reitern′–Rol′tsberg′*, St Petersburg, 1913, pp. 168–73; Diego Merry del Val, 'José de Ribas: un genio military al service de la zarina', *Clio Revista de historia*, 78, 2008, pp. 74–79.

[38] On Bobrinskii, see P. M. Maikov, 'Bobrinskoi, Aleksei Grigor′evich', *Russkii*

as governors to some of the Russian nobility's most eminent families since the 1770s and, crucially, were often entrusted with guiding young noblemen on lengthy Grand Tours of Europe.[39] Significantly, Massenet and Tieman endeavoured to introduce their respective charges — in this case M. A. Golitsyn and Bobrinskii — to the particular Martinist milieu promoted by Willermoz in Lyon, which in 1784, as mentioned, began to be profoundly influenced by animal magnetism. What is more, as will be demonstrated, Tieman himself introduced a form of animal magnetism into St Petersburg society in 1786, after returning to the Russian capital after his Grand Tour with Bobrinskii.

Mikhail Andreevich Golitsyn may rank as the first Russian directly to observe a demonstration of magnetic somnambulism. This notable occasion took place on 22 July 1784, when the second of three famed demonstrations of animal magnetism took place at Lyon Veterinary College.[40] The goal of the event was to show that the two magnetizers — Jean-Jacques-François Millanois, a lawyer and politician, and Jean Dutreich, a surgeon at the veterinary college — were able correctly to diagnose the internal ailments of a sick horse without recourse to any physical examination.[41] Both magnetizers were followers of Barberin and

biograficheskii slovar': Betankur–Biakster, St Petersburg, 1908, pp. 114–16.

[39] On Massenet, see Michel Poulinquen, La vie de Pierre Jean Massenet (1748–1824), grand-pére du compositeur, Chantilly, 2012. On Tieman, see Antoine Faivre, De Londres à Saint-Pétersbourg: Carl Friedrich Tieman (1743–1802) aux carrefours des courants illuministes et maçonniques, Milan, 2018. On the role of Massenet and Tieman (and other Frenchmen) as governors to young Russian noblemen in the late eighteenth century, see V. S. Rzheutskii, 'Frantsuzskie guvernery v Rossii XVIII v.', Frantsuzskii ezhegodnik, 2011, pp. 59–80; Vladimir Berelovich, 'Guvernery v sem'e Golitsynykh 1760–1780 gg.', ibid., pp. 190–99; A. S. Stroev, '"Vybor guvernera": Fridrikh Tsezar' Lagarp, Fridrikh Mel'khior Grimm i Karl Fridrikh Timann', ibid., pp. 218–232. On Grand Tours of young Russian noblemen in France in the late eighteenth century, see Wladimir Berelowitch, 'La France dans le "Grand Tour" des nobles russes au cours de la seconde moitié du XVIIIe siècle', Cahiers du monde russe et soviétique, 34, 1–2, 1993, pp. 193–209.

[40] Both Massenet and Golitsyn are named in the description of the demonstration of animal magnetism. See Expérience Magnétique. Procès-verbal de l'expérience faite à l'Ecole Vétérinaire de Lyon, le jeudi 22 Juillet 1784, Lyon, 1784, p. 2.

[41] Millanois is listed as being a member of La Bienfaisance Lodge. In 1781–82, for example, he is listed in the membership table as being second orator of the lodge. See Tableau des freres composant la Respectable Loge de la Bienfaisance [...] pour l'année 5782, Lyon, 1782. Millanois was a leading political figure in Lyon in the 1780s and early 1790s. He was the royal Seneschal to Lyon and a deputy for the city at the Estates-General Assembly in 1789. He was executed by the revolutionary authorities in Lyon in 1793. See Maryannick Lavigne-Louis, 'Millanois Jean-Jacques', in Dominique Saint-Pierre (ed.), Dictionnaire historique des académiciens de Lyon 1700–2016, Lyon, 2017, pp. 880–82. Dutreich (or Dutreik, Dutreih) is listed in the table of members for 1786, recorded on 27 December 1785. See Tableau des frères composant la Respectable Loge de la Bienfaisance [...] pour

belonged to the recently established Société de la Concorde, devoted to the pursuit of magnetic somnambulism, and to the Masonic La Bienfaisance lodge in Lyon.[42] Indeed, many of the leading Masons of the lodge and Société de la Concorde, including Willermoz, were also in attendance at the demonstration.[43] After placing the horse in a somnambulistic state, the two magnetizers indicated that the animal was suffering from lung disease and that it also had obstructions in its liver and spleen. An autopsy was subsequently performed that confirmed this diagnosis.[44]

Golitsyn had arrived in Lyon at least ten days earlier, in the company of Massenet, his governor, and as the first destination of note on the itinerary of his Grand Tour. Having Massenet as a preceptor opened many doors for the young Golitsyn, not least of which was the possibility to witness the innovative form of animal magnetism that had emerged in Lyon in the summer of 1784.[45] Massenet had arrived in Russia in 1770, on the

l'année 5786, Lyon, 1786. For a description of Dutreich's collaboration with Barberin, see Dampierre, Réflexions, pp. 14–31.

[42] Barberin, Dutreich and Pierre Paul Alexandre de Monspey Vallière established the Société de la Concorde in Lyon in April 1784. Monspey was initiated into La Bienfaisance in 1780. See Tableau des frères composant la Respectable Loge de la Bienfaisance [...] pour l'année 5780, Lyon, 1780. According to Harmonia Universalis, a prosopographical database managed by Bruno Belhoste and David Armando, the Société de la Concorde only had eleven known members. All eleven — Barberin, Dutreich, Monspey, Millanois, Willermoz, André de Bory, Jean Antoine de Castellas, Pierre-André de Grainville, Jean Paganucci, Claude Polycarpe de Rachais and Antoine Louis Sabot de Pizay — were Masons of La Bienfaisance. On the Société de la Concorde, see 'Société de la Concorde de Lyon', in Harmonia Universalis <https://harmoniauniversalis.univ-paris1.fr/#/institution/58dc28d125f595563d000005> [accessed 15 March 2023]. For information on the Masonic membership of all eleven, see Paris, Bibliothèque Nationale de France (hereafter, BNF), FM Fichier Bossu (281). All entries are arranged alphabetically by surname.

[43] The description of the experiment conducted on 22 July 1784 states that Willermoz, Paganucci and Gaspard Guillaume de Savaron were also in attendance. All three were leading members of La Bienfaisance. See Expérience Magnétique, p. 1; BNF, Fichier Bossu (281).

[44] The promotion of magnetic somnambulism, according to the theories of Barberin, to eminent guests also occurred eighteen days later, on 9 August 1784, when Millanois and Dutreich demonstrated their skills at Lyon Veterinary College to Prince Henry of Prussia (travelling incognito as the Comte d'Oels). See Procès verbal de l'Expérience Magnétique faite à l'Ecole Vétérinaire de Lyon, le lundi 9 Août 1784, Lyon, 1784.

[45] Golitsyn was already well-educated at the time of Massenet's appointment as his tutor in March 1784. Along with his brothers, Boris Andreevich and Aleksei Andreevich, Golitsyn entered The University of Leiden in 1780, where he was resident until the autumn of 1783. For an examination of Russian students who studied in Leiden in the eighteenth century, see Nicholas Hans, 'Russian Students at Leyden in the 18th Century', Slavonic and East European Review, 35, 85, 1957, pp. 551–62. Hans includes a list of Russian students with information about their years of study, matriculation, subject and faculty, drawn from the university register. For the Golitsyn brothers, see p. 561. For a discussion of M. A. Golitsyn's time in England and Wales in the summer of 1785, accompanied with the publication of a letter he wrote from London to Mikhail Andreevich Iusupov, see

recommendation of his tutor, Johann Daniel Schöpflin, after graduating from the University of Strasbourg. He took up a position as a professor of *belles-lettres* at the Imperial Land Gentry Cadet Corps (Imperatorskii sukhoputnyi shliakhetnyi kadetskii korpus) in St Petersburg and, in order to boost his income, he soon began to serve as a preceptor for eminent Russian noble families. Alongside his professional career, Massenet also immersed himself in the burgeoning world of Masonic sociability in St Petersburg. Significantly, he was a founding member of the Apollo Lodge in St Petersburg in 1771, which was established by Johann Gottfried von Reichel and was the first in Russia to work under the high-degree (and esoteric) Zinnendorf Rite.[46] Thus, by the time Massenet and Golitsyn arrived in Lyon in July 1784, the former was an experienced and well-connected Illuminist Freemason.

Recognition of Massenet's seniority within Willermoz's Rectified Scottish Rite came in January 1784, when he was initiated as a *grand profès* — the highest degree — in Turin.[47] Massenet was admitted by Dr Sebastiano Giraud, who had received a recommendation from Bernard-Frédéric de Turckheim, a prominent member of the Rectified Scottish Rite and a resident of Strasbourg.[48] As Pierre-Yves Beaurepaire notes:

> Giraud knew [...] how to make the most of the position of Savoy and Piedmont as a strategic crossroads [...] to sound out travellers who were

L. Iu. Savinskaia, 'Puteshestvie Mikhaila Andreevicha Golitsyna po Anglii. 1785 g. (K istorii obrazovatel'nogo puteshestviia brat'ev Mikhaila, Borisa i Alekseia Golitsynykh po Evrope. 1780—1788 gg.)', in E. E. Rychalovskii (ed.), *Rossiia v XVIII stoletii, vypusk II*, Moscow, 2004, pp. 262–89. For an informative account of the education enjoyed by Boris Andreevich and Aleksei Andreevich in Strasbourg, under the tutelage of Christophe Guillaume Koch from 1784, see Rodolphe Baudin, 'Préface. Christophe Guillaume Korch et la Russie', in Rodolphe Baudin and Wladimir Berelowitch (eds), *Histoire de Russie avec sa partie politique par Mr. Koch, Professeur à Strasbourg suivie de la Constitution de L'Empire de Russie*, Strasbourg, 2018, pp. 7–77 (pp. 26–77).

[46] On Massenet's role as a founding member of Apollo Lodge, see, Andrei Serkov, *Russkoe Masonstvo, 1731-2000*, Moscow, 2001, p. 960. Johann Wilhelm Kellner von Zinnendorf (1731-82), a Prussian physician, established the Grand Landlodge of the Freemasons of Germany (Große Landesloge der Freimaurer von Deutschland) in 1770. On the foundation of this rite in Russia, under the supervision of Reichel in late 1770, see A. Semeka, 'Russkoe masonstvo v XVIII veke', in S. P. Mel'gunov and N. P. Sidorov (eds), *Masonstvo v ego proshlom i nastoiashchem*, vol. 1, Moscow, 1914, p. 141. For a brief explanation of the key attributes of the Zinnendorf Rite, see de Hoyos, 'Masonic Rites and Systems', pp. 363, 366.

[47] Pouliquen, *La vie de Pierre Jean Massenet*, pp. 65–66.

[48] Antoine Faivre, 'Une collection maçonnique inédite: Le fonds Bernard-Frédéric de Turckheim', part 2, *Revue de l'histoire des religions*, 175, 2, 1969, pp. 170–71. On Turckheim and his links to the Rectified Scottish Rite, see Roland Edighoffer, *La dynastie des Turckheim au temps de Goethe*, Paris, 2002, pp. 28-32.

Freemasons [...] and excite their curiosity about the Lyonnais reform
[the Rectified Scottish Rite-RC] before sending them to Jean-Baptiste
Willermoz.[49]

Moreover, by 1784 Giraud had become the foremost proponent of animal
magnetism, initially as a follower of Mesmer, in the Italian peninsula.[50]
Hence, he was the perfect individual to whet Massenet's appetite for the
unique Masonic milieu being cultivated in Lyon by Willermoz.

Massenet wintered in the capital of the Savoyard state with M. A.
Golitsyn and his two younger brothers, where he instructed them in
chemistry. In March 1784, Massenet was entrusted with the education
— in the form of a grand tour — of Mikhail, at the behest of the family
patriarch, Aleksandr Mikhailovich Golitsyn, whom he had served as
secretary. Both Massenet and Giraud must have been delighted at this
opportunity. After all, Massenet was at liberty to plan the entire itinerary
of his young princely ward, who hailed from one of the most eminent
houses of the Russian nobility. Thus, it is wholly unsurprising that
Massenet chose to begin the Grand Tour of M. A. Golitsyn by travelling
across the Alps to visit Lyon, the epicentre of the Willermozian Masonic
rite. That Massenet sought to bring the young Russian prince into this
particular Masonic fold is testified by the fact that Golitsyn was initiated
into La Bienfaissance during his stay in Lyon in 1784.[51] Golitsyn and
Massenet's arrival in Lyon also coincided with the sudden emergence
of magnetic somnambulism as a pivotal preoccupation of the leading
Masons of La Bienfaissance. Indeed, Massenet and Golitsyn arrived in
Lyon only several days after Millanois and Dutreich had first tested the

---

[49] Pierre-Yves Beaurepaire, 'La baquet entre l'équerre et le compass. Luttes d'influence
maçonnique autour du magnétisme animal et des Sociétés de l'Harmonie', *Annales
Historiques de la Révolution Française*, 1, 2018, p. 118.

[50] For evidence of Giraud's practice of animal magnetism in Turin in 1784 and 1785, see
F. Alessio, 'Nuovi Documenti sul Giraud', *Bollettino storico-bibliografico subalpino*, 1901,
pp. 355–61. For a short biography of Giraud and an overview of his activities as an animal
magnetist, see 'Sebastiano Giraud', in *Harmonia Universalis* <https://harmoniauniversalis.
univ-paris1.fr/#/personne/53d5ea736a6a5c563d000001> [accessed 15 March 2023].

[51] See *Tableau des freres composant la Respectable Loge de la Bienfaisance à l'Orient
de Lyon*, Lyon, 1785. The table of members for 1785 was approved on 27 December 1784
and published on 13 February 1785 (see the last page of the publication). Golitsyn's name
appears on the penultimate page of the membership table in the section devoted to
affiliated non-resident members of the lodge. The young Russian nobleman (who was only
eighteen or nineteen years old when he was initiated in Lyon) is listed as 'Le Prince Michel
Galitzin', from Moscow, who had entered the grade of apprentice (*apprentif*).

techniques of magnetic somnambulism developed by Barberin.[52] Hence, they witnessed only the second demonstration of this new form of animal magnetism.

As mentioned, the rapid emergence of magnetic somnambulism in Lyon in 1784 seems to have gone unnoticed by the Russian authorities. Consequently, five months after Golitsyn observed the work of Lyon magnetizers, the empress's own son, Bobrinskii, was also fêted by the same group. As with Golitsyn, Bobrinskii's encounter with Lyon magnetizers in December 1784 was not serendipitous. Since 1776, the education of Bobrinskii in Russia had been overseen by Ribas at the Imperial Land Gentry Cadet Corps in St Petersburg, where the latter was employed. Moreover, Ribas was entrusted with planning Bobrinskii's learning as a young man when he graduated from the Cadet Corps in 1782.[53] This educational role occurred at a time when Ribas was intensely preoccupied with Masonic affairs in Russia. In short, Ribas was the preeminent representative in Russia of Willermoz's Rectified Scottish Rite, which emerged as the dominant form of Strict Observance Freemasonry after the Convent of Wilhelmsbad held in July 1782.[54]

Ribas was greatly aided in his efforts to establish Willermoz's rite in St Petersburg by Tieman, who hailed from the Electorate of Saxony and who had been employed in Russian service as a governor since 1776. It was during his first Grand Tour in Russian service, when he accompanied the Livonian nobleman Gotthard Andreas Manteuffel, that he had been initiated in France into Willermoz's rite of Freemasonry.[55] In April 1783, Tieman wrote to Willermoz that 'we have a society of friends here, small

[52] For a description of the first experiments conducted by Millanois and Dutreich, at the beginning of July 1784, see *Expérience Magnétique*, p. 1.

[53] Maikov, 'Bobrinskii', p. 114; Samuel M. Smucker, *Memoirs of the Court and Reign of Catherine the Second, Empress of Russia*, New York, 1855, p. 172.

[54] On the Convent of Wilhelmsbad in 1782 and its importance in the emergence of the Rectified Scottish Rite, see Ludwig Hammermayer, 'La crise de la franc-maçonnerie européenne et le Convent de Wilhelmsbad', *Dix-Huitième Siècle*, 19, 1987, pp. 73–95. On the Masonic endeavours of Ribas in Russia, in which he acted as the chief representative of Willermoz's Rectified Scottish Rite after 1782, see Faivre, *De Londres à Saint-Pétersbourg*, pp. 79–88. In a letter to Willermoz, written from St Petersburg on 6 April 1783, C. F. Tieman remarked that Ribas was at the head of a choice company advancing the Masonic doctrine of the Rectified Scottish Rite. See Lyon, Bibliothèque Municipale de Lyon (hereafter, BMdL), Ms. 5866, no. 72. See also, Faivre, *De Londres à Saint-Pétersbourg*, pp. 380–82. For contemporary discussion of the tension engendered by Ribas's espousal and promotion of this rite among rival Masonic leaders in Russia, see the letter of N. N. Trubetskoi to A. A. Rzehevskii, written in Moscow on 23 June 1783. See Ia. L. Barskov, *Perepiska moskovskikh masonov XVIII-go veka 1780–1792 gg.*, Petrograd, 1915, pp. 251–54.

[55] Faivre, *De Londres à Saint-Pétersbourg*, pp. 12–28.

in number but select, with Ribas at our head: our great desire is to open up and work according to the light established at Wilhelmsbad'.[56]

It would seem that the role of a governor, who accompanied young, impressionable Russian noblemen on formative Grand Tours of Europe, was valued highly by Ribas and Willermoz: the Masonic governor enjoyed tremendous license, away from the prying eyes of their employer, to mould the worldview of their ward as they saw fit. With this in mind, it is telling that Ribas ensured that Tieman would escort Bobrinskii on his Grand Tour when the latter departed the Russian Empire in late 1783.

Bobrinskii and Tieman spent much of 1784 in Italy, but by 7 December the pair had arrived in Lyon. Bobrinskii's diary provides fascinating descriptions of his encounters with the Mason-magnetizers of Lyon during his time in the city. It is clear, from these journal entries, that animal magnetism served as the principal means to woo the Russian nobleman. On 9 December, for example, Bobrinskii indicated that Tieman had written him a note stating that 'a person would come to him regarding magnetization'.[57] This individual was none other than Willermoz, who then took them to the same Veterinary College that had been the site of the famous demonstrations of animal magnetism five months earlier. Here, Bobrinskii and Tieman were not as fortunate as Golitsyn and Massenet, as they were not treated to a live magnetization of horses. Instead, Willermoz showed them an anatomical cabinet containing the carcass of a dead horse that had been experimented on eight days earlier. At this point, Bobrinskii may well have been unaware of the link between the dead horse and animal magnetism, as he merely commented that an awful stench emanated from the carrion.[58]

The following day, Bobrinskii describes a day largely devoted to animal magnetism. At lunch, he, Tieman and Willermoz 'spoke a lot about magnetism'. Then, later in the afternoon, Willermoz took them to observe a demonstration of animal magnetism that evidently drew on Mesmer's method of treatment. Bobrinskii describes how Willermoz led them into a room, where he saw between fifteen and seventeen people, mostly women,

---

[56] Tieman to Willermoz, 17 April 1783. See Faivre, *De Londres à Saint-Pétersbourg*, p. 381.

[57] S. A. Kozlov (ed.), *Russkii puteshestvennik epokhi prosveshcheniia*, vol. 1, St Petersburg, 2003, pp. 421–22. For a redacted edition of Bobrinskii's diary, which omits his dalliance with animal magnetism in Lyon, see A. G. Bobrinskii, 'Dnevnik grafa Alekseiia Grigor'evicha Bobrinskago, vedennyi v kadetskom korpuse i vo vremia puteshestviia po Rossii i za granitseiu', *Russkii arkhiv*, kn. 3, vyp. 10, 1877, pp. 116–65. For the original diary, see RGADA, f. 1412, op. 1, d. 9.

[58] Kozlov (ed.), *Russkii puteshestvennik epokhi prosveshcheniia*, pp. 421–22.

sat around an oval table that was enclosed by boards above and on the sides. Ropes protruded from the sides and were tied around the bodies of the patients, who were all experiencing some form of convulsions. This was 'a very strange sight' for Bobrinskii, who was then led to a separate room. Here, the Russian nobleman was presented to the most sensitive young woman of the group, who was enclosed within a marked circle from which she could not leave or even lift her legs. Bobrinskii was then given the chance to try and lift the woman, who, to him, seemed much heavier than in normal circumstances. The diary entry then finishes with Bobrinskii proclaiming that Millanois was the best of all the magnetizers he met.[59]

Bobrinskii appears to have been shown a conventional, Mesmerist, form of animal magnetism. However, by December 1784 the Lyon Mason-magnetizers had begun to explore the clairvoyant and prophetic potential of young, female visionaries — Jeanne-Gilberte-Rosalie Rochette, Marion Blanchet and a Mademoiselle Bergé — whom they initially placed in a state of somnambulism to treat various medical ailments, including nervous agitation and catalepsy.[60] Significantly, in his correspondence with Willermoz, Tieman indicates that he was acquainted with Marion Blanchet and Bergé and may even have magnetized them in Lyon at this time. On 9 March 1785, for example, he wrote, from Paris: 'If Marion needs help, tell me; you will have given her, I hope, what I intended for her.'[61] Four months later Tieman enquired whether 'Marion needs my help' and beseeches Willermoz to 'greet her whilst waiting for me', before asking him to pass on his 'compliments to Mlle Bergé' and to 'tell her that I often think

[59] Ibid., p 422.

[60] The identity of three young women and a girl are known: Marion Blanchet, known as Mion, was magnetized and treated by Willermoz and a thirteen-year-old girl, called Novellet, was treated for paralysis. Two young women were believed to possess the gift of clairvoyance and visions: a certain Mademoiselle Bergé, who was magnetized by Millanois, and Mademoiselle Jeanne-Gilberte-Rosalie-Rochette, who was treated by Jean Antoine de Castellas. For the notes relating to the magnetic somnambulism of Rochette by Castellas in 1785, see Jean-Baptiste Willermoz, *Sommeils*, ed. Émile Dermenghem, Paris, 1926. For the original manuscript, see BMdL, 'Le Sommeils de Jeanne Rochette', Ms. 5478. For analysis of the treatment and visions of Jeanne Rochette during her magnetic somnambulism, which particularly centred on the belief that she could communicate with the deceased relatives of Willermoz and Castellas, see Joly, *Un Mystique lyonnais*, pp. 215–56; Edelman, *Voyantes, guérisseuses et visionnaires en France*, pp. 21–39. See also, Christine Bergé, *L'Odyssée de la Mémoire*, Paris, 2010, pp. 148–53.

[61] C. F. Tieman to J.-B. Willermoz, 9 March 1785. BMdL, Ms. 5868, no. 54. See also, Faivre, *De Londres à Saint-Pétersbourg*, pp. 111, 113. On the emergence of magnetic somnambulism in France from 1784, see Nicole Edelman, 'Les liens entre magnétiseurs et somnambules magnétiques (1784–années 1840)', in Maren Sziede and Helmut Zanders (eds), *Von der Dämonologie zum Unbewussten*, Berlin, 2015, pp. 133–48.

of her'.[62] Moreover, on 29 September 1785, prior to departing from Paris to St Petersburg, Tieman sent Willermoz a four-page account of a vision he experienced when he was thirteen or fourteen years old. This text was given to Jeanne Rochette, who apparently sent Willermoz a response.[63]

It is also worthy of note that Bobrinskii met Cagliostro, the controversial adventurer, Freemason and supposed sage of occult philosophy, at the latter's hotel apartment during his stay in Lyon. In his diary, Bobrinskii notes that this meeting took place in the afternoon of 15 December 1784 and that a lively conversation between them lasted for two hours. According to Bobrinskii, Cagliostro proclaimed to the young Russian nobleman that he had been alive since ancient times.[64]

By March 1785, Tieman and Bobrinskii had arrived in the French capital, where they spent several months. Whilst Bobrinskii's journal makes no direct reference to animal magnetism during this time, Tieman's correspondence is awash with references to his immersion in the subject.[65] Crucially, Tieman became something of a disciple of Barberin during his time in Paris. Indeed, Antoine Faivre recently demonstrated that Tieman was the author of one of two manuscript copies of *Mémoires du Chevalier de Barbarin*,[66] which records a remarkable series of dialogues that took place from March until September 1785 between Barberin (the magnetizer) and three women in a state of magnetically-induced somnambulism.[67]

---

[62] Tieman to Willermoz, 8 July 1785, BMdL, Ms. 5868, no. 58.

[63] Tieman to Willermoz, 29 September 1785, BMdL, Ms. 5868, no. 61. For a full reproduction of Tieman's description of his teenage vision, see Faivre, *De Londres à Saint-Pétersbourg*, pp. 319–21.

[64] Kozlov (ed.), *Russkii puteshestvennik*, p. 423. On Cagliostro's time in Lyon, which lasted from 20 October 1784 until 15 January 1785, see J.-B. Bricaud, 'Cagliostro et la franc-maçonnerie lyonnaise', *Revue d'histoire de Lyon*, 1910, pp. 363–76.

[65] See, for example, Tieman to Willermoz, 6 January 1785, BMdL, Ms. 5868, no. 53; Tieman to Willermoz, 9 March 1785, BMdL, Ms. 5868, no. 54.

[66] See Erlangen, Friedrich-Alexander-Universität, Institut für Kirchengeschichte (hereafter EFAU), Fonds Johann Friedrich von Meyer, 33b, 'Mémoires du Chevalier de Barbarin'. For a discussion about Tieman being entrusted with producing a written document of Barberin's experiments in magnetic somnambulism and as the author of the biographical introduction, see Faivre, *De Londres à Saint-Pétersbourg*, pp. 114–17. See also, Grenoble, Bibliothèque Municipale de Grenoble (hereafter BMdG), Fonds Prunelle de Lière, cote T/4, 188. This manuscript version draws on notes written down by Louis-Claude de Saint-Martin. For an edited publication of Barberin's journal, see A. P. L. de Barberin, 'Auszug aus dem magnetistischen Tagebuch des Ritters von Barberin', *Blätter für höhere Wahrheit*, 1, 1818, pp. 208–42. This copy was translated from the French manuscript presented to Tieman and contains the brief biographical sketch by the Saxon. For a discussion of Barberin's experiments in magnetic somnambulism based on a journal he wrote in 1785, see Edelman, *Voyantes*, pp. 21–39.

[67] The three women magnetized by Barberin are named in the *Memoires* as Madame de

Moreover, Tieman wrote a brief biographical introduction to the *Mémoires*, as well as testifying about Barberin's remarkable ability. According to Tieman, Barberin was 'the only one of the true magnetizers [...] who has pushed his art so far as to see, by interior sight, all the ailments of the body that he treats'.[68]

Tieman's documentation of the dialogues that ensued between Barberin, the magnetizer, and his three somnambulists also highlights how the latter had come to believe that he could induce a state whereby his patients became divinely inspired. As Alice Joly notes, Barberin's innovative embrace of the spiritual potential of magnetic somnambulism owed a great debt to Louis-Claude de Saint-Martin. In close contact in Paris in 1785, Saint-Martin helped Barberin to think of animal magnetism as a form of divine influx, which a few privileged people could transmit to certain no less rare subjects. Saint-Martin and Barberin came to believe that magnetic fluid could momentarily transform material nature, restoring to it some of the pristine qualities present before the Adamic Fall. They believed that such qualities included lucidity, clairvoyance and the power to communicate with spirits and even with God. Magnetic somnambulism to them seemed to offer a means of achieving the cherished goal of reintegration of humankind to prelapsarian abilities and spiritual wholeness.[69] Thus, the three somnambulists — de Montméril, de La Saumès and de La Blache — magnetized by Barberin were supposedly capable of divinely-inspired

Montméril (Marie Élisabeth Deslon de Montméril, née Montdamère de La Melière), the Comtesse de La Saumès (Madeleine de Chanaleilles de La Saumès, née Gerbier), and the Comtesse de La Blache (Charlotte Marie, née Gaillard de Beaumanoir). See EFAU, Fonds Johann Friedrich von Meyer, 33b, 'Mémoires du Chevalier de Barbarin'. Willermoz also wrote the same names on the back of a letter he received from Barberin, dated 6 November 1785. See BMdL, Ms. 5868, no. 6. Interestingly, Jean Goulin, a physician and editor of *Gazette de santé*, referred to the countesses de La Saumès and de La Blache as being two of the female patients of Charles Deslon in the summer of 1784 during which time they were observed by the members of the two royal commissions. According to Goulin, both were convulsionists and de La Blache, in particular, experienced 'extraordinary crises'. See Reims, Bibliothèque Carnegie de Reims, Ms. 1063, fol. 34, Jean Goulin, 'Note sur le magnétisme animal, sur l'initiation de Goulin, en 1784, et sur les séances de magnétisme où il a assité'. For a discussion of the reaction to Deslon's demonstrations of animal magnetism to the royal commissioners in 1784 and the observations of Goulin, see Belhoste, 'La condamnation du mesmérisme revisitée', pp. 187–214. In his memoirs, Paul Thiébault also mentioned that de La Blache was a patient of Charles Deslon and even occupied a part of Charles his house in Paris. See Paul Thiébault, *Mémoires du Général Bon Thiébault*, 1, Paris, 1893, pp. 86–87. Madame de Montméril was the wife of Calixte Deslon de Montméril, the brother of Charles Deslon.

[68] EFAU, Fonds Johann Friedrich von Meyer, 33b. See also, Faivre, *De Londres à Saint-Pétersbourg*, p. 116.

[69] Joly, *Un Mystique lyonnais*, p. 230.

utterances whilst in their trances. Moreover, Barberin too, in a position of power as magnetizer, was also privy to obtaining profound spiritual insights. Hence, in his first session with Madame de Montméril in March 1785, he sought answers about the nature of good and evil. For example, he asked the following questions: 'How can man, who was created by an immense, just and good being do evil'? and 'where does the idea of evil come from'?[70]

The remarkable documentation by Tieman of a profoundly spiritual form of magnetic somnambulism conducted by Barberin in 1785 is a valuable historical document in recording the emergence of such a branch of animal magnetism in France at this time. However, it also demonstrates the privileged position afforded to Tieman vis-à-vis his designated role as a preserver and potential disseminator of the distinctive Barberinian system. As will be discussed below, this is of considerable importance in regard to the introduction of animal magnetism in Russia. After all, Tieman ranks as the earliest known practitioner of animal magnetism in St Petersburg in 1786, on his return to the Russian Imperial capital. Moreover, the only other known practitioner at this time in Russia — Major Blanckennagel — seems to have embraced a form of magnetic somnambulism redolent of the Barberinian system. However, before we examine how Tieman and Blanckennagel introduced animal magnetism into Petersburg society in 1786, attention will turn to one further Russian nobleman — Vasilii Nikolaevich Zinov'ev — who embraced the Lyonnaise form of magnetic somnambulism between 1785 and 1787.

The crucial role played by Dr Giraud in Turin, in terms of promoting the trans-European network of the Rectified Scottish Rite, has already been noted above in relation to Massenet and M. A. Golitsyn. However, his guidance and sway arguably had an even more profound impact on the spiritual and Masonic odyssey of V. N. Zinov'ev in Western Europe between 1783 and 1788.[71] Zinov'ev experienced a profound spiritual crisis

[70] BMdG, Fonds Prunelle de Lière, cote T/4, 188, p. 17.

[71] For a redacted version of Zinov'ev's travel journey, see V. N. Zinov'ev, 'Zhurnal puteshestviia po Germanii, Italii, Frantsii i Anglii', ed. N. P. Baryshnikov, *Russkaia starina*, vol. 23, 1878, pp. 207–40, 399–440, 593–607. For a short memoir, written by Zinov'ev in 1806, see V. N. Zinov'ev, 'Vospominaniia V. N. Zinov'eva', ed. N. P. Baryshnikov, *Russkaia starina*, vol. 23, 1878, pp. 613–30. For an unredacted manuscript of Zinov'ev's journal, see St Petersburg, Institut russkoi literatury Rossiiskoi akademii nauk (Pushkinskii Dom), Rukopisnyi otdel, Q. 265, op. 1, No. 21. For a short biography of Zinov'ev, see A. G., 'Zinov'ev, Vasilii Nikolaevich' in *Russkii biograficheskii slovar': Zhabokritskii–Zialovskii*, Petrograd, 1916, pp. 397–99. On the tour of V. N. Zinov'ev in Europe between 1783 and 1788, see Raffaella Faggionato, 'La Maschera e lo Specchio. Cronaca del Viaggio in Occidente

in 1783, after the deaths of first his sister, Ekaterina Nikolaevna Orlova and then his brother-in-law and mentor, Grigorii Grigor′evich Orlov. Indeed, he later wrote in his memoir that he 'wished to flee' what he saw as 'this place of tribulations and sins' in order to become a true, sincere Christian by seeking out people 'who would annihilate' all his 'doubts'.[72] Those people he sought out across Europe were Freemasons.[73]

It was through using Masonic networks that Zinov′ev first met Dr Giraud in Turin in the autumn of 1785. More specifically, Zinov′ev was guaranteed a warm reception by Giraud on account of possessing a personal (Masonic) reference from Duke Ferdinand of Brunswick, the Grand Master of the Strict Observance Rite.[74] Zinov′ev relayed to Giraud his desire to travel to Lyon so that he could be initiated into the Rectified Scottish Rite of Willermoz. This soon came to pass, but not before Giraud, whom Zinov′ev refers to as 'a zealous magnetizer', demonstrated 'the miraculous effects of this force' to him in Turin.[75]

In his memoir the Russian nobleman does not elaborate on what exactly was demonstrated to him by Giraud in the autumn of 1785. However, it is known that by this time Giraud had fully embraced the magnetic somnambulism practised by his fellow Masons in Lyon. His principal patient-somnambule from 1785 was Adélaïde Diane de Cossé, duchesse de Brissac. As Alice Joly notes, Giraud devoted all his energies to the duchess, 'whom he cared for and whom he introduced into the circles of his [Masonic-RC] colleagues and friends, so that they might contribute to

di un Illuminista Russo', *Europa Orientalis*, 17, 2, 1998, pp. 7–53; Sara Dickinson, 'The Trajectory of a Freemason: Vasily Zinoviev', in Dickinson, *Breaking Ground: Travel and National Culture in Russia from Peter I to the Era of Pushkin*, Amsterdam, 2006, pp. 59–64; N. G. Morozova, 'Putevye dnevniki XVIII veka: "Zhurnal puteshestviia" V. N. Zinov′eva', *V mire nauchnykh otkrytii*, 2010, pp. 36–38; Grażyna Czerniak and Jolanta Kowalik, 'Turystyka kulturowa, rozważania a wyjazdy. Europa Zachodnia oczami XVIII-wiecznego podróżnika Wasila Zinowiewa', *Turystyka Kulturowa*, 2, 2016, pp. 135–45.

[72] Zinov′ev, *Vospominaniia*, p. 614.

[73] Zinov′ev is recorded as visiting the Royal York of Friendship Lodge (Royal York zur Freundschaft) in Berlin on 29 October 1783, where he received the Master's Degree, the third degree in the Strict Observance Rite. See Karlheinz Gerlach, *Die Freimaurer im Alten Preußen 1738–1806*, Innsbruck, Vienna and Bozen, 2014, pp. 571, 575.

[74] The Russian nobleman then travelled to Brunswick to obtain an audience with Duke Ferdinand of Brunswick. Zinov′ev resided for six months in Brunswick, during which time Duke Ferdinand furnished him 'with a true understanding of this Order' and then on his departure provided him with 'with many letters of recommendation, for various members, partly scattered in France, partly in Italy'. See Zinov′ev, *Vospominaniia*, pp. 615–16.

[75] Ibid.

her cure and her mystical instruction'.[76] Hence, it is probable that Zinov'ev first witnessed some form of magnetic somnambulism in Turin in late 1785. Irrespective of what sort of animal magnetism Zinov'ev initially witnessed, he later professed that he had a 'grand désir pour le magnétisme' until the end of 1787.

This initial 'grand désir' was sparked by Giraud, whom Zinov'ev came to regard as his 'benefactor'.[77] However, it was almost certainly fuelled by his first visit to Lyon, where he arrived on 19 December 1785.[78] Six days later Zinov'ev was initiated into La Bienfaisance. Thenceforth he could partake in the unique Masonic milieu of the lodge, which at the time was so closely entwined with a profoundly esoteric form of magnetic somnambulism in which it was possible to communicate with the spirits of deceased ancestors. For nearly three weeks Zinov'ev enjoyed the company of Willermoz, Millanois and other leading members of La Bienfaisance, as well as Louis-Claude de Saint-Martin, with whom he then travelled to Paris at the turn of 1786.

Zinov'ev subsequently spent much of 1786 in Britain before returning to France in early 1787. At the end of June Zinov'ev was reacquainted with his 'benefactor' Giraud, at the country residence of the Duchess de Brissac near Ermenonville.[79] By early November, Zinov'ev and Giraud had returned to Lyon, where the pair rented an apartment in a hotel. At the beginning of his six-month stay in Lyon, Zinov'ev met Willermoz, Millanois and Pierre-André Grainville on a daily basis.[80] On 18 November, Zinov'ev wrote an intriguing entry in his journal in regard to how Grainville had convinced him of the folly of his previous 'grand désir pour le magnétisme'.[81] According to Zinov'ev, he attended mass on this day 'with dear Giraud'. However, on the walk back to his apartment he had entered into conversation with Grainville, who apparently gave him 'a clearer meaning about somnambulists'. Evidently Grainville had also forsaken his previous enthusiasm for magnetic somnambulism by the end of 1787. It is entirely possible that Zinov'ev was simply swayed by Grainville's arguments out of respect for the venerated status of the latter within the Martinist milieu of the age.[82]

---

[76] Joly, *Un Mystique lyonnais*, p. 256.

[77] Zinov'ev, 'Zhurnal puteshestviia', pp. 602, 599.

[78] Ibid., p. 230. In the redacted publication, the editor erroneously writes that Zinov'ev arrived in Lyon on 19 December 1784.

[79] Ibid., p. 599.

[80] Ibid., p. 602.

[81] Ibid.

[82] According to Jean Bossu, Grainville had been initiated into Freemasonry in 1748.

Yet, in his journal Zinov'ev also seems to hint that his renunciation of animal magnetism may have also been influenced by Giraud's conduct. Hence, immediately after remarking that Grainville had persuaded him to disavow his 'grand désir' for animal magnetism, Zinvov'ev adds the following: 'I must note two extraordinary incidents that happened to dear Giraud: first — an individual who found him in a village unknown to him, and the second — a woman, who was in a state of somnambulism, and who was in service in the office of a notary.'[83] Zinov'ev provided no further detail in his journal, yet clearly felt the need to state these 'extraordinary incidents' in the context of what appears to be his sudden renunciation of animal magnetism. It is impossible to prove that Giraud's moral propriety or medical expertise as a magnetist was called into question by these two incidents. Yet, Zinov'ev's journal entry would seem to allude to such an eventuality playing some part in extinguishing what had been his 'grand désir' for animal magnetism.

Animal magnetism in St Petersburg in 1786
The influence of Barberin on Tieman, discussed above, is highly significant as by December 1785 the latter was once again resident in St Petersburg, where he was to remain until the summer of 1786. Tieman's return to the Russian capital coincided with growing interest among the nobility in forms of Illuminism. He wrote to Willermoz, with notable excitement, on 14 October 1786, that the translation of Saint-Martin's *Of Errors & Truth*, which had recently been published in Russian by Ivan Lopukhin, had caused 'so great an effervescence in the minds in St Petersburg and Moscow that there are more than 3,000 Martinists'.[84]

Furthermore, in September 1785, the Chevalier de la Colinière, an attaché to the French Embassy in St Petersburg, wrote to Gilbert Romme from Moscow and described how 'Mesmerism takes the greatest credit' after the appearance of an unnamed collection on animal magnetism

See BNF, Fichier Bossu (281), Grainville, Pierre-André, de. In 1767, Grainville became a founding member of the Order of Knight-Masons Elect Priest of the Universe (Ordre des Chevaliers Masons Élus Coëns de l'Universe), often referred to as the Élus Coëns, under the leadership of Martinez de Pasqually (c.1727–74). Grainville also introduced Saint-Martin into the Élus Coëns in 1768. For more on Grainville as a pivotal figure in the early development of Martinism, see Gérard van Rijnberk, *Martines de Pasqually, un thaumaturge au XVIIIe siècle*, Hildesheim, Zurich and New York, 1982, *passim*. See also, Papus, *Louis-Claude de Saint-Martin*, Paris, 1902, *passim*.

[83] Zinov'ev, 'Zhurnal puteshestviia', pp. 602–03.

[84] See BMdL, MS 5869, no. 32. See also, Faivre, *De Londres à Saint-Pétersbourg*, pp. 430–32. For the Russian translation, see Louis-Claude de Saint-Martin, *O zabluzhdeniiakh i istinne*, Moscow, 1785.

and that it had 'converted many unbelievers'.[85] Thus, it was amidst this burgeoning general interest among the Russian nobility that Tieman evidently thought it timely to introduce animal magnetism into Petersburg society. We know this, as in the same letter to Willermoz, written on 14 October 1786, he disclosed that he had undertaken two attempts at animal magnetism in the Russian capital. We do not know the identity of the first person magnetized by Tieman. The second experiment had been very successful, in Tieman's mind, and had been carried out on Princess Aleksandra Nikolaevna Volkonskaia, the daughter of Nikolai Vasil´evich Repnin. Tieman boasts of making her 'most painful attacks of periodic convulsions disappear'. Significantly, he stresses to Willermoz that Volkonskaia did not enter into a state of somnambulism and, importantly, he had not attempted to do this.[86] Why was this so? Perhaps he deemed it prudent to tread carefully when practising such a novel technique among such eminent personages? After all, Volkonskaia was a Russian princess and the daughter of one of the most powerful Freemasons in the country, who was known to be one of the foremost exponents of Martinism within Catherine II's realm.[87] Yet, given the maligned reputation of the Mesmeric technique of animal magnetism in France at the time, in which close physical contact had given rise to accusations of sexual impropriety, Tieman risked potential scandal in St Petersburg.

It is therefore unsurprising that to mitigate any potential for reproach Tieman treated the daughter of a prominent Martinist Freemason, thereby tapping into one of his trusted Masonic networks. This enabled Tieman to undertake his novel demonstration of what was a controversial technique within a relatively safe associational milieu. Nonetheless, this was not an

[85] Jean Alexandre Charette de La Colinière to Gilbert Romme (8 September 1785). Moscow, Gosudarstvennyi Arkhiv Rossiiskoi Federatsii, f. 728, op. 1, d. 342.

[86] 'J'ai fait deux essais de magnétisme à St Petersbg. dont l'un m'a parfaitement réussi. C'était sur une Princesse [Aleksandra Nikolaevna] Volkonsky, que j'ai retabli[e] en peu de tems en faisant disparaitre les plus pénibles accès de convulsions periodiques: mais il ne s'est point présenté de somnambulisme que d'ailleurs je ne cherchais pas de produire.' See BMdL, Ms. 5869, f. 32. See also, Faivre, *De Londres à Saint-Pétersbourg*, p. 432.

[87] In February 1786, Johann Georg Ritter von Zimmermann, Catherine II's long-time correspondent, wrote to the Russian Empress to inform her that Repnin was the provincial head of the Illuminists in Russia and that this 'cabalistic sect was very strong in Moscow'. What is more, Repnin was labelled 'an enthusiast' of Saint-Martin's *Of Errors & Truth*. See H. M. Marcard, *Zimmermanns Verhähaltniss mit der Kayserin Catharina II und mit dem Herrn Weikard*, Bremen, 1803, pp. 134–35. Zimmermann's exposé of Repnin as a leading Freemason of a decidedly Martinist hue was accurate. On Repnin and his status as a Martinist and Rosicrucian in Russia in the 1780s and 1790s, see A. N. Pypin, *Russkoe masonstvo XVIII i pervaia chetvert´ XIX v.*, Petrograd, 1916, *passim*; G. V. Vernadskii, *Russkoe masonstvo v tsarstvovanie Ekaterinyi II*, Moscow, 1999, *passim*.

Fig. 1. Portrait of Aleksandra Nikolaevna Volkonskaia in the 1780s. Magnetized by C. F. Tieman in St Petersburg at some point between December 1785 and July 1786. Source: Image in the public domain, courtesy of Alamy.com.

esoteric ritual performed in secret, but a treatment with the potential to arouse the curiosity of a broader swathe of the Russian nobility outside the exclusive space of the lodge. To be sure, Tieman does not seem to have courted attention to his use of animal magnetism, only revealing that he had undertaken the treatment of two patients in a letter to J.-B. Willermoz.

The relative restraint shown by Tieman in not openly flaunting his use of animal magnetism before he departed for western Europe in July 1786 was not replicated by Major Blanckennagel, a Baltic German in Russian service. He began to attract attention in October 1786 in St Petersburg for performing magnetic somnambulism on various members of the nobility. Two contemporary noblemen — Nikolai Aleksandrovich L'vov and Andrei Timofeevich Bolotov, who rank among the most talented polymaths in Russia's Age of Enlightenment — provide us with invaluable insights into Blanckennagel's brief foray into magnetic somnambulism in the autumn of 1786. It must be stated however, that a degree of ambiguity remains as to the precise identity of Blanckennagel, as L'vov simply refers to him as 'M[iste]r' (G[ospodi]n) and Bolotov names him as a Major. Bolotov's inclusion of rank is helpful here as it strongly suggests that the magnetizer in question was Georg von Blanckennagel (Egor Ivanovich Blankennagel'), who did indeed hold the rank of major in 1786 in the Corps of Engineers (Inzhenernyi korpus) in Moscow.[88]

Like Barberin and Puységur in France, Blanckennagel was a military man with no medical expertise whatsoever. More specifically, he was a hydraulic engineer who had graduated from the Artillery and Engineering Gentry Cadet Corps (Artillersiiskii i inzhenernyi shliakhetskii kadetskii korpus) in St Petersburg in 1770.[89] Blanckennagel went on to enjoy a

[88] See *Mesiatsoslov s rospis'iu chinovnykh osob v gosudarstve*, St Petersburg, 1786, p. 60. At the time Georg's half-brother, Magnus Johann (Ivan Ivanovich in Russian), who died in 1817, held the lower rank of Second Major in the Ingermanland Infantry Regiment. See *Spisok voinskomu departamentu na 1787 god*, St Petersburg, 1787, p. 136. Blanckennagel also had another half-brother, Aleksandr (d. 1804), who achieved the rank of Major at some point in the 1790s. Aleksandr Ivanovich von Blanckennagel does not feature in any official published records of officials in the Russian Empire in the 1780s. In 1793–94 A. I. Blanckennagel undertook an expedition from Orenburg to Khiva, in the Khanate of Khiva (in modern-day Uzbekistan), in order to try and cure the blindness of Fazil bi, the elderly brother of the leading Qungrat Inak, the de facto rulers of the khanate. According to Blanckennagel, he ended up treating hundreds of local inhabitants. His extensive notes on his experiences in the Khanate of Khiva were presented to the State Council in St Petersburg in 1797 and 1798. See RGIA, 'Po zapiskam otstavnogo maiora Blankennagelia: 1) o puteshestvii ego v Khivu i 2) o sposobakh k ovladeniiu Khivoiu; 1797–1800 gg. Protokoly: 2, 9, 16 i 23 iiulia, 29 oktiabria, 7, 14 i 21 dekabria 1797 g. i 18 i 22 marta 1798 g.', Sovet pri vysochaishem dvore, f. 1146, op. 1, d. 155. For a published version of the report (written in French) submitted to the State Council in 1797, and Blanckennagel's subsequent responses to queries, see pp. 623–52. For the manuscript version of Blanckennagel's travel journey of his expedition to Khiva, see GIM, 'Primechaniia maiora Blankennagelia na Puteshestvie ego v Khivu', f. 92, op. 1, ed. kh. 12. For a published version, see V. V. Grigor'ev (ed.), *Zamechaniia maiora Blankennagelia vposledstvie poezdki ego iz Orenburga v Khivu*, St Petersburg, 1858. For archival material on A. I. Blanckennagel, who held the rank of court councillor (*nadvornyi sovetnik*), see RGADA, Gerol'dmesterskaia kontora, f. 286, op. 2, kn. 128, ll. 101–06.

[89] On his involvement in the planning and building of the Neglinnyi Canal in Moscow in 1792, see Mariia Besedina, *Moskva Akuninskaia*, Moscow, 2007, p. 194. For a brief

Fig. 2. Portrait of Georg von Blanckennagel (d. 1813). Source: Moscow, Gosudarstvennyi Istoricheskii Muzei (hereafter, GIM), inventory number: I I 2683.

highly successful career as a military engineer and was awarded the Order of St George (4th class) in 1795.[90] He is undoubtedly best known, however, as being the co-founder of the first sugar beet factory in the Russian Empire that was established in a village in Tula province in 1802.[91] Indeed, as only the second ever sugar beet factory in the world,

biography of Blanckennagel, see 'Blanknagel´ (Blankennagel´), Egor Ivanovich', *Bol´shaia sovetskaia entsiklopediia*, vol. 5, Moscow, 1950, p. 290.

[90] Rossiiskaia gosudarstvennaia biblioteka, Moscow, OR f. 32, k. 19, ed. 21, 'Reskript na imia polkovnika Blankennagelia o nagrazhdenii ego ordenom sv. Georgiia'.

[91] For more on this endeavour, which Blanckennagel undertook in collaboration

Blanckennagel's scientific entrepreneurialism, in which he displayed considerable chemical expertise, was noted at the time across Europe.[92]

Nothing is known about how Major Blanckennagel came to view himself as a magnetic somnambulist. It is redolent of a contemporaneous trend that was being advocated by Johann Caspar Lavater, the famed Swiss physiognomist and theologian from Zurich. From the autumn of 1785 Lavater began to extol a form of magnetic somnambulism infused with religious elements.[93] There is no documentary evidence of Tieman teaching Blanckennagel (or anyone else) the form of magnetic somnambulism developed by Barberin in Lyon and Paris in 1784–85. Tieman would seem the most likely candidate given the form of magnetic somnambulism embraced by Blanckennagel was still a rare pursuit in Europe in 1786. Yet, Tieman mixed and demonstrated his skills as an animal magnetism

with Iakov Stepanovich Esipov, see F. F. Reis, *Opisanie sveklo-sakharnago zavoda, osnovannago g. general-maiorom Blankennagelem, Tul'skoi gubernii Chernskago uezda v sel'tse Aliab'eve*, St Petersburg, 1808. For the initial decree (*ukaz*) issued by Emperor Alexander I in October 1802, see 'O nabliudenii za proizvodstvom vydelyvaemago iz sveklovitsy sakharu i spirity na zavode General-Maiora Blankennagell', *Polnoe sobranie zakonov rossiiskoi imperii s 1649 goda*, vol. 27, St Petersburg, 1830, pp. 934–36.

[92] The following report, for example, featured in a British newspaper in March 1802: 'The Russian Proprietors of land, among others Major-General Blankenagel, and Colonel Jessipow, are causing sugars to be made from beet root from their estates in the Government of Moscow; they have brought the method of preparation to great perfection, and have sent to his Imperial Majesty specimens of their beet-root sugar, of which he has testified his high approbation.' See *General Evening Post*, 25 March 1802, pp. 1–2. It should also be noted that Blanckennagel was an agronomical pioneer in the Russian Empire in the 1790s. From 1792, he introduced innovative techniques of grass cultivation on his estate near Zvenigorod, west of Moscow, that were commented upon favourably by his peers. See, for example, Andrei Vasil'evich Roznotovskii, *Novoe zemledelie*, Moscow, 1794, pp. 346–58. He also attempted to innovate methods to settle peasants on his land and to collect income from them more efficiently from 1798. See *Usad'by ili novyi sposob selit' krest'ian i sobirat' s nikh pomeshchichii dokhod*, St Petersburg, 1801.

[93] On Lavater's embrace of magnetic somnambulism that was strongly imbued with religious elements, see his contemporary correspondence. See, for example, a letter he wrote to Heinrich Matthias Marcard (1747–1817) on 10 September 1785, in which he discusses his treatment of his wife, Anna, using magnetic somnambulism. See 'Schreiben des herrn Diakonus Lavater an herrn hofmedicus Marcard', *Berlinische Monatsschrift*, vol. 6 (November 1785), pp. 434–38. See also, Dietrich G. Kieser, ed., 'J. C. Lavater's bisher ungedruckte Briefe und Aufsätze über thierischen Magnetismus', *Archiv für thierischen Magnetismus*, vol. 8 (1820), pp. 1–60. On Lavater's influence on the Bremen physicians Arnokld Wienholt, Heinrich Wilhelm Olbers and Georg Bicker in terms of their subsequent embrace of magnetic somnambulism enthused with religious elements, see Tilmann Hannemann, 'Das Reich Gottes: Pragmatische Anpassungen und experimentelle Ausblicke', in Hannemann, *Religiöser Wandel in der Spätaufklärung am Beispiel der Lavaterschule 1770–1805*, Göttingen, 2017, pp. 207–82. See also, Gantet, 'The Dissemination of Mesmerism in Germany', pp. 768–69.

within a Masonic milieu and it would appear that Blanckennagel was not a member of any lodge within the Russian Empire.[94]

Whatever the case, from surviving descriptions it is clear that Blanckennagel was practising a distinctly similar form of magnetic somnambulism in the Russian capital in the autumn of 1786. In a letter addressed to G. P. Derzhavin, for example, dated 1 November 1786, the polymath Nikolai Aleksandrovich L'vov complained that Blanckennagel — to whom he refers as an *odnodvorets* — had 'arrived with his magnetism and made both the court and city talk about him without exception' with the help of 'powerful eloquence'.[95] More specifically, L'vov related how 'the whole city is only speaking about the wife of *gospodin* Kovalenskii, who, being lulled to sleep by Blanckennagel by means of the power of magnetism, spoke things in her sleep, that, when she awoke she not only did not know, but could not have known'.[96]

The woman magnetized by Blanckennagel was Nadezhda Mikhailovna Kovalenskaia (neé Matsneva), the wife of Mikhail Ivanovich Kovalenskii (Mykhailo Ivanovich Kovalyns'kyi in Ukrainian).[97] Kovalenskii is best known for his *Life of Hryhorii Skovoroda*, about the renowned philosopher, with whom he had been a close friend since 1762.[98] In his own right, Kovalenskii was a talented poet and translator, having been educated in Strasbourg between 1772 and 1775.[99] According to a contemporary,

---

[94] Blanckennagel's brother, Magnus Johann, is listed as being a member of Isis Lodge in Revel (Tallinn) in 1782. See Henning von Wistinghausen, *Freimaurer und Aufklärung im Russischen Reich. Die Revaler Logen 1773–1820*, vol. 1, Cologne, 2016 p. 384.

[95] N. A. L'vov, *Izbrannye sochineniia*, St Petersburg, 1994, p. 331. In referring to von Blanckennagel as an *odnodvorets*, which literally translates as 'smallholder', L'vov may be highlighting the Baltic German's lack of official noble status within the Russian Empire. On the complex status of *odnodvortsy* in the Russian Empire in the late eighteenth century, see Thomas Esper, 'The Odnodvortsy and the Russian Nobility', *Slavonic and East European Review*, 45, 1967, pp. 124–34; Alfred J. Rieber, 'Social Identity and Political Will: The Russian Nobility from Peter I, "The Great," to 1861', in Rieber, *The Imperial Russian Project: Autocratic Politics, Economic Development, and Social Fragmentation*, Toronto, 2017, pp. 299–336.

[96] Ibid.

[97] The Kovalenskiis married in 1778 and were resident in St Petersburg in the 1780s, with the husband working in the chancellery of G. A. Potemkin from the middle of the decade.

[98] See M. I. Kovalenskii, *Zhitie Skovorody*, Kyiv, 1886. For a recent edition, see Mikhailo Kovalins'kyi, 'Zhizn' Grigoriia Skovorody', in *Hryhorii Skovoroda. Povna akademichna zbirka tvoriv*, ed. Leonid Ushkalov, Edmonton, Toronto and Kharkiv, 2011, pp. 1343–386.

[99] For a short biography of M. I. Kovalenskii, see M. P. Lepekhin, 'Kovalenskii (Kovalinskii) Mikhail Ivanovich', in *Slovar' russkikh pisatelei XVIII veka*, ed. A. M. Panchenko, vol. 2, St Petersburg, 1999, pp. 82–84.

Kovalenskii was 'a bit of a mystic'.[100] This is reinforced by Sergei
Mikhailovich Solov'ev, a descendant of Kovalenskii, who begins his
memoir with a description of his distant relative based on access to his
private archival material: 'Although Mikhail Ivanovich was close to
Potemkin, moved among the students of Diderot's *Encyclopaedia* and
even went to Ferney to see Voltaire, his mood was entirely determined by
Skovoroda and, perhaps, the Freemasons and Swedenborg.'[101]

Drawing on Kovalenskii's diary and letters, Solov'ev also attests that his
relationship with Nadezhda Mikhailovna was 'tender and poetic'.[102] Whilst
Solov'ev's account provides valuable snippets of information regarding the
family life of the Kovalenskiis, he discloses nothing about the character and
disposition of Nadezhda Mikhailovna. However, an extant postscript she
wrote to Skovoroda in 1779 reveals that she too enjoyed a close friendship
with the philosopher. As with her husband, she calls Skovoroda 'Meingard'
and writes of her love and respect for him, ending the letter in French with
'Adieu, mon ami!'[103] In short, this postscript reveals a warm, eloquent and
educated individual.

The brief contemporary description offered by L'vov of the interaction
between Blanckennagel and Kovalenskaia was considerably embellished
in 1796 by the memoirist Andrei Timofeevich Bolotov. He notes that
Blanckennagel performed animal magnetism on several members of the
nobility in 1786, but that his treatment of Kovalenskaia was especially
renowned. According to Bolotov, Blanckennagel successfully placed her in
a magnetic form of somnambulism on several occasions. The services of
Blanckennagel were initially called upon to treat Kovalenskaia's eight-year-
old son, Mikhail, who was not responding to the conventional methods
of their family physician. Blanckennagel brought the boy to a state of
somnambulism several times in order for the patient to self-diagnose his
illness and how to treat it. The boy apparently spoke when somnambulized,

[100] S. P. Zhikharev, *Zapiski sovremennika*, ed. B. M. Eikhenbaum, Moscow and
Leningrad, 1955, p. 22. The similarity of Kovalenskii's world-view with the Martinist circle
of Nikolai Novikov has been the subject of a recent article by Serhii Yosypenko. See Serhii
Yosypenko, 'Skovoroda, Kovalyns'kyi i Meinhard', *Filosofs'ka dumka*, 4, 2022, pp. 27–53.
[101] S. Solov'ev, *Vospominaniia*, Moscow, 2003, p. 36.
[102] Ibid., pp. 37–40.
[103] She also informs Skovoroda that she is sending him parmesan and Dutch cheese,
as well as a violin and pipes. See G. P. Danilevskii, 'Grigorii Savich Skovoroda (s 1722
po 1794 g.)', *Ukrainskaia starina: materialy dlia istorii ukrainskoi literatury i narodnogo
obrazovaniia*, Kharkiv, 1866, p. 47. See also, Hryhorii Skovoroda, *Povne zibrannia tvoriv*,
vol. 2, Kyiv, 1973, p. 477. On the meaning of 'Meingard', used by the Kovalenskiis in their
correspondence with Skovoroda, see Yosypenko, *Skovoroda*, pp. 27–53.

but Blanckennagel was not satisfied and concluded that his patient was too young.

Instead, he turned to the mother, who was entirely healthy, and somnambulized her so that she could attempt to diagnose what was wrong with her son and how to cure him. As Bolotov describes, her somnambulistic abilities were so great that she was able to detect whether anyone present was ill. According to Bolotov, these purported abilities were displayed at semi-public spectacles, as many of Kovalenskaia's acquaintances were invited to attend her being magnetized by Blanckennagel and entering into a state of somnambulism. Whereas Tieman had earlier been reticent to openly demonstrate magnetic somnambulism in Petersburg in 1786, this was not the case with Blanckennagel. Indeed, in his letter to Derzhavin, L'vov foresaw that Blanckennagel's brazen demonstrations of magnetic somnambulism among the Petersburg nobility would soon be publicised in the city's gazettes.[104]

One such attendee was Count Petr Vasil'evich Zavadovskii, who was informed that he urgently needed to seek treatment for an illness of which he was unaware. The presence of Zavadovskii — a former private secretary and favourite of Catherine II and a privy councillor (tainyi sovetnik) — is indicative of the éclat (albeit brief) enjoyed by Blanckennagel in 1786 among the upper echelons of the Petersburg nobility.[105]

More astonishing still, Bolotov describes how Kovalenskaia would pass judgement, when questioned by the magnetizer, on acquaintances who were 'absent and located several hundred versts away' as to whether they were 'healthy or sick and how to cure them'.[106] Another remarkable feature of Kovalenskaia's somnambulistic state, as attested by Bolotov, was that she also wrote 'beautiful verses, although they did not resemble verses in the least'. On such occasions a pencil and paper were placed by the side of a bed on which she was lying in a state of somnambulism. Bolotov provides an example from 24 October 1786, which is brimming with religious fervour and is reminiscent of the visionary utterances of the French prophetesses who were somnambulized by Barberin in Paris the preceding year:

---

[104] L'vov, *Izbrannye sochineniia*, p. 331. There would appear to be no evidence to attest that Blanckennagel's demonstrations of magnetic somnambulism were advertised in the gazettes of St Petersburg at this time.

[105] 'Zavadovskii, Petr Vasil'evich', *Russkii biograficheskii slovar': Zhabokritskii–Zialovskii*, Petrograd, 1916, pp. 137–43.

[106] A. T. Bolotov, *Pamiatnik pretekshikh vremian, ili Kratkie istoricheskie zapiski o byvshikh proisshestviiakh i nosivshikhsia v narode slukhakh*, Moscow, 1990, pp. 124–25.

24 октября я была в сомнамбулизме, а послезавтра опять буду.
Чувствие живое, чувствие истины, чувствие премудрости! ты, которое
никогда не умираешь! которое есть жизнь человеков! Буди мне всегда
вождь в пути жития! Да слышит сердце мое глас твой непорочный! —
О вы, предстоящие и с удивлением взирающие на спящего человека!
отжените от себя движения телесные, чувствования преходящие,
ощущения временные, понятия земные, низу поникшие помышления!
Упразднитесь от суетных занятий! Уразумейте, что есть Бог!

On 24 October I was somnambulized, and the day after tomorrow I shall
be again. The feeling is alive, a feeling of truth, a feeling of wisdom! Thou,
who never dies! who is the life of the people! Always be my leader in the
path of life! May my heart hear your chaste voice! O you [addressing the
onlookers], who stand in front of and behold with amazement the sleeping
person! Divorce yourselves from bodily movements, transient feelings,
temporary sensations, earthly notions, lowly considerations! Set yourself
aside from idle pursuits! Comprehend what God is![107]

Bolotov provides a scathing commentary on Kovalenskaia's somnambulistic
prophecies and stresses that her predictions did not come to pass.
Irrespective of their accuracy, it is fascinating to note that Blanckennagel
and Kovalenskaia were replicating the form of magnetic somnambulism
developed in 1784 and 1785 by Barberin and championed by Tieman and
the Lyon Mason-magnetizers.

This form of animal magnetism offered educated women a degree of
agency otherwise denied them in European and Russian society. Indeed, in
many ways, the female somnambule of the mid 1780s, such as Kovalenskaia,
can be viewed as a precursor of the plethora of female spiritualist mediums
of the second half of the nineteenth century. Much has been written
about how these later women mediums used the opportunity afforded by
spiritualist séances to voice all manner of opinions (religious, romantic,
political) that were essentially prohibited in other public and private
spaces.[108] Yet, as Kristen Friedman has astutely noted vis-à-vis female
somnambules in the United States in the early nineteenth century, these
women also 'spoke publicly about religion and acted in ways that defied the

---

[107] Bolotov, *Pamiatnik*, p. 125. The last sentence can also be translated as 'Comprehend
that there is God'.

[108] See, for example, Alex Owen, *The Darkened Room: Women, Power and Spiritualism
in Late Victorian England*, Philadelphia, PA, 1990; Ann Braude, *Radical Spirits: Spiritualism
and Women's Rights in Nineteenth-Century America*, 2nd edn, Bloomington, 2001.

social limitations placed on female agency'.[109] Thus, although Bolotov was wholly dismissive of Kovalenskaia's abilities, he did deem them worthy of recording for posterity. Hence, even when mediated via the male gaze of Bolotov, Kovalenskaia's state of artificial somnambulism can still be seen to offer a theatrical spectacle that blurred all manner of boundaries but did provide her with a voice that resonated with strength for a short period among the nobility of St Petersburg.

It is important to emphasize Blanckennagel was at the forefront, albeit for a short period of time, of a wider European movement towards a spiritual form of magnetic somnambulism. In this regard, it is significant that Bolotov adds that the magnetic somnambulism of Blanckennagel caused such a sensation that Catherine II ordered him to abandon his occupation, 'or be ready to go to such a place where he forgets his magnetism and somnambulism'.[110] Whereas some among the Petersburg nobility viewed Blanckennagel's embrace of magnetic somnambulism as a curative wonder, the Russian Empress held a starkly different opinion: to her it was perceived in terms of being a highly contagious disease that necessitated swift action to eradicate the danger it posed. Such decisive action by the Empress is entirely unsurprising. After all, the form of magnetic somnambulism practised by Blanckennagel was essentially an expression of something that Catherine II had quickly come to regard as a pernicious influence; namely Martinism.

It was at this time that the Russian monarch unleashed a wide-ranging attack on what she perceived to be the growing threat of Martinists within her realm — broadly understood as any type of Illuminist Freemason and the practitioners of esoteric pursuits (alchemy, Christian Cabbala, astrology and animal magnetism) — among her nobility. To be sure, Catherine II's anger would have been redoubled if she had become aware at this time that her own son had been recently introduced to the very dangers — Martinists, magnetists and even Cagliostro — that she found abhorrent. Irrespective of whether she knew of her own son's dalliance with these very people in Lyon, her scorn and vitriol was heaped upon such perceived enthusiasts and charlatans in 1786.

[109] Kristen Anne Keerma Friedman, 'Soul Sleepers: A History of Somnambulism in the United States, 1740–1840', unpublished PhD thesis, Harvard University, 2014, pp. 7–8, 289. Alison Winter also touches upon issues of gender in terms of the increased popularity of Mesmerism in Victorian Britain, particularly in regard to Ada Lovelace in the 1840s. See Alison Winter, *Mesmerized: Powers of Mind in Victorian Britain*, Chicago, IL, 1998, pp. 214–15, 230–38, 244–45.
[110] Bolotov, *Pamiatnik pretekshikh vremian*, p. 125.

Most famously, this year saw the premieres in St Petersburg of three comedies written by the empress — *The Deceiver* (*Obmanshchik*), *The Deceived* (*Obol'shchennyi*) and *The Siberian Shaman* (*Shaman sibirskii*) — that are commonly referred to as simply being anti-Masonic, but which more accurately constituted a broader attack against the Russian nobility's rising fascination in all strands of Western esotericism.[111]

Catherine II continued her attack on Martinists in July 1786, when she anonymously published a short piece entitled 'A household note about the contagion of a newly-fashionable heresy and about the means to be healed from it'.[112] Herein she recounts how a sect of new heretics had recently emerged in Russia known as '*Martyny*' or '*Martyshki*'. Indeed, the author confesses that they had nearly become infected with the disease after reading 'the book about truths and errors', that is Saint-Martin's most-famed work, written in 1775 and first published in Russian, as mentioned above, by Lopukhin in 1785.[113] The author was only saved from this supposedly insidious Martinist infection by the intervention of a doctor, who carried out a five-step curative treatment plan. The final stage of this treatment involved the removal of works by Swedenborg and Saint-Martin from the patient's library, as well as other 'heretical' books, which were subsequently burned.[114]

This year also saw the beginning of a concerted attack on the publishing activities of Nikolai Ivanovich Novikov, the foremost proponent of Martinism in Moscow. All 461 books on sale in the shop of Novikov's private typography were sequestered and examined by Archbishop Platon and an Ecclesiastical Commission and the activities of his publishing

---

[111] On 17 February 1786, Catherine II wrote to Friedrich Melchior von Grimm and explained that the character of *The Siberian Shaman* was envisaged as a comedic representation of 'a theosophist who carries out all the charlataneries of the confrères of Paracelsus' and was explicitly based on the definition of a *théosophe* contained in *L'Encyclopédie*. Notably, this included freemasons *and* 'fashionable sects'. See Catherine II, *Pis'ma Imperatritsy Ekateriny II k Grimmu*, p. 374. For the characterization of a theosophist contained in *L'Encyclopédie*, see Denis Diderot and Jean Le Rond d'Alembert (eds), *L'Encyclopédie*, vol. 16, Paris, 1751, pp. 253–61. For the reproduction of the scripts of all three plays, see Catherine II, Empress of Russia, *Sochineniia imperatritsy Ekateriny II*, vol. 1, ed. Aleksandr Nikolaevich Pypin, St Petersburg, 1901, pp. 247–88 (*Obmanshchik*), pp. 289–346 (*Obol'shchennyi*), pp. 347–419 (*Shaman Sibirskii*). The plays premiered in The Hermitage Theatre in St Petersburg on 4 January, 2 February and 24 September (all Old-Style dates) respectively. See A. V. Khrapovitskii, *Dnevnik A. V. Khrapovitskago 1782–1793*, ed. Nikolai Varsukov, St Petersburg, 1874, pp. 5, 6, 16.

[112] 'Domovaia zapiska o zaraze novo-modnoi eresi i o sredstvakh iztseliaiushchikh ot onoi', *Rastushchii vinograd*, July 1786, pp. iii–vii.

[113] Ibid., p. iii.

[114] Ibid., p. vii.

house were suspended. The latter body picked out only twenty-two works that were deemed to be suspect and heretical.[115] These offending publications were not burned, but in March 1786 Catherine II did order Iakov Aleksandrovich Brius, the Governor-General of Moscow, to warn Novikov to 'beware of publishing books filled with similar strange philosophizing, or, better to say, sheer delusions'.[116] Alongside this explicit warning vis-à-vis Novikov's printing endeavours, pressure seems to have been exerted by Brius on Masonic lodges in Moscow, as they ceased to operate in this year.[117]

Thus, on the one hand, Blanckennagel's rather brazen promotion of magnetic somnambulism, which was so closely associated with French — and by extension Russian — Martinists, appealed to a significant section of the Petersburg elite who had recently been drawn to what Catherine II regarded as a 'newly-fashionable heresy'. On the other hand, however, the timing of Blanckennagel's emergence as the preeminent exponent of magnetic somnambulism in the capital of the Russian Empire occurred at a wholly inopportune moment. After all, he began to attract attention in St Petersburg when the activities of Martinists, and particularly Novikov, had come to be regarded by the state as decidedly suspicious. Furthermore, his magnetic treatments of members of the Petersburg nobility came to the fore only a month after the premiere of *The Siberian Shaman*. In this play, Catherine II continued to ridicule both the fraudulent pursuits of exotic quacks and charlatans *and* the attraction of many of her nobility to Martinism and strands of mysticism.[118]

Significantly, a direct association between those mocked in *The Siberian Shaman* and the practitioners of magnetic somnambulism was made in May 1787 by Johann Georg Zimmermann, the Swiss writer and physician and correspondent of Catherine II. After visiting Strasbourg, Zimmermann published an article, written on 29 May of this year, in the

[115]   See M. N. Longinov, *Novikov i moskovskie martinisty*, Moscow, 1867, pp. 255–76; W. Gareth Jones, *Nikolay Novikov Enlightener of Russia*, Cambridge, 1984, pp. 186–91; Gary M. Hamburg, 'Novikov and the Moderate Enlightenment', in Hamburg, *Russia's Path Toward Enlightenment: Faith, Politics, and Reason, 1500–1801*, New Haven, CT, 2016, pp. 623–27.

[116]   The official edict (*ukaz*) of Catherine II to Brius is reproduced in N. I. Novikov, *N. I. Novikov Izbrannye sochineniia*, ed. G. P. Makogonenko, Moscow and Leningrad, 1951, p. 587.

[117]   Longinov, *Novikov i moskovskie martinisty*, p. 272.

[118]   See Lurana D. O'Malley, 'The Monarch and the Mystic: Catherine the Great's Strategy of Audience Enlightenment in *The Siberian Shaman*', *Slavic and East European Journal*, 41, 2, 1997, pp. 224–42.

German press in which he expressed his disdain for all members of the city's Société harmonique des amis réunis, who adhered to Puységur's method of magnetic somnambulism. He concluded his scathing denunciation of the Société harmonique of Strasbourg by proclaiming that he would be 'just as pleased to be initiated into [this] harmonious or magnetic society [...] as into the society of Siberian shaman'.[119] Catherine II was delighted with Zimmermann's comparison between the magnetic somnambulists of the Société harmonique of Strasbourg and a society of Siberian shaman. In a letter to Zimmermann, penned on 1 July 1787, she wrote with glee that 'I flatter myself that soon we will bring some [Siberian shaman] from this country to those that have such a decided taste for such kinds of charlatan'.[120]

Major Blanckennagel may well have been prepared to brush-off any comparisons drawn by readers or spectators of *The Siberian Shaman* between himself, as a 'quack' practitioner of magnetic somnambulism and the charlatanry of the play's protagonist, Amban-Lai. However, the direct offstage warning he purportedly received from Catherine II was another matter entirely. The punitive measures directed at Novikov and Moscow Freemasons more generally sent out a clear signal that the Russian Empress was no longer prepared to tolerate any activity that promoted Martinism in any guise. Thus, in the case of Blanckennagel, and animal magnetism more broadly, the shot across the bow issued by the empress seems to have been highly effective in the short term: there were no documented demonstrations of any form of animal magnetism in the Russian Empire from the autumn of 1786 until the end of the Napoleonic Wars.

Yet, Catherine II's cauterization of animal magnetism in 1786 did not ultimately eradicate what she believed to be a disease that encouraged delusional enthusiasm among her nobility. The infection was certainly stymied — aided in the Russian Empire and across Europe by the tumultuous events that unfurled in France from 1789 — but many of the underlying reasons behind the fashion for animal magnetism among the Russian (and European) nobility in the mid 1780s merely lay dormant.

[119] Johann Georg Zimmermann, Erklärung gegen eine Unwahrheit', *Berlinische Monatsschrift*, July 1787, pp. 78–79. For a redacted summary of Zimmermann's article, see *Darmstädter Zeitung: amtliches Organ der Hessischen Landesregierung*, 5 June 1787, n.p. Vera Proskurina has recently noted that the comedy was aimed at the fashionable European fascination for magnetism among Masons and healers. See Vera Proskurina, *Imperiia pera Ekateriny II: literatura kak politika*, Moscow, 2017, pp. 8–9.
[120] *Zimmermanns Verhältnisse mit der Kayserin Catharina II un mit dem Herrn Weikard*, ed. H. M. Marcard, Bremen, 1803, p. 355.

In essence the brief dalliance with forms of animal magnetism in 1786 foreshadowed (as did early expressions of romanticism) the more sustained challenge to Enlightenment ideals that occurred in the post-Napoleonic era in the Russian Empire and Europe as a whole: a spiritual curiosity and anxiety that emboldened individuals to seek unorthodox and personal channels to the divine; a heightened sense of the unexplored potential of the realm of the unconscious within the human mind; and a willingness to embrace unconventional methods of healing that drew on older theories of occult philosophy. An understanding of this initial, albeit fleeting, attraction to animal magnetism among the Russian nobility in the 1780s provides an essential grounding for further studies that can examine the resurgence of interest in the varied forms of animal magnetism in the decades after 1815, which has yet to receive in-depth scholarly attention.[121] To be sure, such a study is long overdue, as it has the potential to broaden our understanding of the nuanced attitudes to religion, science, medicine and the human mind in the Russian Empire in the decades after the Napoleonic Wars.

[121] For a recent study of the revival of animal magnetism in France after 1815, see Sean M. Quinlan, 'The Mesmerist Undercurrents and Testing the Limits of Scientific Authority', in Quinlan, *Morbid Undercurrents: Medical Subcultures in Postrevolutionary France*, Ithaca, NY, 2021, pp. 176–216. See also, Gauld, *A History of Hypnotism*, pp. 99–162; Adam Crabtree, *From Mesmer to Freud: Magnetic Sleep and the Roots of Psychological Healing*, New Haven, CT, 1993, pp. 109–70; Bell, 'Romanticism and Animal Magnetism', pp. 167–207. For the best study to date on animal magnetism in the Russian Empire after 1815, see Kondakov, 'Zhivotnyi magnetism v Rossii', pp. 161–200.

East-West Cultural Exchange in the Coldest Years of the Cold War: A Case Study of Poland and the Netherlands (1950–1956)

MICHAŁ WENDERSKI

FOR more than forty years the metaphorical Iron Curtain impeded political, personal and cultural relationships and exchanges in post-war Europe. In this difficult Cold War reality, music, art, literature, dance and science often created the sole possibility for individuals to cross this dividing line and come into contact with peoples and cultures from 'the other side'. This article explores the realms of such international East-West cultural exchange between 1950 and 1956, as exemplified by bilateral relations between the Kingdom of the Netherlands and the 'People's Poland'[1] that have so far gained limited scholarly attention.[2] Poland and

Michał Wenderski is an assistant professor in the Faculty of English at the Adam Mickiewicz University, Poznań and in 2023/2024 guest researcher at the Research Institute for Cultural Inquiry at Utrecht University.

Research for this article was supported by the Polish National Science Centre under Grant number 2018/31/B/HS2/00121.

[1]   The term 'People's Poland' (Polska Ludowa) was a semi-official reference to the Polish state under Communism. The country's official name after the war was Rzeczpospolita Polska (Republic of Poland), which was changed in June 1952 to Polska Rzeczpospolita Ludowa (Polish People's Republic).
[2]   The existing literature devoted to Polish-Dutch relations rarely mentions cultural exchange before 1956, mostly limiting it to weak contacts in the field of music or personal mobility. See Peter Krug, 'Culturele en economische betrekkingen tussen Nederland en Polen door de eeuwen heen', *Ons Erfdeel*, 23, 1981, pp. 495–508; Lucia Thijssen, *1000 jaar Polen en Nederland*, Zutphen, 1992; Duco Hellema, 'The Cold War Years 1945–1975', in Duco Hellema, Ryszard Żelichowski and Bert van der Zwan (eds), *Poland and the Netherlands: A Case Study of European Relations*, Dordrecht, 2011, pp. 123–40; Anna Sikora-Sabat, *Teksty kultury niderlandzkiej w Polsce (1945–1989). Przekłady literackie, polityka wystawiennicza i kulturalna*, Poznań, 2013; Ryszard Żelichowski, *Stosunki polsko-holenderskie w Europie pojałtańskiej*, Warsaw, 2014. The author's recent work devoted to Polish-Dutch cultural relations at the outset of the Cold War indicates, however, that the issue in question is more

the Netherlands serve as examples of the so-called 'smaller powers' in the Cold War conflict.[3] Although it lay in the Soviet sphere of influence, Poland remained one of the most West-oriented countries, 'independent at heart', whilst the Netherlands was seen as one of the most zealous members of NATO, with a strict anti-Communist policy. They thus represented two opposing stances when it came to East-West cultural relations, with Poland attempting to foster them and the Netherlands remaining very restrained.

The case study of Polish-Dutch cultural relations needs to be placed in the broader context of the so-called 'Cultural Cold War', with culture intentionally used by state governments for their political purposes — not only to achieve mutual understanding, but also as a weapon, a means of penetration, infiltration and propaganda.[4] This battle for hearts and minds has, over the years, received more and more scholarly attention: from works predominantly concentrated on the binary opposition of the two blocks and the Soviet-American cultural rivalry,[5] to more nuanced accounts devoted to the previously overlooked players, both European and worldwide, with their own agendas and political interests.[6] Scholars have

complex. See Michał Wenderski, 'Art Versus Politics: Polish-Dutch International Cultural Relationships at the Outset of the Cold War (1947–50)', *Cold War History*, 22, 1, 2022, pp. 103–21, and the forthcoming monograph, *Art and Politics during the Cold War: Poland and the Netherlands*, London and New York, 2024. This article presents and elaborates on a case study of the history of Polish-Dutch Cold War cultural relations delineated in the forthcoming book.

[3] For an outline of the term 'smaller powers', see Laurien Crump and Susanna Erlandsson (eds), *Margins for Manoeuvre in Cold War Europe: The Influence of Smaller Powers*, London and New York, 2020.

[4] Numerous theoretical notions have been applied to studies on cultural relations during the Cold War, ranging from public and cultural diplomacy to soft and smart power. They are, however, often used vaguely and interchangeably, and their proper definition and application are not always evident. See Martina Topić and Cassandra Sciortino, 'Cultural Diplomacy and Cultural Imperialism: A Framework for the analysis', in Martina Topić and Siniša Rodin (eds), *Cultural Diplomacy or Cultural Imperialism*, Frankfurt, 2012, pp. 9–48, and Melissa Nisbett, 'Who Holds the Power in Soft Power?', *Arts & International Affairs*, 1, 1, 2016, pp. 110–48 for an outline of relevant terms and approaches.

[5] See Walter Hixson, *Parting the Curtain: Propaganda, Culture, and the Cold War*, New York, 1997; Francis Stonor Saunders, *The Cultural Cold War*, New York, NY, 1999; Yale Richmond, *Cultural Exchange and the Cold War: Raising the Iron Curtain*, University Park, PA, 2003; David Caute, *The Dancer Defects: Struggle for Cultural Supremacy during the Cold War*, Oxford, 2003; Gilles Scott-Smith and Hans Krabbendam, *The Cultural Cold War in Western Europe 1945–1960*, London, 2003; Greg Barnihsel, *Cold War Modernists: Art, Literature, and American Cultural Diplomacy*, New York, 2015.

[6] See Óscar J. Martín García and Rósa Magnúsdóttir (eds), *Machineries of Persuasion: European Soft Power and Public Diplomacy during the Cold War*, Berlin and Boston, MA, 2019, pp. 1–5. Other studies that go beyond the binary superpower opposition include the following: Antoine Fleury and Lubor Jílek (eds), *Une Europe malgré tout, 1945–1990. Contacts et réseaux culturels, intellectuels et scientifiques entre Européens dans la guerre,*

gradually reframed the very concept of the Cold War,[7] and dismantled the symbolic meaning of the Iron Curtain which came to be perceived more as a 'semi-permeable membrane' or a 'nylon curtain', instead of a nonporous and insurmountable divide.[8] East-West cultural relations also came to be recognized as one of the few opportunities for 'smaller powers' to appear on the international scene and to broaden their margins for manoeuvre in a global conflict induced by the two superpowers. By appealing to an image of Europe with its shared identity and common values, and by making use of ruptures in their respective blocs and hegemonic relations, smaller states managed to obtain some room for individual actions.[9]

Scholarly analyses based on the superpower dichotomy imply that during the first decade after the Second World War, East-West cultural exchange hardly existed: out of suspicion and fear of propaganda, the Western world refrained from cultural endeavours with the Communists, while Soviet cultural diplomacy — with full control exerted on most aspects of international cultural exchange — was directed at the consolidation of its control over Central and Eastern Europe.[10] When it came to American-

Brussels, 2009; Peter Romijn, Giles Scott-Smith and Joes Segal (eds), *Divided Dreamworlds? The Cultural Cold War in East and West*, Amsterdam, 2012; Kim Christiaens, Frank Gerits, Idesbald Goddeeris and Gilles Scott-Smith, 'The Low Countries and Eastern Europe during the Cold War: Introduction', *Dutch Crossing*, 39, 3, 2015, pp. 221–31; Simo Mikkonen, Gilles Scott-Smith and Jari Parkkinen (eds), *Entangled East and West: Cultural Diplomacy and Artistic Interaction during the Cold War*, Berlin and Boston, MA, 2019.

[7] See Odd Arne Westad (ed.), *Reviewing the Cold War: Approaches, Interpretations, Theory*, New York, 2011, and 'The New International History of the Cold War: Three (Possible) Paradigms', *Diplomatic History*, 24, 4, 2000, pp. 551–65; Joel Isaac and Duncan Bell (eds), *Uncertain Empire: American History and the Idea of the Cold War*, New York, 2012; Federico Romero, 'Cold War Historiography at the Crossroads', *Cold War History*, 14, 4, 2014, pp. 685–703; Nils Gilman, 'The Cold War as Intellectual Force Field', *Modern Intellectual History*, 13, 2, 2016, pp. 507–23.

[8] See Michael David-Fox, 'The Iron Curtain as Semi-Permeable Membrane', in Patrick Babiracki and Kenyon Zimmer (eds), *Cold War Crossings: International Travel and Exchange across the Soviet Bloc*, College Station, TX, 2014, pp. 14–39, and György Péteri, 'Nylon Curtain – Transnational and Transsystemic Tendencies in the Cultural Life of State-Socialist Russia and East-Central Europe', *Slavonica*, 10, 2, 2004, pp. 113–23 respectively.

[9] For recent accounts of the history and role of 'smaller powers' in the development of the Cold War, see Crump and Erlandsson (eds), *Margins for Manoeuvre*; Holly Case, *Between States: The Transylvanian Question and the European Idea During World War II*, Redwood City, CA, 2009; Laurien Crump, *The Warsaw Pact Reconsidered: International Relations in Eastern Europe, 1955–1969*, London and New York, 2015; Theodora K. Dragostinova, *The Cold War from the Margins: A Small Socialist State on the Global Cultural Scene*, Ithaca, NY, 2021.

[10] Existing analyses devoted to the mechanisms of Communist public diplomacy at the outset of the Cold War are scarce. See, for instance, Nigel Gould-Davies, 'The Logic of Soviet Cultural Diplomacy', *Diplomatic History*, 27, 2, 2003, pp. 193–214; Greg Castillo, *Cold War on the Home Front: The Soft Power of Midcentury Design*, Minneapolis, MN,

Soviet cultural relations, for instance, it was not until the mid 1950s that artistic and cultural exchanges between Washington and Moscow could take place, even though in other Western countries, Soviet artists, scholars and athletes had been able to perform several years earlier.[11] Mutual relations and growing tensions between the two superpowers certainly had a major impact on bilateral relations between Poland and the Netherlands in the analysed period. Yet, to what extent are such histories of East-West cultural relations similar to one another?

By scrutinizing the history of Polish-Dutch cultural relations, I wish to determine how the authorities of such 'smaller powers' reacted to international tensions and shaped their individual international cultural policies. Did they manage to develop mutual cultural relations despite global political tensions and a climate of distrust towards one another? What room for manoeuvre did the actors of Polish-Dutch cultural exchanges have before the 1956 thaw, and what was the scale and nature of such exchanges? Answers to these questions will shed some light on ways in which the field of culture coped with obstacles and limitations imposed by the field of power during the first half of the 1950s, one of the coldest moments of the Cold War.

At the end of the 1940s, with the Truman Doctrine in force, the Berlin Blockade and the West-German rearmament, the Cold War seemed to be a real threat to world peace. The first years of the next decade were a period of major tensions that only gradually lessened, leading to a 'small détente' and a relaxation of international relations around 1955/56, with the Geneva Summit and the process of de-Stalinization in Eastern Europe accelerated by the publication of Khrushchev's 'Secret Speech'. In the history of Poland, 1956 marked a particularly important moment — the so-called October Thaw. At that moment, radical shifts took place within the Polish Communist Party that allowed for the end of the Stalinist era in Poland and a certain degree of liberalization, opening a new chapter in the country's Cold War history. Given the radical change in Poland's relations with the West after the October Thaw, 1956 has been treated as a closing date for this analysis.[12]

2010; Cadra Peterson McDaniel, *American–Soviet Cultural Diplomacy: The Bolshoi Ballet's American Premiere*, Lanham, MD, 2014, and Patryk Babiracki, *Soviet Soft Power in Poland: Culture and the Making of Stalin's New Empire, 1943–1957*, Chapel Hill, NC, 2015.

[11] Jimmy Dwain Parks, *Culture, Conflict and Coexistence: American-Soviet Cultural Relations, 1917–1958*, Ann Arbor, MI, 1980, p. 262.

[12] See David Curp, 'The Revolution Betrayed? The Poznan Revolt and the Polish Road to Nationalist Socialism', *The Polish Review*, 51, 3/4, 2006 pp. 307–24, and Tony Kemp-Welch, 'Dethroning Stalin: Poland 1956 and Its Legacy', *Europe-Asia Studies*, 58, 8, 2006,

This article reflects on the institutionalized sphere of Cold War cultural exchange, and employs the term 'culture' to connote the domains of so-called 'high culture': the fine arts, literature, theatre, music and dance.[13] Particular attention is paid to art exhibitions which were one of the most spectacular and complex forms of cultural exchange across the Iron Curtain, as they needed to be preceded by protracted preparatory measures on various levels, including intergovernmental arrangements. It has also been argued that analysing the history of Cold War exhibitions allows for various influences and power relations imposed on culture to be identified and mapped.[14] Other forms of cultural exchange will also be explored, such as literary translations, personal mobility and — last but not least — informal diplomacy.[15] Not only organizational aspects of such initiatives will be scrutinized, but also purely political factors that had a considerable impact on the nature, scale and intensity of bilateral cultural relations in the period under discussion. Attention will also be paid to non-state actors of international cultural relations, cultural mediators such as art historians, literary scholars, translators and museum directors, who played an important complementary role in mutual relations, bridging official and political gaps.[16]

pp. 1261–84 for a more detailed analysis of this issue.

[13] Needless to say, high culture has lost its privileged scholarly status and the definition of culture has been extended to include popular culture and everyday life practices and artefacts. See Gordon Johnston, 'Revisiting the Cultural Cold War', *Social History*, 35, 3, 2010, pp. 290–307, and Siegfried Weichlein, 'Representation and Recoding: Interdisciplinary Perspectives on Cold War Cultures', in Konrad H. Jarausch et al. (eds), *The Cold War*, Berlin, 2017, pp. 19–66 for an in-depth discussion of various concepts of cultures and how they relate to Cold War culture(s) and its historiography. These, however, are intentionally omitted in this analysis.

[14] See Gabriela Świtek, 'The Borderlines of the Thaw: Graphic Art from the Federal Republic of Germany in Warsaw's Exhibition Factory (1956–1957)', *Biuletyn Historii Sztuki*, 82, 1, 2020, p. 131.

[15] Aspects such as personal mobility, student exchange, scientific and technical cooperation were often included under a broader definition of cultural exchange between states at both sides of the Iron Curtain, and incorporated into their official cultural agreements. Such was also the case of the Polish-Dutch cultural agreement signed in 1967.

[16] This analysis is based on archival materials gathered in the following archives: Archiwum Ministerstwa Spraw Zagranicznych in Warsaw: Departament Prasy i Informacji (hereafter, PL_AMSZ_DPI) and Departament II (hereafter, PL_AMSZ_D II); Archiwum Akt Nowych in Warsaw: Ministerstwo Szkolnictwa Wyższego (hereafter, PL_AAN_MSW) and Komitet Współpracy Kulturalnej z Zagranicą (hereafter, PL_AAN_KWKZ); Nationaal Archief in the Hague: Archief van het Nederlands Instituut voor Internationale Culturele Betrekkingen 1955–1959 (hereafter, NL_NA_NIICB); Stadsarchief Amsterdam: Archief van het Stedelijk Museum (hereafter, NL_SA_SM), as well as in Het nationaal veiligheidsarchief – Stichting Argus (hereafter, NL_NVA-SA). I would like to thank Dorota Pawlicka for her help in the collection of relevant archival materials.

The Nederland–Polen Association

In the first half of the 1950s, all cultural exchange between Poland and the Netherlands essentially ran through the Nederland–Polen Association, launched in Amsterdam on 8 February 1947 as one of the so-called 'friendship societies' between Communist and capitalist states. It was also in 1947 that the Nederland–USSR Association was formed, and later Nederland–Joegoslavië. Nederland–Polen was in fact a front organization of the Polish Legation, and an important vehicle of propaganda and cultural diplomacy for the Polish authorities. Officially, the Association was meant to help strengthen cultural, scientific and economic cooperation between both countries. It taught a course on Polish as a foreign language, issued propaganda flyers and published a magazine that praised the achievements of the People's Poland. It also launched a Cultural Club that organized film evenings, exhibitions, lectures and concerts that were meant to promote Polish culture in the Netherlands.

These initiatives were in fact indirectly supported by the Polish envoy, who for instance supplied the Association with materials necessary for its publications.[17] Although the Association was not an official organ of the Communist government in Poland, it did not take long for its true character to become obvious, and numerous Dutch intellectuals soon withdrew their support. Dutch newspapers, too, quickly ceased to use materials published in the *Nederland–Polen* magazine, and foreign diplomats warned each other of the Association's pro-Communist character.[18] The predominantly anti-Communist Polish community in the Netherlands similarly distanced itself from both the Association and the Legation, and rarely participated in their activities.

Bilateral relations between Poland and the Netherlands in the first half of the 1950s were far from smooth. From the late 1940s — following the events of the Czechoslovak coup d'état, the Berlin Blockade, the introduction of the Truman Doctrine and the Marshall Plan — Dutch policy towards Eastern Europe became more and more rigid, and Poland came to be perceived as part of the enemy camp, which had a major impact on cultural exchange between the two countries. According to the Polish envoy at The Hague, Dutch intellectuals were forced to refrain from supporting Polish initiatives in order to avoid accusations of promoting Communism.[19]

[17] See Górzyński's letter to the Ministry of Information and Propaganda from 15.09.1946 (inv. nr. 21–625–43, PL_AMSZ_DPI).
[18] Political report for January–February 1952 (inv. nr. 8-325-25, PL_AMSZ_D II), and an undated note nr. 64482 (inv. nr. OD 618, NL_NVA-SA). See also, Żelichowski, *Stosunki polsko-holenderskie*, pp. 275–95.
[19] Nederland–Polen report for 1952 (inv. nr. 8-459-35, PL_AMSZ_D II).

Nevertheless, the central authorities in Warsaw kept insisting that the contents of the *Nederland–Polen* magazine be more politically driven so that they could be used for the sake of Communist propaganda. According to Warsaw, articles on Polish science and culture should reflect political issues, and 'inspired responses' to negative publications on Poland should be included in *Nederland–Polen*.[20] Hence, when the December 1952 issue was marked by a much more visible and nearly absurd political tint, Warsaw judged it as 'significant and profitable'.[21] The counter-productiveness of such a policy still seemed not to disturb Warsaw.

Cultural exchange during the coldest period of the Cold War
Tensions between East and West grew and grew in the period under discussion. Even after Stalin's death, the Dutch anti-Communist policy seemed not to alter. The Dutch press regularly reported on worrisome events in Poland, for example on the alleged protests in Poland and other satellite countries in July 1953,[22] actions against Roman Catholic priests in September 1953,[23] or the creation of Warsaw Pact in May 1955.[24] At the same time, other issues were ignored, such as the unexpected Polish support action after the 1953 North Sea flood in the Netherlands,[25] the Peace Race,[26] or the International Youth Festival in Warsaw in 1955.[27] Not surprisingly,

---

[20] Kowalikowa's letter to Polish Legation at The Hague from 25.11.1952 (inv. nr. 21-604-42, PL_AMSZ_DPI).

[21] Mendel's memo from 20.01.1953 (inv. nr. 21-606-42, PL_AMSZ_DPI).

[22] It concerns the first campaign for freedom behind the Iron Curtain, namely the East-German uprising of 17 June 1953 that ended after only a few days. Surprisingly, at that moment West German secret services started to spread false news that similar protests were taking place elsewhere in the Eastern Bloc, hoping that, after Stalin's death, others would stand up and try to free themselves from Soviet control. This did not happen, however, but the Dutch media took the bait and for several days extensively reported on the subject. See Legation's report for July 1953 (inv. nr. 8-457-35, PL_AMSZ_D II).

[23] A wave of anti-Catholic persecutions swept Poland throughout 1953, with mass trials and imprisonment of priests, including primate Stefan Wyszyński, and bishops Antoni Baraniak and Czesław Kaczmarek.

[24] The Treaty of Friendship, Cooperation and Mutual Assistance, known as the Warsaw Pact, was signed in Warsaw in May 1955 between the Soviet Union, Albania, Bulgaria, Czechoslovakia, East Germany, Hungary, Poland and Romania. It was established in reaction to the integration of West Germany into NATO, as a balance of power to NATO.

[25] The North See flood of 1953 took place during the night of 31 January/1 February in the Netherlands, Belgium, England and Scotland. Known as *Watersnoodramp* in the Netherlands, it caused more than 1,800 deaths and enormous damage.

[26] The Peace Race (a.k.a. Friedensfahrt, Course de la Paix, Vredestour and Wyścig Pokoju) was a bicycle race held throughout the Cold War in Czechoslovakia, Poland and East Germany, gathering the best cyclists from Communist states as well as guest teams from non-Communist countries. See Jakub Ferenc, *Sport w służbie polityki*, Warsaw, 2008.

[27] The World Festival of Youth and Students was held throughout the Cold War as an

these circumstances did not facilitate cultural exchange between Poland and the Netherlands that had to face growing tensions and unfriendly attitudes. Despite the political situation, the Polish authorities kept trying to exploit the field of culture for the sake of their Communist propaganda and policy. Various cultural and artistic events held behind the Iron Curtain were meant to propagate socialist ideology and to improve the image of Poland in the West. Most of them, however, could hardly be described as successful.

A series of exhibitions, for instance, was organized by Nederland–Polen. They were devoted to a wide range of issues, such as Polish literature, press, history, women's issues, sport and leisure. I will concentrate on two initiatives, namely the *Het kind in Polen* and *De Zeester en Poolse schilderessen* exhibitions, which illustrate how delicate an issue East-West cultural exchange was in the early years of the Cold War. As these two exhibitions show, this was particularly the case for non-state actors who were insufficiently informed about the profile of organizations such as Nederland–Polen, and unaware of the contents of the exhibition that they had agreed to house.

The *Het kind in Polen* (The Child in Poland) exhibition was organized in April–May 1950 on the premises of a privately owned company, Gerzon's Modemagazijnen in Amsterdam. The exhibition featured works related to the social, medical and cultural upbringing of children aged 7–15 years in post-war Poland. Its propagandist character was obvious. It included, among others, child drawings which were given odd titles and descriptions, supposedly by the Polish children themselves. Oozing with 'grown-up' Marxist labour discourse, they in fact revealed the artificiality and coarseness of the display, making it clear to visitors what the real agenda behind this exhibition was, and thwarting the propaganda efforts of the exhibition organizers and Communist policymakers.

The board of directors of Gerzon's Modemagazijnen had not been informed about either the exhibition's contents or the profile of Nederland–Polen, which caused them some trouble. Suspicions of 'sympathy towards Soviet policy in Poland' fell on the company and its workers, who were put on the secret service's radar.[28] Those who had decided to host the exhibition on the company's premises claimed in fact that it had resulted from a series of misjudgements. It was the Polish envoy who had asked them to house an

event of anti-war and anti-imperialist youth solidarity. Initiated as a neutral and pluralist event, it soon became an outlet for Communist propaganda. See Joel Kotek, *Students and the Cold War*, London, 1996.

[28] Note from S.T. to BVD (*Binnenlandse Veiligheidsdienst*) from 31.05.1950 (inv. nr. OD 618, NL_NVA–SA).

exhibition devoted to children in Poland, which seemed to be a safe topic. With a green light from the city council, the company agreed to organize the exhibition on its premises.[29] It does not seem that the exhibition attracted large numbers of visitors and it received little attention in Dutch society. Limited, but critical, press coverage indicated that its propagandist message failed: 'The exhibition reveals the joyless results of state upbringing and women's labour', stated one of the major Dutch newspapers.[30] This in turn illustrates that Polish public diplomacy remained ineffective and cumbersome. In particular, with regard to smaller Western states such as the Netherlands, it lacked coherence and a systematic strategy.[31]

It was not only cumbersome Communist soft power, but also the weaknesses of contemporary Polish art in the eyes of the Western public that hindered the organization of Polish cultural activities behind the Iron Curtain. Polish culture, in particular art and literature, was constrained in this period by the doctrine of socialist realism that until 1956 remained the official national style.[32] This can be exemplified by the *De Zeester en Poolse schilderessen* (De Zeester and Polish Female Painters) exhibition held at Museum Fodor in February–March 1952. De Zeester was a group of female artists established in Amsterdam early in 1950, but their exhibitions did not find much appreciation among Dutch art critics. The same was true of the exhibition in question, for which De Zeester had decided to invite Polish female artists whose works did not turn out to be entirely to the liking of Dutch artists.

---

[29] Note nr. 1537-'50 from 7.07.1950 by secret service agent E-3 (inv. nr. OD 618, NL_ NVA–SA).

[30] Terlingen, Lia. 1950. 'Kindertekeningen zeggen de (treurige) waarheid: "Als ik speel, werkt mijn vader", maar… mijn moeder is dan evenmin thuis', *de Volkskrant*, 10 May 1950, p. 5.

[31] This becomes especially visible when compared with the subtler and non-coercive Western manner of exercising public diplomacy, for instance the Books in Translation programme or modernist art exhibits and jazz tours in Communist countries orchestrated by the US State Department.

[32] Recently, however, increasing attempts are being made to reassess the value and nature of socialist realist art. Museums across the former Eastern Bloc have come to treat Soviet aesthetics as integral to national and European twentieth-century art history. Recent exhibitions and scholarly publications shedding new light on art from this period re-examine the traditional view of socialist realism as the antipode to modernism, which have resulted in this large aspect of European art history being almost entirely absent from Western critical discourse and museum collections. See, for instance, Irina Gutkin, *The Cultural Origins of the Socialist Realist Aesthetic 1890–1934*, Evanston, IL, 1999; Agata Pyzik, 'Get Real: Why Socialist Realist Painting Deserves Another Look', *The Calvert Journal*, 2014; Magdalena Moskalewicz, 'Rethinking Socialist Realism', *Art in America*, 108, 6, 2020, pp. 72–77; Katarzyna Chmielewska, 'Socialist Realism in a New Perspective: A Proposal of Literary History Analysis', *Studia Litteraria et Historica*, 8, 2019.

Both local critics and members of De Zeester judged the quality of the seventeen works sent by Polish artists as very low in both technical and artistic terms. Dutch newspapers published negative reviews of the exhibition, criticizing works from both countries, and even claiming that the De Zeester artists were aghast when they saw the Polish works. Reflecting on the doctrine of socialist realism, and art produced in accordance with it, the Dutch press also described the exhibition as proof that when the state interferes with the process of artmaking, when art cannot develop in a free manner but instead is subject to propaganda, artistic poverty can be the only result.[33] Such a negative reception must have been disappointing for Polish officials — the envoy himself, along with the head of the Polish Committee for Cultural Cooperation with Foreign Countries (hereafter, C.C.C.F.C.), admitted that the exhibition had failed to convey the desired message beyond the Iron Curtain.[34]

The question of Dutch official patronage and support, or lack thereof, is particularly interesting in relation to events staged by Communist front organizations such as Nederland–Polen. Exhibitions organized under the auspices of Nederland–Polen caused embarrassment to the directors of Gerzon's Modemagazijnen, and members of De Zeester faced accusations of promoting Communism in the Netherlands. Dutch officials, who were often approached by representatives of the Association or the Legation, had to struggle with similar difficulties. The mayor of Amsterdam, for instance, was invited by the Polish envoy to open the *Het Hoger Onderwijs in Polen* (Higher Education in Poland) exhibition, as he had been for *Het kind in Polen*. In this case, however, the mayor refused to attend the opening, for fear that his official support for such an event could cause him trouble. On a similar note, the rector of the University of Amsterdam refused to distribute posters promoting the exhibition on university premises.[35]

---

[33] Press relations quoted in Findziński's exhibition report from 12.04.1952 (inv. nr. 2/175/0/6.1/250, PL_AAN_KWKZ). In this context it is worth mentioning that in May 1955 the Polish envoy sent the following request to Warsaw: 'Faced with the claim, spread by local reactionists, that in the socialist system the Party hampers artists in their creative work and imposes its artistic direction, the Legation requests an article [to be published in *Nederland–Polen*] indicating artistic freedom in any field as well as an article on the possibility and liberty of press critique, with examples.' Findziński's letter to the Department of Press and Information (D.P.I.) from 8.05.1955 (inv. nr. 21-606-42, PL_AMSZ_DPI).

[34] Findziński's exhibition report from 12.04.1952 (inv. nr. 2/175/0/6.1/250, PL_AAN_KWKZ), and C.C.C.F.C. report from 29.05.1953 (inv. nr. 2/175/0/1.1/7, PL_AAN_KWKZ, p. 27).

[35] Korzeniowski's exhibition report from 24.05.1952 (inv. nr. 2/317/0/1.14/501, PL_AAN_MSW).

In fact, from mid 1951 Dutch officials declined to attend cultural events organized directly or indirectly by diplomats of Communist states. Hence, no representative of Dutch universities accepted the invitation to attend the opening of the *Het hoger onderwijs in Polen* exhibition. The Polish envoy maintained that this decision had to do with a growing fear of expulsion for showing one's affinity towards countries from behind the Iron Curtain, and claimed that Dutch scholars had visited the exhibition on the sly.[36] It was only in mid 1954, once global political tensions eased, that the mayor of Amsterdam once again accepted invitations and attended an event organized by Nederland–Polen, namely the exhibition of Polish architecture held in May–June 1954 in Amsterdam and Rotterdam. Even the Queen's commissary gave his excuses for not being able to attend the opening, an unprecedented moment.[37]

The presence of Dutch officials at an event organized by the Polish Legation after a four-year gap indicated a clear shift towards a détente in cultural relations between the Netherlands and the Eastern Bloc. This shift is also visible in Dutch responses to other Polish initiatives, such as the Chopin Competition or the Peace Race that had so far been overlooked.[38] Similarly, Dutch cultural institutions also reopened their doors to artists from behind the Iron Curtain. The Stedelijk Museum in Amsterdam was ready to hold another exhibition of Polish art, the director of the Royal Theatre Carré suggested that a Polish artistic group could appear on its stage, whilst Dutch radio for the first time in years broadcast a programme devoted to Poland.[39] However, such manifestations of Polish cultural achievements meant they would be subject to critical assessment in the Netherlands, for which the Polish authorities needed to be prepared. The Polish envoy therefore warned that meticulous planning for Polish cultural initiatives was crucial.[40] Understandably, the Legation, at the time of the first cultural thaw between both countries, chose to steer clear of potential setbacks such as *De Zeester en Poolse schilderessen* or *Het hoger onderwijs in Polen* exhibitions.

(Not) exhibiting Dutch art in Poland
Although Polish initiatives could still take place in the Netherlands in the coldest period of the Cold War, the Dutch authorities remained sceptical

---

[36] Political reports from 5.12.1951 and 1.03.1952 (inv. nr. 8-325-25, PL_AMSZ_D II).
[37] Legation's report from 2.06.1954 (inv. nr. 8-457-35, PL_AMSZ_D II).
[38] Ibid.
[39] Legation's report from 9.10.1954 (inv. nr. 8-457-35, PL_AMSZ_D II).
[40] Legation's report from 2.06.1954 (inv. nr. 8-457-35, PL_AMSZ_D II).

and deliberately refrained from organizing official cultural events in Poland. As mentioned above, in the late 1940s the Netherlands adopted a defined anti-Communist policy and refused to participate at large-scale events in Communist countries, limiting East-West cultural exchange to private visits and initiatives. In fact, in the first decade after the Second World War no official Dutch cultural event took place in Poland, which seems to contradict the general assumption regarding Cold War cultural relationships: that each side sought to explore the other's territory while denying access to its own.[41]

Among the most spectacular and effective forms of such exchange, art exhibitions were one of the most important. From the mid 1940s Warsaw made numerous attempts to hold Western art exhibitions in Poland, and Poland was in fact the first country of the Communist bloc to host art exhibitions from the other side of the Iron Curtain. For Communist decision-makers, holding Western exhibitions in Poland was intended to prove that the Iron Curtain did not make it impossible for Polish people to get acquainted with artworks that were not in line with socialist realism. At the same time though, they could see with their own eyes that even the most prominent artists such as Léger or Matisse had evolved from non-figurative art towards realism. 'Organizing such exhibitions, showing that in all countries only realist art has the potential to grow, is a factor accelerating the evolution of our artists', claimed the head of C.C.C.F.C.[42]

Interestingly, Western figurative art was also used by the Polish authorities to promote socialist realist art among its citizens. Various travelling exhibitions were organized, such as the 1950–51 exhibition, *Realiści wieku XVII* (The Seventeenth-Century Realists), composed of works by Dutch masters from Polish museum collections, and *Wystawa prac postępowych artystów plastyków* (Exhibition of Progressive Artists) from early 1954. The latter gathered c.400 graphic works by 140 artists from fifteen non-Communist countries. Even though Dutch officials refused to engage in cultural exchange with the Communist bloc, the organizers of the 1954 exhibition managed to obtain fifty-eight works by nineteen Dutch artists. In fact, artworks received from the Netherlands constituted the largest part of the exhibition.

[41] Nigel Gould-Davies, 'The Logic of Soviet Cultural Diplomacy', *Diplomatic History*, 27, 2, 2003, pp. 192–214 (p. 212).

[42] C.C.C.F.C. report from 29.05.1953 (inv. nr. 2/175/0/1.1/7, PL_AAN_KWKZ, p. 28). This was probably the reason why painter Chris Beekman — a Leftist painter who had been related to *De Stijl* but later abandoned its abstract ideals and went back to figuration — had been invited to Poland in 1951. See Lieske Tibbe, *Chris Beekman (1887–1964) en De Stijl. Afvallig en Strijdbaar*, Amsterdam, 2017 for more details on the life and *oeuvre* of Beekman.

The mid 1950s brought a gradual improvement in East-West relations. Following the death of Stalin, the end of the Korean War, the conclusion of the Austrian State Treaty, and the Geneva Summit of 1955, international tensions eased, and the potential for international cultural exchange increased .[43] This can be illustrated by the fact that in 1956 the first official post-war exhibition of Dutch art, *Rembrandt i jego krąg* (Rembrandt and His Circle), opened in Poland, marking the 350th anniversary of the birth of the Dutch Golden Age artist Rembrandt van Rijn. It had taken four years to come to fruition. In November 1952, Warsaw approached the Legation with the idea of organizing an exhibition of Dutch paintings in Poland. However, due to the Dutch authorities' reluctance to send such valuable works to Poland, the idea was quickly abandoned in favour of an exhibition of Dutch graphic art. Envoy Findziński claimed that it might be possible to organize an exhibition of Dutch graphic or applied art, but nothing materialized. Instead, two years later, in November 1954, Poland began to inquire about the possibility of receiving Rembrandt's drawings and graphic works for an exhibition commemorating the anniversary of the painter's birth.[44]

Plans to hold an exhibition of Rembrandt's works met with a positive reaction from Dutch decision-makers, and in May 1955 the head of the cultural department of the Dutch Ministry of Foreign Affairs approved the idea. Consequently, when Stanisław Lorentz, director of the National Museum in Warsaw, approached Dutch museums later that year, inquiring about the possibility of showing Rembrandt's works, the responses were affirmative.[45] This demonstrated a notable shift in Dutch policy towards cultural relations with Communist countries, and meant that the long-awaited exhibition of Dutch art could finally take place in Poland. In return, the Polish authorities agreed to send some of the Polish Rembrandts for a big retrospective exhibition planned to open in May 1956 in the Rijksmuseum in Amsterdam.[46]

---

[43] See Findziński's report from 27.02.1956 (inv. nr. 8-684-51, PL_AMSZ_D II).

[44] Kowalikowa's and Mencel's letters to Polish Legation at The Hague from 25.11.1952 and 22.10.1953 respectively, Findziński's letter to D.P.I. from 19.12.1953 (inv. nr. 21-604-41, PL_AMSZ_DPI); Kowalikowa's letter to Chabasiński from 29.11.1954 (inv. nr. 2/175/0/1.3/63, PL_AAN_KWKZ).

[45] Findziński's political report from May 1955 (inv. nr. 8-607-46, PL_AMSZ_D II); Lorentz's letters to Sandberg from 10.06.1955 and 16.11.1955; Van Schendel's letter to Sandberg from 28.11.1955; Jaffe's letter to Lorentz from 13.02.1956 (inv. nrs. 2186, 2191 and 2194, NL_SA_SM).

[46] 'Tekeningen uit Polen naar ons land', *Het Parool*, 26 April 1956, p. 13; 'Hoe komen vóór 16 mei tachtig Rembrandts bij elkaar?', *de Volkskrant*, 14 April 1956, p. 11.

The *Rembrandt i jego krąg* exhibition was held at the National Museum in Warsaw between 15 March and 30 April 1956. Its opening attracted various cultural representatives, including a delegation from the Dutch museums, garnering much attention in the Polish press. Despite featuring a relatively small collection of only twelve paintings and approximately fifty drawings by Rembrandt, the exhibition attracted a substantial number of visitors. Besides Rembrandt's paintings, of which only three showcased his artistic mastery, the exhibition also included circa twenty reproductions of paintings that had once been part of Polish collections but were lost during the Second World War, as well as works by other artists active in Rembrandt's artistic circle.[47]

Prior to the event, extensive archival research was conducted in various Polish institutions in order to ensure an exhibition of the highest quality. This effort led to a remarkable discovery at the Wawel Castle in Kraków, where twenty-eight drawings, previously thought to have been lost during the war, were found.[48] As part of the Rembrandt anniversary, in April–July 1956, the National Museum in Poznań also organized an exhibition of seventeenth-century Dutch portraits, drawing on works from Polish collections and featuring three paintings by Rembrandt. Following the success of the Warsaw exhibition, in June 1958 an educational exhibition, *Wie was Rembrandt?* (Who was Rembrandt?) was shown in twenty Polish cities. It included a biographical film and twenty-two panels presenting the painter's life and work, attracting over 50,000 visitors.[49]

Even the Dutch Queen was impressed by this intensifying of Polish-Dutch cultural relations. During the Polish envoy's annual meeting with Queen Juliana in February 1956, they discussed cultural relations between the two countries, in particular the Netherlands' contribution to the Rembrandt exhibition in Poland. According to Findziński's report, the Queen seemed positively surprised that such a lively cultural exchange had taken place,[50] which might well have been genuinely unexpected given how reluctant her foreign policy-makers were to foster relations with Communist countries during the first decade after the Second World War.

---

[47] Michał Walicki, 'Rembrandt w Polsce', *Biuletyn Historii Sztuki*, 18, 3, 1956, pp. 319–48; Sikora-Sabat, *Teksty kultury niderlandzkiej*, pp. 33–41.

[48] 'Tekeningen van Rembrandt in Polen teruggevonden', *De Telegraaf*, 2 March 1956, p. 7. Not all of these drawings, though, turned out to have been made by Rembrandt. See Anna Kozak, *Rembrandt rysunki i ryciny w zbiorach polskich*, Warsaw, 2006.

[49] Van Woerden's letters to the Dutch Institute for International Cultural Relations from 26.06.1958, 18.11.58 and 19.01.1959 (inv. nr. 795, NL_NA_NIICB)

[50] Findziński's report from 11.02.1956 (inv. nr. 8-681-51, PL_AMSZ_D II).

The power of literature

In order to commemorate the 100th anniversary of the death of the Romantic dramatist and poet, Adam Mickiewicz, the Polish authorities designated the period from November 1955 to December 1956 as the Adam Mickiewicz Year. A wide range of celebrations and events was envisaged both in Poland and abroad, aiming to underscore Mickiewicz's profound influence on the formation of Polish national identity and to recognize his contribution to global culture. Plans included the translation and publication of works written by and about Mickiewicz, official galas, lectures and exhibitions.[51] Beyond the Iron Curtain, the coordination of these events fell under the purview of Mickiewicz Year Committees established through local 'friendship societies'. In the Netherlands, these efforts faced various challenges, primarily because Mickiewicz's works remained relatively unknown, and because of internal organizational problems within the Nederland–Polen Association. Eventually, it proved possible to bring together thirty-five individuals for the Dutch Committee, including renowned writers, scholars, critics and journalists.[52]

In contrast to other Western countries, the scale of the celebrations in the Netherlands was relatively limited.[53] They included official ceremonies, lectures, and articles in literary periodicals such as *Kroniek van Kunst en Kultuur* and *Streven*. There were also plans for a Dutch-language publication featuring selected works by Mickiewicz and also a biography.[54] The latter was to be written by Siegfried van Praag, head of the Nederland–Polen Association, translator and promoter of Polish literature in the Netherlands. Regrettably, this project never came to fruition because of van Praag's sudden death in March 1958. Notwithstanding, a selection of Mickiewicz's works was translated into Dutch and published in Amsterdam in 1957. A total of twenty-six works were included, translated by notable Dutch writers such as Hella Haasse and Paul Rodenko, and compiled in a modest volume titled *Het levende lied* (A Living Song). The title was taken from the famous 'Great Improvisation', drawn from one of Mickiewicz's most renowned poems, *Dziady* (*Forefathers' Eve*), in which the character Konrad expresses his love for his homeland:

---

[51] Adam Mickiewicz was made patron of the Poznań University in 1955.
[52] Nederland–Polen report for December 1955 (inv. nr. 2/175/0/4.1/195, PL_AAN_KWKZ).
[53] See documents regarding Mickiewicz Year activities planned in capitalist countries (inv. nr. 2/175/0/1.7/80, PL_AAN_KWKZ).
[54] Mickiewicz Year report from 23.12.1955 (inv. nr. 2/175/0/1.7/81, PL_AAN_KWKZ).

Ja bym mój naród jak pieśń żywą stworzył,
I większe niż Ty zrobiłbym dziwo,
Zanuciłbym pieśń szczęśliwą!

I will make my land a pride,
A living song more marvellous than thine
Own works. For I will sing of happiness divine![55]

The choice of this title carries an intriguing ambiguity. On the one hand, the volume was published under the auspices of the Communist front organization, Nederland–Polen, and included translations of Mickiewicz's socialist-oriented texts, originally published by the Leftist newspaper, *La Tribune des Peuples*, that he himself edited. On the other hand, a direct reference to Konrad's monologue expressing his love and longing for a homeland that no longer existed could have been interpreted as a negative comment against Communist Poland. In other words, it might have implied that the real, free and independent Poland was yet to emerge on the post-war map. Whether this was indeed the intention of those who chose these words for the book's title remains uncertain. What is clear, however, is that the 'Great Improvisation' — a pivotal part of *Dziady III* — was not included in the Dutch volume. Similarly, other significant works written by Mickiewicz were omitted from the publication, despite having been translated into Dutch.[56] This selective approach to Mickiewicz's *oeuvre*, particularly in the case of *Dziady*, is not surprising, as it could be interpreted as anti-Russian and liberationist, which the Communist authorities could not allow.[57]

---

[55] Translated by Dorothea Prall Radin, quoted in Michał Masłowski, 'Mickiewicza modele uniwersalności', *Kwartalnik Polonicum*, 2, 2006, p. 9.

[56] Nederland–Polen report for December 1955 (inv. nr. 2/175/0/4.1/195, PL_AAN_ KWKZ). In fact *Dziady*, as well as *Pan Tadeusz* and 'Oda do młodości', were subject of harsh censorship at the time of their publication. See Małgorzata Rowicka, *Wydawnicze i cenzuralne losy twórczości Adama Mickiewicza w okresie zaborów*, Warsaw, 2014 for a detailed analysis of Mickiewicz's struggle with censorship during the Partitions of Poland.

[57] At this point it is worth mentioning that putting *Dziady* on stage often caused a great deal of trouble. In 1948 president Bolesław Bierut banned it because of its visible anti-Russian message, and it was not until 1955 that the play could appear on stage, albeit harshly censored. In 1968 Władysław Gomułka's decision to remove Kazimierz Dejmek's version from the stage triggered large-scale protests against censorship in Poland (known as the March Events). Even the most recent interpretation of *Dziady* (directed by Maja Kleczewska in 2021) caused much upheaval among the Polish populist right-wing government. The play was judged as anti-Polish and anti-nationalist, which has led to suspending ministerial subvention for Słowacki Theatre in Kraków.

The decision of the Communist authorities to celebrate the life and works of Adam Mickiewicz, the Polish national bard, might appear odd at first glance. After all, the tradition of Polish Romanticism, marked by its religiosity and anti-Russian sentiments, stood in stark contrast to Communist ideology. The Mickiewicz Year mirrors similar instances in other Communist states, such as the celebration of Aleksandr Pushkin in Soviet Russia. In these cases, the inclusion of such iconic writers in national identity discourse was driven more by strategic calculations than a genuine interest in their work. For pragmatic reasons, Communist rulers could not afford to overlook or openly deprecate Mickiewicz's accomplishments. Consequently, in order to align him with official agenda, it was necessary to 'reshape' the poet's biography and the discourse on Romanticism, just as had been the case with Pushkin and the lavish celebration of his jubilee in 1937. Such celebrations were meant to reinvent the Romantic tradition in the interest of political legitimacy and to create a sense of unity within the new Socialist system. The figure of national bard was therefore irrevocably appropriated and institutionalized by the state.[58] In the case of Mickiewicz, publications bearing meaningful titles such as 'Mickiewicz as a Socialist' or 'Mickiewicz as a Revolutionary' were meant to represent the poet first and foremost as a political activist, revolutionary and a forebear of socialism. Mickiewicz's works also received a very selective interpretation. In order to influence their post-war reading, 'proper' comments and footnotes were added to new editions of Mickiewicz's writings that channelled them in a direction that was far from the poet's original intentions.[59]

Of the lectures on the life and work of Mickiewicz organized in the Netherlands, Wacław Kubacki's visit in March–April 1956 had an unexpected impact. Kubacki, a literary critic specializing in Mickiewicz, gave several lectures, in which he expressed very negative opinions about post-war Poland, to the dismay of Polish officials. Envoy Findziński admitted that although he had been hoping to use Kubacki's visit to improve Polish-Dutch cultural relations, it actually turned out that his actions had had the opposite effect. Kubacki criticized the situation in Poland and talked about the low level of Polish culture, higher education

[58] See Stephanie Sandler, *Commemorating Pushkin: Russia's Myth of a National Poet*, Redwood City, CA, 2004; Jonathan Brooks Platt, *Greetings, Pushkin! Stalinist Cultural Politics and the Russian National Bard*, Pittsburgh, PA, 2016.

[59] See John Bates, 'Cenzura w epoce stalinowskiej', *Teksty Drugie*, 1/2, 2000, pp. 95–120; Mariusz Zawodniak, '"Żywy Mickiewicz". Socrealistyczny obraz wieszcza', in Edward Balcerzan and Włodzimierz Bolecki (eds), *Osoba w literaturze i komunikacji literackiej*, Warsaw, 2000, pp. 177–85, as well as Anna Artwińska, *Poeta w służbie polityki: o Mickiewiczu w PRL i Goethem w NRD*, Poznań, 2009.

and living standards. According to Findziński, progressive Netherlanders did not believe Kubacki's words, but those who were anti-Communist took them at face value, even though they were surprised that someone from behind the Iron Curtain would criticize his or her country to that extent. This case illustrates that even individuals, who the authorities believed would be good conveyors of the desired message, did not always fulfil their designated task. Such instances, as well as interpersonal affairs, had a major impact on the functioning of the Communist propaganda machine.[60]

The example of Mickiewicz illustrates the role which literary translations could play in cultural diplomacy and propaganda.[61] In the first half of the 1950s, several Polish literary works were translated into Dutch, and vice versa. Poland mainly published translations of works by Dutch Communist writers, such as Theun de Vries and Nico Rost, and not surprisingly, the primary focus of the Polish authorities was to translate and publish pro-Communist works in the Netherlands.[62] From the beginning of the Cold War Warsaw exerted pressure on the Polish Legation at The Hague to publish Dutch translations of works such as Leon Kruczkowski's *Niemcy* (Germans), Tadeusz Borowski's *Muzyka w Herzenburgu* (Music in Herzenburg) or Jerzy Andrzejewski's *Wielki Tydzień* (Holy Week).[63] Until 1955, a slightly modified version of *Niemcy* was distributed in Polish bookstores. Kruczkowski, under pressure to take a clear political and propagandist stance, added an epilogue that gave the play a defined anti-fascist tone. Although the Dutch edition from 1953 included the epilogue, it included the following note:

> The Redaction of Wereldbibliotheek [the publisher] finds it worth stating that we perceive this drama written by a contemporary Polish writer as a

---

[60] In order to avoid similar misunderstandings in the future, the envoy pointed out that subsequent guests from Poland would have to receive precise instructions as to the aim of their visit, i.e. what to do, whom not to approach, etc. See Findziński's memo from 5.05.1956 (inv. nr. 8-686-51, PL_AMSZ_DII).

[61] See Iana Popa, *Traduire sous contraintes. Littérature et communisme (1947–1989)*, Paris, 2010 for a detailed analysis of the mechanisms of literary translations in times of Cold War.

[62] For a detailed bibliography, see Ronald Pieters et al., 'Poolse literatuur in Nederlandse vertaling', *Slavica Gandensia*, 4, 1977, pp. 51–92. See also, Jerzy Koch, 'Przypływy. Uwagi o obecności literatury niderlandzkiej w Polsce 1945–1990', and 'Nadzieja polskich scen? O powojennej recepcji naturalistycznego dramatu Hermana Heijermansa', in Jerzy Koch and Piotr Oczko (eds), *Widzę rzeki szerokie... Z dziejów literatury niderlandzkiej XIX i XX wieku*, Poznań, 2018, pp. 481–97 and 499–517 for a broader analysis of post-war editions of Multatuli's and Heijermans's works in Poland.

[63] See Mencel's letter to the Polish Legation at The Hague from 18.04.1952 and Findziński's letter to Kowalikowa from 20.01.1953 (inv. nr. 21-604-42, PL_AMSZ_DPI).

theme play carrying a message of peace, and not political propaganda. We are convinced that it was not the author's intention to describe any factual but fictional events that, in particular in relation to the Epilogue, should not be perceived as a reference to any particular events such as those that have taken place in our country.[64]

In response to pressure from Warsaw to increase the number of Polish books published in the Netherlands, envoy Findziński put forward a noteworthy solution. In order for the Legation to be able to contribute to the financing of such publications, which could not happen in the open, Findziński suggested that the Legation buy a certain number of copies from the publisher. Given that heavily propagandist books were not particularly popular among Dutch readers, by providing such indirect financial support and ensuring guaranteed sales rates, the Legation would be able to introduce politically-loaded books into the Dutch market, which would otherwise be unfeasible and unprofitable.[65] This case serves as an interesting example of how the Communist field of power sought to influence the Dutch field of culture, as it were in velvet gloves, so as to avoid exposure of their involvement and propaganda efforts.

Informal diplomacy through personal mobility
With time, the Polish authorities gradually came to focus their propaganda efforts on selected individuals and groups that might serve as mouthpieces to convey the idea of an open and prosperous socialist society. At the same time, C.C.C.F.C. reported on increasing interest from capitalist societies in the social, cultural and economic achievements of East European countries. Polish officials attempted to leverage this interest to reach out to progressive representatives of the Western cultural field, and to invite them to Poland. The purpose of these invitations was to 'at least partially "defalsify" information regarding the People's Poland and to present its achievements'.[66] At first, individuals and intellectuals supportive of Communist ideals, often members of 'friendship societies', were invited. However, this approach proved to be unsuccessful, since these individuals were little known in their own national cultural and intellectual circles. On a similar note, the C.C.C.F.C.'s efforts to send Communist-oriented representatives of the Polish cultural field to the West were met with reluctance from Western authorities. Ultimately, only renowned musicians

---

[64] Leon Kruczkowski, *Czytelnik*, Warsaw, 1953, p. 109.
[65] Findziński's letter to D.P.I. from 19.12.1953 (inv. nr. 21-604-42, PL_AMSZ_DPI).
[66] C.C.C.F.C. report from 29.05.1953 (inv. nr. 2/175/0/1.1/7, PL_AAN_KWKZ).

from Communist countries managed to secure invitations to perform beyond the Iron Curtain.

The 1954 shift in bilateral relations was also visible in terms of personal mobility from capitalist countries. Not only did the number of visitors from beyond the Iron Curtain grow by nearly 40 per cent in one year, but also individuals who held politically-neutral views, or even those with 'a serious ballast of prejudices against people's democracies' received invitations to visit Poland.[67] This opened up opportunities for the Communist authorities to reach out to new targets. Western specialists and scholars were afforded the most attention, yet their links to post-war Poland were established on a completely apolitical basis, for example, on the occasion of the Mickiewicz Year. Foreign visitors first underwent thorough screening to assess their 'ability to use what they learn for the [Polish] cause',[68] and upon arrival were granted full freedom of movement and permission to engage openly with local inhabitants, although they were carefully monitored to ensure they conveyed the desired message to the West. Such a strategy aimed to provide these visitors with first-hand exposure to Poland's economic and cultural growth, as well as to the freedoms of religion and movement that Poles supposedly enjoyed. An underlying goal was to make them 'aware of the mendacity of hostile [Western] propaganda',[69] which would then contribute to the creation of a positive image of Poland in the West. Western guests did often reflect on these freedoms during press conferences or articles that appeared in Western periodicals after their return, yet the outcomes of these visits tended to be rather short-lived. Notwithstanding their claims, the Polish authorities actually displayed limited interest in maintaining contact and furthering cooperation with these visitors.[70]

In September 1950 four representatives of the Dutch cultural field (Willem Sandberg, Jacobus Bot, Marius Flothuis and Leendert Braat) visited Poland, constituting an interesting example of Polish-Dutch personal mobility. The choice of these individuals appears deliberate, as all four had actively participated in the Dutch resistance movement, had strong anti-fascist and Leftist beliefs and were connected to progressive

---

[67] Report on cultural exchange with capitalist countries for 1954 (inv. nr. 2/175/0/1.3/63, PL_AAN_KWKZ, p. 41).

[68] Propositions for furthering the cultural relations between People's Poland and Western Europe by Anema, 23.01.1955 (inv. nr. 2/175/0/4.1/194, PL_AAN_KWKZ).

[69] Report on cultural exchange with capitalist countries for 1955 (inv. nr. 2/175/0/1.3/63, PL_AAN_KWKZ, p. 189).

[70] Report on cultural exchange with capitalist countries for 1954 (inv. nr. 2/175/0/1.3/63, PL_AAN_KWKZ, pp. 42-43, 45).

newspapers and intellectual circles. This, presumably, was why the Polish authorities viewed them as potential intermediaries in cultural exchange with the Netherlands.

Sandberg was an important actor in Polish-Dutch cultural exchange. As curator of the Stedelijk Museum he adopted a progressive policy and did not refrain from exhibiting artworks from behind the Iron Curtain.[71] Because of his activities in this field, he had been approached by the director of the Dutch International Institute for Social History with a request to intervene on the issue of the Dutch archives deported by the Nazis in 1944 and temporarily stored in Kraków. Their letters indicate that official diplomatic channels between Polish and Dutch decision-makers failed to return the archives to the Netherlands, hence the 'informal diplomat' Sandberg was asked to use his visit to Poland and hold unofficial personal talks with Polish officials. Sandberg discussed this issue with a representative of the Polish Ministry of Culture and Art during his stay, yet it was only in 1956/57 that the archives finally found their way back to the Netherlands.[72]

Another noteworthy example of citizen diplomacy concerns the so-called Wawel Arrases which Poland tried to regain from Canada, where they had been sent shortly after the Second World War broke out. After 1945 Poland made numerous attempts to regain its national treasures, leading to a diplomatic struggle between Warsaw and Ottawa.[73] Besides using

[71] See Ewa Banach and Andrzej Banach, *Odkrycie Amsterdamu*, Kraków, 1975, for a personal account on Sandberg's involvement and attitude towards the cultural contacts with Poland. For a more general outline of Sandberg's cultural diplomatic activities see Claartje Wesselink, 'De reizende jonkheer. Museumdirecteur Willem Sandberg als cultureel diplomaat', *Virtus*, 22, 2015, pp. 171–88.

[72] Letters between Posthumus and Sandberg from 11.09.1950 and 8.10.1950; Sandberg's letter to Janczewski from 12.01.1950 (inv. nr. 863, NL_SA_SM).

[73] The arrases are sixteenth-century tapestries made in the Low Countries for the Jagiellonian royal dynasty to decorate the Wawel Castle in Kraków. At the outbreak of the Second World War, together with other Polish National Treasures, the arrases had been transported to Canada in order to keep them safe from the Nazis. In 1945, however, the Polish government in exile convinced the Canadian curators of the collection that the Communist regime in Poland had no right to it, and that it should not be returned to Stalinist Poland. In 1948 the arrases were moved to the Quebec Provincial Museum by Maurice Duplessis, the province premier and a fierce anti-Communist. He did this behind the back of the Canadian government causing a long-lasting stalemate, since the federal authorities had no legal grounds to move the treasures from the Provincial Museum. This impasse lasted until the mid 1950s when Władysław Gomułka's government was formed, which appeared to be independent from Moscow. It triggered a new round of negotiations between Poland and Canada, facilitated by Duplessis's death in September 1959. Finally, the Wawel Arrases returned to Poland in 1960. See Gordon Swoger, *The Strange Odyssey of Poland's National Treasures, 1939–1961: A Polish-Canadian Story*, Toronto, ON, 2004 for

traditional diplomatic channels, the Communist authorities also resorted to public diplomacy aiming to influence international public opinion and put pressure on the Canadian authorities. This tactic is exemplified by the Polish reaction to an invitation received from the Dutch Legation in 1952 to participate at the Seventeenth Art Historian Congress in Amsterdam. In an effort to take advantage of this opportunity, Polish officials decided to delegate 'someone who could bring up the issue of the Arrases to throw a proper spotlight on it'. Particularly significant was the fact that the Organization Committee included Professor Jan Gerrit van Gelder who, according to the Polish authorities, had 'progressive' political views and held an interest in the issue, and could therefore lobby for the Polish case. In the end, it appears that no one was sent to the Congress.[74] Instead, Nederland–Polen published a brochure describing the issue of 'Polish artworks stolen by Canada' which was sent to various Dutch museums and officials in order to give this issue more coverage in the Netherlands.[75]

These two examples illustrate the function that non-state actors have in public democracy, and show that informal diplomacy/citizen diplomacy can indeed 'play a critical role in this process, easing relations when they are strained, re-brokering them for changed times, and establishing fresh links in uncharted waters'.[76] The history of diplomacy shows that a country's diplomatic interests could be advanced not only by means of official channels or through large-scale, state-inspired programmes of public diplomacy (e.g. 'Books in Translation' or jazz tours in Communist countries orchestrated by the US State Department), but also by individual representatives from the field of culture who were often engaged to safeguard these interests, at times as a last resort.[77]

a detailed analysis of this issue.

[74] Kowalikowa's letters from 29.04.1952 and 27.05.1952 (inv. nr. 2/175/0/4.1/194, PL_ AAN_KWKZ). The second letter has a hand-written comment stating that Poland should not participate at the congress, but only send propaganda materials. In fact, the conference proceedings make no note of any Polish participant at the congress. See Murk Daniël Ozinga et al. (eds), *Actes du XVIIme Congrès International d'Histoire de l'Art*, La Haye, 1955.

[75] Nederland–Polen report for 1952 (inv. nr. 2/175/0/4.1/195, PL_AAN_KWKZ). This attempt, however, proved unsuccessful, and no mention of the issue appeared in Dutch national newspapers until the new round of negotiations with Canada began after the October Thaw in Poland.

[76] Kirsten Bound, Rachel Briggs, John Holden and Samuel Jones, *Cultural Diplomacy*, London, 2007, p. 52.

[77] This phenomenon has been observed since antiquity. See Andrzej Dudziński, 'Dionizjusz I i Ateńczycy. Ludzie kultury w służbie dyplomacji', in Sławomir Sprawski (ed.), *Człowiek w świecie antycznym*, Kraków, 2012, pp. 57–73. See also, Richard Langhorne, 'The Diplomacy of Non-State Actors', *Diplomacy & Statecraft*, 16, 2, 2005, pp. 331–39 for a more detailed analysis of non-state actors diplomacy.

Conclusions

The aim of this article has been to explore the realms of Polish-Dutch cultural exchange during one of the coldest periods of the Cold War, namely the first half of the 1950s. The first decade of the Cold War was without doubt a period of escalating international tensions and mutual mistrust. Once Stalin gained complete domination in Eastern Europe and the vision of a divided world became a reality, the Netherlands adopted a clear pro-American and anti-Communist strategy. Dutch policy-makers, suspicious of Communist propaganda, refused to play an active role in any mutual exchange with Poland and other Communist states. This did not, however, signify absolute stagnation. Even though in the first years of the 1950s, official institutions refrained from holding cultural manifestations originating from the other side of the Iron Curtain, this did not mean that bilateral cultural exchanges did not develop at all before the 1956 thaw. As discussed above, a number of initiatives could and did take place: small-scale exhibitions, events, occurrences of personal mobility and informal diplomacy. It was only in the mid 1950s, when global East-West relations started to improve, that larger official events could be organized, for example the Mickiewicz Year celebrations in the Netherlands, or the first official post-war exhibition of Dutch art in Poland — the 1956 *Rembrandt i jego krąg* exhibition in Warsaw.

Nevertheless, it is not evident how we should classify cultural relations between Poland and the Netherlands in relation to the global setting. On the one hand, in this truly cold period of the Cold War, the Netherlands adopted one of the harshest strategies of the West, refusing to hold any official cultural events in Poland, just as Washington had with Moscow. This approach, however, was not ubiquitous, as other Western states remained more open when it came to cultural exchanges with the Eastern Bloc, for instance France or Belgium. Poland, on the other hand, seemed to look Westwards as much as it did Eastwards, and — regardless of the Iron Curtain — made numerous and determined attempts to develop cultural relations with Western counties, including the Netherlands. Worth emphasizing is the fact that The Hague did not really block Warsaw in these attempts, and neither did Dutch citizens who wished to foster relations with Communist states despite official reluctance.

Naturally, between 1950 and 1956 the organization of cultural events of Polish provenance in the Netherlands was linked with issues of a purely political nature. Most initiatives undertaken by Polish officials were propagandist and aimed at spreading Communist ideology beyond the

Iron Curtain. As the examples analysed in this article indicate, however, such attempts were rarely successful, and Dutch cultural and intellectual circles distanced themselves from most initiatives launched by the Polish Legation under the auspices of the Nederland–Polen Association. In fact, until 1956 Poland did not shape its international cultural policy very effectively.[78] Hence, this aspect of soft power could actually have been of use for the Dutch had they not missed an opportunity by refusing to exert their international cultural policy behind the Iron Curtain. After all, as historians of the so-called Cultural Cold War have shown, cultural exchanges also functioned as a proxy for propagandist and political objectives for Western countries.[79] It was only after the mid 1950s that Dutch decision-makers altered their approach to cultural relations with the Eastern Bloc, and started actively to shape it.

In this setting, cultural mediators such as Willem Sandberg or Stanisław Lorentz played a very important role in fostering mutual relations, as they were often much more open to East-West dialogue and exchanges in the field of art and culture than political decision-makers. It was often due to their willingness and persistence that East-West cultural exchanges took place in the early period of the Cold War. These non-state actors, however, needed to act within the official frameworks of their respective institutions and positions, and had to seek out room for manoeuvre so that cultural relations could develop between states from both sides of the Iron Curtain. On the other hand, on several occasions use was also made of such individuals and their networks by the authorities who, unable to reach their goals through traditional diplomatic channels, resorted to citizen diplomats such as museum directors and scholars. All in all, even though the international climate and local political circumstances formed a major obstacle for Polish-Dutch exchanges, representatives of both fields of culture did manage to cultivate bilateral relations, albeit on a smaller scale and often with propagandist intentions. It was partly due to these efforts that Polish-Dutch relations could later develop at quite a rapid pace, once a 'small détente' in East-West relations and the 1956 thaw in Poland took place.

---

[78] Adam Koseski and Andrzej Stawarz (eds), *Polska dyplomacja kulturalna po roku 1918*, Warsaw, 2006, pp. 117–18.

[79] See, for instance, Barnihsel, *Cold War Modernists*, and Paweł Zajas, 'Literatur und auswärtige Kulturpolitik: Thesen zu einem Spannungsverhältnis', *Internationales Archiv für Sozialgeschichte der deutschen Literatur*, 44, 1, 2019, pp. 66–99.

Reviews

Ilchuk, Yuliya. *Nikolai Gogol: Performing Hybrid Identity*. University of Toronto Press, Toronto, ON, Buffalo, NY and London, 2021. xvi + 268 pp. Illustrations. Tables. Appendices. Notes. Bibliography. Index. $74.00.

Nikolai Gogol: Performing Hybrid Identity is an important scholarly contribution to Gogol´ studies and the examination of identity performance. It came out between Russia's invasions of Ukraine in 2014 and 2022, and it speaks to two issues of urgent importance: Ukrainian identities and Russian imperial mindsets. Gogol´ has been at the nexus of debates over identity since he emerged on the literary scene in the late 1820s and he continues to be treated as a political football between Ukrainian and Russian nationalists today. Yet it is his significance for both national literary traditions that makes his life, works and legacy an excellent lens through which to study how Ukrainians and Russians have navigated their national and imperial identities from the nineteenth century onwards. In her book, Ilchuk sidesteps the never-ending debate about whether Gogol´ is a Ukrainian or a Russian writer, instead arguing for a hybrid identity, one which spanned both his self-fashioning in society and his literary works.

Over six distinct yet complementary chapters her book covers: 1) the formation of Russian and Ukrainian national identities; 2) Gogol´'s self-fashioning in the imperial capital of St Petersburg; 3) his use of a hybridized, Ukrainian-influenced Russian language; 4) his theories of language and identity; 5) the development of different drafts and versions of his writing; and 6) the posthumous treatment of his stories and their translation into Ukrainian. Ilchuk deftly moves between examinations of broad socio-historical contexts to close readings of portraits, letters and literary works. Woven through the book are examples of Gogol´'s idiosyncratic use of language. In chapter three the reader is presented with lexical and morphological calques from Ukrainian into Russian from Gogol´'s Ukrainian tales (pp. 74–76), while a table in chapter four shows how Gogol´ continued this linguistic inventiveness when playing with Russian idioms in his later writing in *Dead Souls* and *The Inspector General* (p. 112). Digital tools also provide the means for performing comparisons: Ilchuk contrasts drafts of the same stories, showing how the changing socio-linguistic contexts of his lifetime prompted Gogol´ to revise or have others rework earlier stories (chapter 5). In the afterword she compares Gogol´'s lexical choices in his published works with those of other writers of Russian, Ukrainian and Polish ethnic origin, showing that Gogol´ falls between writers of Russian and Ukrainian origin in his word choices (p. 169).

It is as a contribution to postcolonial studies that *Nikolai Gogol: Performing Hybrid Identity* really makes its mark. Postcolonial approaches came late to Slavonic Studies, with the Russian imperial situation falling outside traditional Western European models of understanding empire. Though there has been interest in recent decades in examining the particularities of the Russian imperial example, such as Alexander Etkind's influential *Internal Colonization: Russia's Imperial Experience* (Cambridge and Malden, MA, 2011), this remains an understudied area to which Ilchuk's book adds another dimension. The strength of this work lies in its extensive engagement with theory and scholarship from Ukrainian and Russian studies and beyond. The main theoretical strands include performance and speech-act theories, as well as postcolonial ideas of mimicry and hybridity. In the introduction, Ilchuk traces the evolution of theories of hybridity, from Frantz Fanon to Homi Bhabha to more recent scholarship critical of the notion (pp. 4–6). In Ilchuk's conceptualization of hybridity, she avoids the idea prevalent in other studies 'that Gogol had internalized a colonial mode of behavior' (p. 7), instead arguing that his hybridity created ambivalent 'in-between' spaces in which he could perform creative and subversive identities. In doing so, she builds on Mikhail Bakhtin's concept of the 'in-betweenness of languages', which, she asserts, lays important groundwork for understanding 'Gogol's crossing the border of Russian and Ukrainian, which led to [...] semantic shifts, unusual collocations, neologisms, and new compounds — all of which deterritorialize and reterritorialize discursive and social systems of the imperial culture' (p. 94).

Gogol´ was writing at a time when national identities were becoming an important part of how people thought about themselves all over Europe. It has also become commonplace to refer to this time as the period when a national Russian literature began to take shape. Ilchuk's book calls into question the idea of an independent Russian national literature, instead demonstrating the complexities of an imperial culture in which Russian and Ukrainian literatures and identities informed and shaped each other, with Gogol´ playing a key role in these processes. Although this book is not a comprehensive examination of Gogol´'s writing — it does not include, for instance, analysis of some of his most famous stories such as 'The Nose' or 'The Overcoat' — it is an extremely rich work that should appeal to a wide range of readers, some of whom may read it purely for its historical contextualization of an important writer, while others will engage more fully with its strong theoretical foundations. *Nikolai Gogol: Performing Hybrid Identity* is essential reading for scholars and students eager to decolonize their nineteenth-century Russian literature curricula or to set Gogol´ and his writing in their imperial contexts.

University of Bristol   DANIEL GREEN

Stanevičiūtė, Rūta and Janicka-Słysz, Małgorzata (eds). *Music and Change in the Eastern Baltics Before and After 1989*. Studies in the History and Sociology of Music. Academic Studies Press, Boston, MA, 2022. 355 pp. Illustrations. Music examples. Figures. Tables. Notes. Bibliography. $149.00.

THIS volume frames the Eastern Baltics as a distinct category, offering fresh insights into the interconnected music histories along the Baltic shore, united by geographical proximity and Soviet hegemony. These connections unveil broader dynamics within the Eastern Bloc and present less-studied musical histories of Lithuania and Latvia in English-language scholarship. The twelve essays, with authors from the US, Lithuania, Poland and Russia, highlight cultural and socio-political entanglement with music criticism, events, promotion, composition and performance. The book is divided into three parts: 1) cultural encounters; 2) musical liberation; and 3) music within political transitions. Overarching themes, including informal networks, cultural exchange, utopian pursuits, models of freedom and generational change, shed light on shared patterns.

One significant shared pattern is the emphasis on scenes, rather than composers or works per se. Kevin C. Karnes (chapter 9) advocates a 'horizontal' approach to Soviet cultural histories, emphasizing local over central dynamics. He explores Hardijs Lediņš's unconventional Soviet discos in Riga during the 1970s and 1980s and notes their USSR-wide fascination, attracting Alfred Schnittke and Arvo Pärt. Unlike Western practices, these educational/stationary discos featured listening-focused lectures and dancing, inviting the public to perceive the Soviet world anew. In the 1980s Lediņš added a multimedia dimension, enabling immersive experience of physical surroundings. He aspired to create a socialist utopia, embodying early Soviet ideals of communality, accessibility and care for others, despite the system's shortcomings. Vita Gruodytė (chapter 8) delves into Lithuania's alternative festivals in 1985 and 1995. These interdisciplinary events rejected hierarchical structures, favouring instead happenings and performances in less monitored and unconventional spaces, including swimming pools. Established Lithuanian composers endorsed these student-led activities due to their common goal of reshaping and de-Sovietizing Lithuanian music. Dominika Micał (chapter 3) explores Baranów Sandomierski's and Sandomierz's meetings that fuelled Polish music scholarship in the 1970s and 1980s. They combined academic discussions with concerts, films, plays and readings, attracting crowds from Poland, Czechoslovakia, Bulgaria and Lithuania. These meetings offered a communal atmosphere outside stringent official super-inspection, yet required friendly relations with sympathetic officials to continue. Subsequently, Andrzej Mądro (chapter 11) observes the formation of the yass scene in the 1990s Poland, a response to both jazz stagnation and institutional conservatism. Yass emerged from the Totart movement, rejecting musical hierarchies and social norms. It advocated free jazz, humour and shock as expressions of freedom.

There is, perhaps predictably, a moment to contemplate the Soviet centre of gravity, handled astutely by Peter J. Schmelz (chapter 10) in particular. He navigates the 1980s US-USSR cultural exchange through tours by the Rova Saxophone Quartet and The Ganelin Trio, highlighting the persistent dominance of the US narrative well into the twenty-first century. Schmelz shows that jazz is a symbol of democratic freedom in the US, which linked with the concept of *glasnost'* (openness) in the Soviet space. While emphasizing the significant role of non-state actors and fluctuating policies, Schmelz also shows touring musicians' freedom of expression and glimpses of transcendence. Most chapters explore memories of transformative events, but Olga Manulkina (chapter 12) captures post-Soviet Russia's short-lived free press. Leonid Desiatnikov's coverage in the 1990s shaped the new music criticism toward balancing tradition and innovation and examining academic and popular aspects, all of which waned with dwindling media independence.

The volume also leans on transnational informal relations, especially around a Polish-driven network. Rūta Stanevičiūtė (chapter 1) studies the intricate Poland-Lithuania musical network in the late 1970s, emphasizing unofficial collaboration and transformation. Małgorzata Janicka-Słysz (chapter 2) highlights common values of freedom in the Polish-Lithuanian scene. Both nations share similar aesthetic tendencies, including the symbolic meaning of music as freedom 'from' imposed Communism and freedom 'for' the spiritual and personal. Kinga Kiwała (chapter 4) discusses Poland's generational fissure during the 1970s. United by resistance to socio-political oppression, composers embraced the Romanticist aesthetic in opposing forms. Generation 33, including Krzysztof Penderecki and Mikołaj Górecki, constructed a collective national ethos while Generation 51 sought individualistic expressions of freedom, often evading religion and nationalism. Freedom aesthetics are further explored in discussions of works by Penderecki (in chapter 5 by Iwona Sowińska-Fruhtrunk) and Górecki (in chapter 6 by Teresa Malecka). Meanwhile, Ewa Czschorowska-Zygor (chapter 7) delves into freedom within Polish film music.

This collection evokes a rich music historiography, underscoring the value of focusing on scenes and local events, notably highlighted by Karnes. It features a methodological emphasis on network-driven analysis, facilitating a comparative exploration of intricate musical interconnections. Furthermore, several discussions, especially by Schmelz, accentuate the perpetual flux in interpretive meanings, particularly regarding concepts such as 'freedom'. They elucidate the continuous reinvention and dynamic nature of these ideas for both scholars and the musicians they study. Collectively, these significant perspectives intertwine, offering a multifaceted lens to comprehend the complex musical narratives within the Eastern Baltics.

Department of Music   Živilė Arnašiūtė
The University of Chicago

Milner-Gulland, Robin. *Andrey Rublev: The Artist and his World.* Medieval
   Lives. Reaktion Books, London, 2023. 152 pp. Illustrations. Notes.
   Bibliography. Index. £16.95.

The icon painter Andrei Rublev (*c.*1360–*c.*1430) did not have an entry in the Brockhaus and Efron encyclopedia (1890–1907), yet in 1918, he was listed among sixty-six candidates for celebration in Lenin's 'Scheme for Monumental Propaganda'. This surprising fact reflects the new aesthetic appreciation of icons that emerged in the late Russian Empire and the recognition of Rublev as a master of the craft. It appears towards the end (p. 114) of Milner-Gulland's short history, but the notion of the duality of icons as both religious objects and works of art underpins the approach throughout.

   Due to the paucity of surviving material, the book is less a chronological biography than a synthesis of historical fragments, historiography and hypotheses. Milner-Gulland's remarks in the Introduction and chapter one that Rublev's history has an imprecise start date (he was born 'no doubt in the 1360s', p. 9) and 'in a broad sense' has no end (p. 16) were confirmed when, in 2023, Vladimir Putin authorized the return of Rublev's famous icon of the Old Testament Trinity to the Trinity Sergius Lavra. The decision flouted the wishes of curators at the State Tretyakov Gallery and was widely debated in the West. It is with this most familiar work that Milner-Gulland, seizing the freedom offered by thin pickings, decides to start. It is one of the few for which attribution is not in doubt.

   Over seven chapters, whose main titles are 'The Trinity', 'Russia, *c.*1400', 'The World of Rublev', 'Life and Works', 'Rublev as Artist', 'Afterwards', and 'Summing Up', the layering of contexts, facts (or myths) and interpretations from various angles creates an imperfect but compelling picture of a life. The helpful postscript 'Note on Icons' could usefully have been worked into the main text. The inevitable repetition of some topics is offset by the author's pedagogical clarity and demystifying tone when covering such a lot of ground, including: Kyivan Rus' culture, Byzantine art tradition and the Mongol Horde; the rise of the monastery; hesychasm; icon painting and training; iconography; scripture; icon painters and historical figures, such as Daniil Chernyi, Feofan Grek, Sergius of Radonezh and Epiphanius the Wise; and later commentators, such as Nikolai Punin, Pavel Florenskii and Viktor Lazarev.

The convergence of text and illustrations in the narrative is a strength of the book. In difficult times, Milner-Gulland has sourced many colour images, some new for Western readers. (A list would have been helpful.) Icons and wall paintings known mainly from monochrome Soviet monographs are given fresh meaning. There are maps and photographs to situate the geography, works in fresco and glass mosaic, panel icons, carved wood and metal icons, embroideries, jewelled *oklady* and illuminated manuscripts. Milner-Gulland takes time to consider open questions, such as whether Rublev painted the Andronikov monastery or the Zvenigorod Dormition Cathedral. As for the Zvenigorod deesis, he is unsure about recent assessments that such long-held Rublev treasures as the luminous Archangel Michael and Christ the Saviour icons are not his. Here and elsewhere, the biographer's difficulty is shared with the reader: can there ever be a definitive account? The book raises as many questions as it tries to answer, and several works that have been attributed to Rublev are not discussed or illustrated.

Other things can be challenged, not least the 'all-Russian' version of history (starting with 'Kiev'), although the author concedes that there are many accounts. Art historians may raise an eyebrow at, among other things, the idea of figures in icons showing 'more than a hint of contrapposto' (p. 100), the notion that a secular tradition of 'palace painting' could have been lost to history (p. 38), or the remark that Igor Grabar´ was a 'Symbolist painter' (p. 118). Footnotes are scant and the short bibliography omits publications including those by Lindsey Hughes, Clemena Antonova and Martin Kemp, as well as Robert Bird's monograph on Tarkovskii's 1966 biopic (but the film is briefly discussed). The use of essays by Natalia Murray and Wendy Salmond in chapter six deserved express credit. And the caption for illustration 18 should reference the Trinity Sergius, not Vladimir Dormition cathedral.

What matters, though, is the commendable aim of bringing Rublev to a wider audience, through the author's careful curation of available sources and the publisher's attention to high-quality production. Milner-Gulland's ability to tell a good story vivifies the elusive artist-monk and his world in ways that should stimulate new interest. The book popularizes the niche subject of religious art in the Slavic lands and could catalyse new research in the West on such important topics. To see Rublev on the cover, paintbrush in hand, atop a ladder in an image from the *Life of St Sergius* (1580s–early 1590s), and to read this vibrant account are just as moving as seeing those final colour scenes of icons in Tarkovskii's eponymous film.

Godalming   LOUISE HARDIMAN

Kaiser, Claire P. *Georgian and Soviet: Entitled Nationhood and the Specter of Stalin in the Caucasus*. Cornell University Press, Ithaca, NY and London, 2022. xv + 275 pp. Maps. Illustrations. Notes. Bibliography. Index. $43.95; $28.99 (e-book).

THE history of Soviet Georgia is a fascinating and under-explored one and also something of a taboo topic for Georgians. The main problem is obvious: the man who was born Ioseb Jugashvili and became Joseph Stalin. The world's most famous Georgian destroyed the nation's cultural intelligentsia and yoked Georgia to Russia. He also promoted a certain kind of Georgianness and granted his native republic favoured status — as much as anyone could be favoured by a regime addicted to violence. Many Georgians remain stubbornly proud of Stalin. A poll commissioned by Carnegie Endowment in 2013 in four countries found that 45 per cent of Georgians harboured feelings of either admiration, respect or approval towards Stalin. (The comparable figure in Russia was 28 per cent.) Georgians also expressed approval for democracy and the Orthodox Church so their belief in Stalin is a complex phenomenon, but it can hardly be described as a healthy one.

The gaps in the Georgian Soviet story are being filled by historians such as Timothy Blauvelt, Ronald Suny and Stephen Kotkin, the latter two having in the last decade published authoritative accounts of Stalin's early years. Claire Kaiser's *Georgian and Soviet* is major contribution to this literature. It is a landmark achievement, bursting with revelations and insights. She draws on archival sources in Georgian and Russian to paint a detailed picture of Georgia's evolution in the seven decades of Soviet rule. It stands alongside Krista Goff's work on Soviet Azerbaijan and its minorities, *Nested Nationalism*, to enrich the study of Soviet-era nation-building in the South Caucasus.

The story of how the Soviet Union cultivated a certain kind of nationalism is now part of the scholarly mainstream. The Union Republics became ethno-nationalist projects whose 'titular' elites were subservient to Moscow but also accrued power and privileges for themselves and their republics. As Kaiser puts it, 'the Soviet institutionalization of nationality equipped national republics and their entitled citizenries with the tools of nationalizing states though the mechanisms of empire' (p. 24). Kaiser prefers the word 'entitled' to 'titular,' and in the Georgian case connects this to the personal patronage of Stalin. Stalin suppressed both the legacy of the Menshevik-led democratic republic of 1918–21 and the independent-minded local Georgian Bolsheviks of the early 1920s. He then blessed policies, implemented by his henchman Lavrenty Beria, which promoted other Georgians to the top of the Soviet hierarchy and privileged the rights of ethnic Georgians in Georgia over those of other national groups, such as Abkhaz and Ossetians.

A particular historical narrative was constructed. Stalin and Beria sponsored a cult of the medieval poet Shota Rustaveli and the seventeenth-century warrior Giorgi Saakadze, the main protagonist of a film released in 1942. The textbook *sakartvelos istoria* (*The History of Georgia*) by Nikoloz Berdzenishvili and Simon Janashia, published in 1943, told a story of Georgian nation-building from ancient times to the early nineteenth century. Kaiser writes, 'The theme and language of struggle (*brdzola*) pervades the textbook's narrative, as various Georgian tribes struggled for independence, unification, and reunification against Persians, Arabs, Mongols, Tamerlane, Iran, and the Ottoman Empire, in rough chronological order' (pp. 55–56). In October 1945 Stalin invited the two historians to his dacha in Sochi and went through the text with them line by line over three days. The two returned to Tbilisi with pages of edits by Stalin which they incorporated into a revised edition, published in Georgian and Russian, in 1946.

Stalin's death threatened to disrupt the Soviet Georgian project. In March 1956 Soviet troops brutally suppressed demonstrations in Tbilisi which were simultaneously pro-Stalin and anti-Soviet, killing dozens of people. The republican elites adapted, however. Free from the threat of arbitrary execution, they took advantage of a much more laissez-faire policy from Moscow towards the national republics and stayed in power for decades. Georgia became prosperous by Soviet standards. In 1958 the official celebration of the 1500th anniversary of the founding of Tbilisi, accompanied by a new wave of construction, relaunched the capital as a self-consciously Georgian 'national' city for the first time.

Along with Goff's book on Azerbaijan, *Georgian and Soviet* re-conceptualizes the Soviet period in what used to be known as the Trans-Caucasus. It is to be hoped that someone can complete the picture with a similarly authoritative study of Soviet Armenia. Reading both Kaiser and Goff, you understand that the legacy of the Soviet era is much more pervasive than first impressions suggest. Elites still show minimal interest in regional cooperation projects and promote notions of national identity in which the titular — or entitled — ethno-national group dominates. They derive legitimation from older narratives of struggle rather than the region's democratic traditions of the early twentieth century. All of this helps perpetuate the persistent conflict and division which the South Caucasus is still unable to shed, thirty years after the actual Soviet Union ended.

Carnegie Europe   THOMAS DE WAAL

Fishel, Eugene M. *The Moscow Factor: US Policy toward Sovereign Ukraine and the Kremlin*. Harvard Series in Ukrainian Studies. Harvard Ukrainian Research Institute and Harvard University Press, Cambridge, MA and London, 2022. xiii + 307 pp. Notes. Bibliography. Index. $59.95; $29.95.

How did we get here? When, in February 2022, the Russian Federation expanded and intensified its invasion of Ukraine (dating back to early 2014), policy-makers and analysts of all stripes, confronted with a full-scale land war on the European continent, were looking for answers.

Long-serving State Department veteran Eugene Fishel lays the blame at the feet of four successive presidents, George H. W. Bush, Bill Clinton, George W. Bush and Barack Obama, who allowed 'the Moscow factor' to cloud their decision-making in European affairs, especially when it came to Ukraine (p. 2). Ukraine and other former Soviet republics took their independence in 1991, Fishel argues, but in the official mind of Washington, it was never truly granted. Russia may have been *de jure* just one of many successor states to the Soviet Union, but it was the *de facto* first among equals in US foreign policy towards the region in the minds of policy makers who frequently — but erroneously — conflated the Soviet Union with Russia.

Fishel shows how a fixation on Moscow shaped the United States' understanding of and policy toward Eastern Europe — for the worse — through four detailed case studies. First, at the end of the 1980s and beginning of the 1990s, the Bush administration suffered from a 'failure of imagination' when it came to the non-Russian republics of the crumbling Soviet Union which led the White House to shore up Mikhail Gorbachev's increasingly precarious position in the Kremlin at the expense of the legitimate independence claims of Ukraine and others (p. 25). Gorbachev was better, to the Bush administration, than what might come in his place: a return to power of the sorts of hardliners who tried to oust the embattled Soviet leader in August 1991. Then, though he had criticized the Bush administration for preferring stability to freedom in Eastern Europe, Bill Clinton continued to fixate on Moscow and overlook Kyiv. His main concern was the denuclearization of Ukraine following the breakup of the Soviet Union. And his main partner was Boris El′tsin, whose slide away from democracy the White House was loathe to broadcast. Ukraine merely acquiesced to the US-Russian policy of denuclearization because Kyiv was 'out of options' (p. 118). George W. Bush fared little better, in Fishel's estimation, adopting a 'non-evidence-based approach to interacting with [El′tsin's successor, Vladimir] Putin' (p. 147). Distracted by the Global War on Terror, the Bush administration failed to appreciate Ukraine's 'strategic importance', instead making a host of regrettable statements about partnering with Russia to fight terrorism (p. 123). And finally, under Barack Obama, the United States continued to make trade-offs. The administration congratulated itself for not defaulting to a 'military solution' in Ukraine in 2014 — even as Russia was in essence implementing exactly that by invading (p. 172). And they continued to talk about a 'crisis in Ukraine' as if it were immaculately conceived even as Russians downed a civilian airliner and murdered all 298 aboard — all the more gallingly, in order to secure Russian assistance removing chemical weapons from Syria, which would later prove to have been in bad faith.

Heroes in this story are few and far between. The diaspora press is one: the *Ukrainian Weekly*'s urging of policy-makers to focus on Kyiv and not only Moscow is frequently cited, with the author lauding the outlet's 'clairvoyance' on Russia policy, particularly its deterioration (p. 108). Some in government, like Secretary of Defense Dick Cheney, who tried to persuade President Bush that the breakup of the Soviet Union and independence of its former constituent republics was in the US national interest, were able to take off their Moscow blinders but not to persuade others to do the same.

Villains, by contrast, abound. Each of the four presidents — 'policy champions' who picked Moscow over Kyiv — falls into this category in Fishel's telling, taking the path of least resistance time and again (p. 219). So too do their advisers who shaped and shared a sunny vision of Russia's democratization and integration into the international community. And the author makes liberal use of italicization to draw the reader's attention to past statements which read as especially regrettable today.

These actors deserve a chance at self-defence, though. Bill Clinton would have a point, for example, in contending that containing the former-Soviet nuclear arsenal lest extraordinarily dangerous materiel fall into the wrong hands was a legitimate policy priority — and that taking it easy on Russia in order to make that happen was not an unacceptably high price to pay. Or a self-aware George W. Bush would note, in response to charges of selling out the Orange Revolution and making common cause with the increasingly dictatorial Putin, that many a compromise was made with unsavoury regimes — Freedom Agenda notwithstanding — in the name of counterterrorism.

The Moscow Factor is passionately and persuasively argued. While the chief obstacle to a Europe whole, free and at peace is the Kremlin's imperial mindset, Fishel offers a pointed reminder that US choices have made that problem worse, not better. Russia's war — and war crimes — in Ukraine show the consequences of both Moscow's mentality and US errors for today. Tomorrow, policy-makers will need to avoid repeating the mistakes of the past.

Sanford School of Public Policy   SIMON MILES
Duke University

Radnitz, Scott. *Revealing Schemes: The Politics of Conspiracy in Russia and the Post-Soviet Region*. Oxford University Press, Oxford and New York, 2021. xiii + 244 pp. Figures. Tables. Appendix. Notes. Bibliography. Index. £64.00; £19.99.

In *Revealing Schemes*, Scott Radnitz explores the politics surrounding the social phenomenon of conspiracy theories that has become so prominent in contemporary times. The Covid-19 anti-vaxxers is perhaps the prime example among many. In his timely book, Radnitz investigates the phenomenon, seeking the answers to two major research questions: what leads political regimes to promote conspiracy claims, and what effects do these claims have on politics and society. Even if the concluding chapter has a broader outlook, the focus of the book is on the former Soviet Union, a region where conspiracy theories seem to be particularly rife.

The book's primary source material comprises an original collection of over 1,500 conspiracy claims about forty-two critical events in Russia and elsewhere in the world during the period between 1995 and 2014. Although this delimitation of the period rules out coverage of the mother of all conspiracism, Covid-19, and obviously also the Russian full-scale attack on Ukraine in February 2022, it does include the Euromaidan and Russia's invasion of Crimea.

Radnitz's sources stem from across the post-Soviet region and have been collected from major newspapers, news websites and radio, chiefly identified through the Integrum database. The approach of isolating the forty-two events — incidents such as the Kursk explosion, the Beslan hostage taking and the Rose Revolution — is innovative. The list is comprehensive, if perhaps also somewhat arbitrarily compiled. In his analysis, Radnitz makes comparisons between countries and, more seldomly, across time, even though the study is subdivided into the periods of 1995–99, 2000–04 and 2005–14. The countries dealt with in depth are Russia, Ukraine, Belarus, Georgia and Kyrgyzstan. Additionally, Radnitz undertook two national surveys and conducted twelve focus groups in Georgia and Kazakhstan, although it is not immediately clear why Kazakhstan is included, as it does not figure in the in-depth analyses.

The focus group material is vividly presented and starkly illustrates the phenomenon of conspiracy thinking and its mechanisms, allowing the reader to get close to the substance. The narrative is attention-grabbing, but there are several instances where Radnitz could have used these accounts to greater effect, and been somewhat less keen on presenting yet another table, graph or diagram to illustrate his argument. While these tools do convey some useful information, an old-fashioned, elaborated verbal account would have done the job just as nicely.

Radnitz consistently argues that political leaders tend to make conspiracy claims to demonstrate their knowledge and authority at moments of uncertainty and threat. Here I would feel inclined to take issue. One could equally well argue that subscription to conspiracy theories is a sign of weakness by rulers who have overstayed their popular mandate and are seeking scapegoats, internal, external or both, to hide their shortcomings. Casting blame is seldom a very constructive way of doing politics, and it does little to convey knowledge and authority. Another area of substance where I would differ somewhat is the notion that populist leaders, due to overuse, risk causing conspiracy fatigue amongst their previously faithful followers. Such effects would no doubt be desirable, but the continued domestic following of leaders such as Putin and Trump indicate the opposite. Some leaders seem to be able to persist with their conspiracist rants year after year and still be believed and rewarded by their followers. Relatedly, Radnitz raises the populist dilemma that the people most prone to believe in conspiracy theories are also the most distrustful of the politicians peddling them. Again, neither Trump nor Putin appear to have had any major problems in selling their pet theories to their electorates, and do so over and over again.

One of Radnitz's main conclusions is that conspiracy theorizing is most prominent where there is some degree of political competition, rather than in closed authoritarian contexts where it is not possible to challenge the regime. However, as he also concedes, Russia is the exception that proves the rule. Putin hardly makes any major address without verbalizing some conspiracy theory, for instance that the war-that-is-not-named-as-such in Ukraine is a consequence of US-led Western scheming against Russia and its people. Importantly, the obligatory barrage of conspiracy theories over the years has been far from mere ritual for the Russian regime. It has meant something, or as Radnitz puts it, 'Russia's seizure of Crimea and its instigation of a proxy war in Ukraine followed logically from and were enabled by the conspiracy claims disseminated piecemeal over the previous decade' (p. 108). As he convincingly shows, the Russian conspiracist stories about Ukraine and the West as breeding grounds of fascism and neo-Nazism were in circulation long before 2022. The insistence suggested a line of action, even if it was long believed to be part of a ranting and basically hollow verbal liturgy.

Words have consequences, and sometimes vast implications for action, and when uttered in authoritarian contexts they often need to be taken seriously. In general, Radnitz's book is as useful as it is topical. It provides a competent analysis of the anatomy of conspiracism and the conditions under which it thrives, and it makes an important contribution to the analysis of how shadowy regimes try to legitimize their rule and sometimes, but not always, get away with it.

Department of Global Political Studies/RUCARR   Bo Petersson
Malmö University

Publications Received

Aleksov, Bojan. *Jewish Refugees in the Balkans, 1933–1945*. Balkan Studies Library, 34. Brill Schöningh, Paderborn, 2023. €101.87 (hardback & e-book).

Baidus, Eduard. *An Unsettled Nation: Moldova in the Geopolitics of Russia, Romania, and Ukraine*. Soviet and Post-Soviet Politics and Society, 252. *ibidem*-Verlag, Stuttgart, 2023. €59.90: $69.00 (paperback).

Bilenky, Serhiy. *Laboratory of Modernity: Ukraine between Empire and Nation, 1772–1914*. CIUS Press, Toronto, ON and Edmonton, AL, 2023. $149.95; $49.95.

Burbank, Jane and Cooper, Frederick. *Post-Imperial Possibilities: Eurasia, Eurafrica, Afroasia*. Princeton University Press, Princeton, NJ and Oxford, 2023. $35.00: £30.00.

Carley, Michael Jabara. *Stalin's Gamble: The Search for Allies against Hitler, 1930–1936*. University of Toronto Press, Toronto, ON and London, 2023. $95.00.

Cooper, David L. *The Czech Manuscripts: Forgery, Translation, and National Myth*. NIU Series in Slavic, East European, and Eurasian Studies. Northern Illinois University Press, an imprint of Cornell University Press, Ithaca, NY and London, 2023. $59.95; $39.99 (e-book).

Duvanova, Dinissa. *Thieves, Opportunists, and Autocrats: Building Regulatory States in Russia and Kazakhstan*. Oxford University Press, Oxford and New York, 2023. £64.00; £19.99.

Edele, Mark. *Russia's War Against Ukraine: The Whole Story*. Melbourne University Press, Carlton, VIC, 2023. AUS$32.00: £25.95 (paperback).

Epstein, Mikhail. *Ideas Against Ideocracy: Non-Marxist Thought of the Late Soviet Period, (1953–1991)*. Bloomsbury Academic, London, New York and Dublin, 2023. £95.00; £28.99; £26.09 (e-book).

Flynn, Molly (ed.). *Ukrainian New Drama after the Euromaidan Revolution*. Methuen Drama. Bloomsbury, London, New York and Dublin, 2023. £75.00; £24.99; £22.49 (e-book).

German, Tracey; Jones, Stephen F. and Kakachia, Kornely (eds). *Georgia's Foreign Policy in the 21st Century: Challenges for a Small State*. Bloomsbury Academic, London, New York and Dublin, 2023. £28.99 (paperback).

Hardy, Jeffrey S. *The Soviet Gulag: History and Memory*. Russian Shorts. Bloomsbury Academic, London, New York and Dublin, 2023. £45.00; £12.99; £11.69 (e-book).

Herrlinger, Page. *Holy Sobriety in Modern Russia: A Faith Healer and His Followers*. NIU Series in Slavic, East European, and Eurasian Studies. Northern Illinois University Press, an imprint of Cornell University Press, Ithaca, NY and London, 2023. $54.95; $35.99 (e-book).

Hornsby, Robert. *The Soviet Sixties*. Yale University Press, New Haven, CT and London, 2023. £25.00.

Jangfeldt, Bengt. *The Nobel Family: Swedish Geniuses in Tsarist Russia*. Translated by Harry D. Watson. Bloomsbury Academic, London, New York and Dublin, 2023. £25.00; £22.50 (e-book).

Japaridze, Tinatin. *Stalin's Millennials: Nostalgia, Trauma, and Nationalism*. Lexington Books, Lanham, MD, Boulder, CO, New York and London, 2022. xii + 157 pp. $105.00: £81.00; $39.99: £30.00; $37.50: £30.00 (e-book).

Malaia, Kateryna. *Taking the Soviet Union Apart Room by Room: Domestic Architecture before and after 1991*. NIU Series in Slavic, East European, and Eurasian Studies. Northern Illinois University Press, an imprint of Cornell University Press, Ithaca, NY and London, 2023. $36.95; $23.99 (e-book).

Meyer, James H. *Red Star over the Black Sea: Nâzım Hikmet and his Generation.* Oxford University Press, Oxford and New York, 2023. £100.00.

Nicolescu, Gabriela. *The Porous Museum: The Politics of Art, Rupture, and Recycling in Modern Romania.* Bloomsbury Visual Arts, London, New York and Dublin, 2023. £85.00; £76.50 (e-book).

Reuter, Anni. *Suomalaiset Stalinin puhdistuksissa.* Kirjokansi, 340. SKS, Helsinki, 2023. €34.00; €14.90 (e-book).

Robinson, Paul. *Russian Liberalism.* NIU Series in Slavic, East European, and Eurasian Studies. Northern Illinois University Press, an imprint of Cornell University Press, Ithaca, NY and London, 2023. $125.00; $26.95; $17.99 (e-book).

Samalavičius, Almantas. *Baltic Postcolonial Narratives: Literature and Power.* Cambridge Scholars Publishing, Newcastle upon Tyne, 2023. £59.99.

Scarborough, Isaac McKean. *Moscow's Heavy Shadow: The Violent Collapse of the USSR.* Cornell University Press, Ithaca, NY and London, 2023. $59.95: $38.99 (e-book).

Scott, Erik R. *Defectors: How the Illicit Flight of Soviet Citizens Built the Borders of the Cold War World.* Oxford University Press, Oxford and New York, 2023. £26.99.

Seifrid, Thomas. *Staging the Absolute: Ritual in Russia's Modern Era.* University of Toronto Press, Toronto, ON and London, 2023. $80.00.

Shelyakhovskaya, Maria A. *Being Grounded in Love: A History of One Russian Family, 1872–1981.* Translated by Christina E. Petrides and Maria A. Shelyakhovskaya. Three String Books, an imprint of Slavica Publishers, Bloomington, IN, 2023. $44.95 (paperback).

Sielska, Alicja (ed.). *Transition Economies in Central and Eastern Europe: Austrian Perspectives.* Routledge Studies in the European Economy. Routledge, Abingdon and New York, 2024. £130.00; £35.09 (e-book).

Sutcliffe, Benjamin M. *Empire of Objects: Iurii Trifonov and the Material World of Soviet Culture.* University of Wisconsin Press, Madison, WI, 202 3. $79.95.

Sutton-Mattocks, Julia. *Cures for Modernity: Medicine in Interwar Russian and Czech Literature and Cinema.* Cultural History and Literary Imagination, 35. Peter Lang, Oxford, Bern, Berlin, Brussels, New York and Vienna, 2023. £48.00 (paperback & e-book).

Taube, Moshe. *The Cultural Legacy of the Pre-Ashkenazic Jews in Eastern Europe.* The Taubman Lectures in Jewish Studies. University of California Press, Oakland, CA, 2023. $34.95; £30.00 (paperback).

Tilley, Terrence W. *The Karamazov Case: Dostoevsky's Argument for His Vision.* T&T Clark Explorations at the Crossroads of Theology and Aesthetics. Bloomsbury, London, New York and Dublin, 2023. £85.00; £76.50 (e-book).

Whitewood, Peter. *The Soviet-Polish War and Its Legacy: Lenin's Defeat and the Rise of Stalinism.* Bloomsbury Academic, London, New York and Dublin, 2023. £85.00; £76.50 (e-book).

Abstracts

Authenticity, Facts and Politics in the Fin-de-Siècle Pushkin Debate by Anna Schur
The article focuses on the Pushkin debate of the 1890s to examine attitudes toward facts and authenticity in fin-de-siècle Russia. It traces the clash between positivist-empiricist methods of enquiry that emphasized facts and authenticity and the neo-romantic intuitivist paradigm that dismissed their importance. While the debaters' modes of engaging with the past might have been impacted by an array of factors (generational preferences, professional habits of mind, matters of aesthetic taste), an important rift also followed ideological lines. The fusion of Pushkin with Russia, typical of nationalist and official patriotic narratives, was aligned with a reliance on subjective intuition as a basis for historical depiction. Conversely, accounts devoid of nationalist fervour and ritualized reverence were grounded in positivist methods of enquiry.

Nabokov's Cinematic Sensibility and Film Strategy in *The Defense* by Barbara Wyllie
This article attempts to address two overlooked aspects concerning Nabokov's treatment of cinema in his work and his relationship to the medium. First, it considers the impact of film on Nabokov during his time in pre-revolutionary Russia, arguing that his cinematic sensibility was formed long before his arrival in émigré Berlin and that these early experiences were foundational to an interaction with cinema that continued throughout his career. Secondly, by way of Nabokov's 1928 poem, 'Kinematograf', the article focuses on his third novel, *The Defense* (*Zashchita Luzhina*), a work that has not yet been explored in terms of cinema, to reveal both contemporary film influences and the ways in which Nabokov deployed cinematic themes, styles and techniques in his portrayal of a protagonist who has until now been considered primarily in terms of chess.

Svalbard in Polish Documentaries (1930s–2020s): A Conceptualized Inventory   by Andrei Rogatchevski and Jacek Szymala
This article presents the first catalogue and analysis of over fifty Polish documentaries about Svalbard, filmed during the ninety years of Polish presence on the archipelago. Four distinct periods of such documentary-making have been identified and characterized: the heroic (in the 1930s), the exotic (in the 1950s–1960s), the routine (in the 1970–1990s) and the ethical (1990s to the present). Common and specific trends for these periods have been detected and comparisons with other nations' films about Svalbard (predominantly Russian and Norwegian) are drawn, while possible future directions and topics for Polish film-making about Svalbard are considered.

A European Entrancement: Animal Magnetism among the Russian Nobility in France and St Petersburg, 1784–1787 by Robert Collis
This article examines the reception of animal magnetism among the Russian nobility in the mid 1780s, at a time when this pseudo-science aroused the curiosity and scorn of many across Europe. The first part of the article focuses on how young Russian noblemen — including Catherine II's illegitimate son, Aleksei Bobrinskii — first encountered animal magnetism in France during Grand Tours, via Masonic networks that were utilized by their governors. Significantly, the Russian noblemen were not only introduced to Franz Mesmer's well-known form of animal magnetism, which sought to cure ailments through physical contact and the use of *baquets*, but they were also exposed to magnetic somnambulism. This strand of animal magnetism purportedly enabled patients to see the cause of ailments within themselves and others. Moreover, practitioners in Lyon believed that magnetic somnambulism offered the potential for a somnambule to obtain powers of clairvoyance and to be able to achieve a higher state of spiritual consciousness. The second part of this article studies how both strands of animal magnetism — Mesmeric and

magnetic somnambulism — briefly flourished in St Petersburg in 1786, the first practitioner being Borbinskii's governor, before Catherine II effectively banned the practice.

East-West Cultural Exchange in the Coldest Years of the Cold War: A Case Study of Poland and the Netherlands (1950–1956) by Michał Wenderski
This article explores international cultural relationships between the Netherlands and Poland in one of the coldest periods of the Cold War, namely the first half of the 1950s. Even though in the analysed period, East-West cultural relations remained overshadowed by growing international tensions, they did exist, as exemplified by the two countries in question and their relations between 1950 and 1956. This case study aims to illustrate how the 'smaller powers' of the Cold War conflict shaped and implemented their international cultural policies, as well as to shed light on the scale and nature of cultural relations that took place across the Iron Curtain at that difficult time.

THE SLAVONIC & EAST EUROPEAN REVIEW

The *Slavonic and East European Review*, the journal of the UCL School of Slavonic and East European Studies, is published quarterly by the Modern Humanities Research Association (MHRA). Issues are numbered serially, the four annual issues constituting a volume. Up to and including 1965 an even-numbered issue (published in December) together with the following and odd-numbered issue (published in June) constituted a volume.

Scholarly contributions are invited on all subjects related to the field of Slavonic and East European Studies. Articles should be between 8,000 and 12,000 words, although contributions falling outside this range may also be considered. Book reviews should be no longer than requested. Other contributions (review articles/essays, marginalia, obituaries, summary notes) should aim at a corresponding and proportionate brevity. Original documents are specially welcome. No correspondence is published in the *Review*.

Contributions should be submitted in English in a form ready for publication and in the final state intended. Contributors should study the leaflet, 'Guide for Contributors', obtainable on request from the Managing Editor, SEER Office, UCL SSEES, Gower Street, London WC1E 6BT (seer@ucl.ac.uk), or online at www.ucl.ac.uk/ssees/publishing/slavonic-and-east-european-review. All contributions must adhere to the *Review*'s house style.

Contributions and other editorial communications should be sent to the Managing Editor. While the editors take every possible care with regard to typescripts, they advise authors to retain duplicate copies. The editors do not consider themselves responsible in the event of the loss of a contribution.

Disclaimer: Views expressed in the content of the *Slavonic and East European Review* are those of the respective authors and contributors and not of the journal editors or of the MHRA. The MHRA makes no representation, express or implied, in respect of the accuracy of the material in this journal and cannot accept any legal responsibility or liability for views expressed or for any errors or omissions that may be made.

Copyright in the individual articles and reviews published in the *Slavonic and East European Review* is vested in the authors. For permission to reproduce material from the *Slavonic and East European Review*, please apply to the Managing Editor.

Further information about the activities of the Modern Humanities Research Association and individual membership may be obtained from the Membership Secretary, email: membership@mhra.org.uk, or from the website at: www.mhra.org.uk. For institutional subscription rates and information, contact subscriptions@mhra.org.uk.

ISSN 0037-6795 (print); ISSN 2222-4327 (online)

THE
SLAVONIC
&
EAST EUROPEAN
REVIEW

INDEX

to

VOLUME 101, 2023

The Modern Humanities Research Association
and The School of Slavonic and East European Studies
University College London

INDEX TO VOLUME 101, 2023